THE PARISH REGISTER

OF MASHAM

THE YORKSHIRE ARCHAEOLOGICAL SOCIETY

PARISH REGISTER SERIES

Volume CLXIX

The Parish Register of Masham

1717 – 1800

Transcribed and edited by
David M. Smith

PRIVATELY PRINTED FOR THE
PARISH REGISTER SECTION

2004

ISBN 1 9035 6415 8

This volume is dedicated
by the editor
to Barbara Holland

Issued to subscribers for the year 2004 by
The Yorkshire Archaeological Society
for the Parish Register Section

CONTENTS

Cleugh
...erham
Abby
Brathwaite Hall
Eastwitton
Mill
Jervaux Abby
WITTON
ound
BROWN RIGG FELL
Newstead
K
Warriner
Moor Coals
Angram Coat
E
Sowdin Buck
Ellingstring
Birkgill
Braun Beck
SLAPSTONES
Constedale
Coal Hill
ASHA CRAGGS
HEALEY PASTURE
Heal Coals
Birks
Pasture House
Goldlith Foot
COLSTERDALE
Burn River
...terdale Hall
River
LLENLITH MOOR
Sprus Beck
Spute gill
S
H
A
SOURMIRE MOOR
M
Towler Hill
Grimes Gill
S
Gredyr Bank
Coal House
H
Leighton Hall
I
R
S
C
H
A
The Hall
Grimesgill Ho.
S
E
Stoyfold
Thrustle flaw
POT MOOR
Summerside
POT
CLINT
Pot beck
Boardenrigg
Ruffells
Agill
Arngill
Twaithouse
here in
BLEASFIELD
Ash
Round Hill

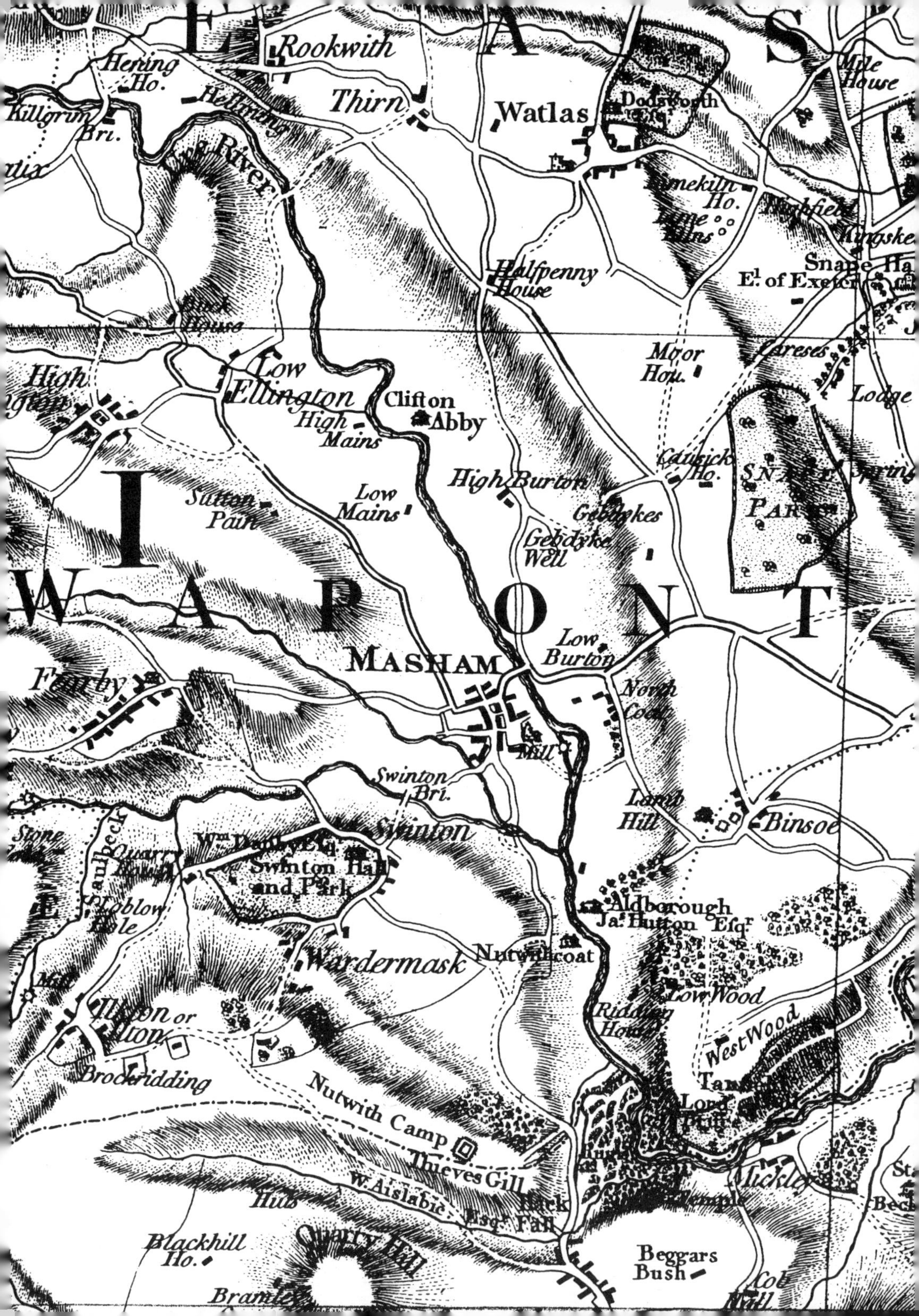

Rookwith
Hening Ho.
Thirn
Watlas
Dodsworth
Killgrim Bri.
River
Mile House
Limekiln Ho.
Lime Kilns
Halfpenny House
Snape Ha
E. of Exeter
Moor Hou.
Lodge
Low Ellington
High
Clifton Abby
High Mains
Low Mains
High Burton
Gebdykes
Gebdyke Well
Sutton Pain
Causick Ho.
W A P O N T
Masham
Low Burton
North Cote
Fearby
Mill
Swinton Bri.
Swinton
Binsoe
Lamb Hill
Swinton Hall and Park
Aldborough
Ja. Hutton Esq.
Nutwithcoat
Wardermask
Low Wood
West Wood
Brockridding
Nutwith Camp
Thieves Gill
W. Aislabie Esq.
Fall
Blackhill Ho.
Quarry Hill
Beggars Bush
Bramley
Temple

INTRODUCTION

The ancient parish of Masham in the North Riding of Yorkshire comprised the market town of Masham with the several townships of Swinton with Warthermarske, Ilton cum Pott, Fearby, Healey with Sutton, High and Low Ellington, Ellingstring, and Burton upon Ure.

The Registers

The earliest register, covering the years 1599 to 1716, was published as volume CLXI in the Yorkshire Archaeological Society Parish Register Section series in 1996. This present volume continues the registers until 1800, and a final volume will cover the years 1801 to 1837. The period 1717 to 1800 is covered, in whole or in part, by four parish registers, now deposited at the North Yorkshire County Record Office at Northallerton. Their descriptions are as follows:

PR/MAS.1/3 (Baptisms and Burials 1717-1730; Marriages 1719-1730)
Paper register, 380 mm. x 240 mm., in parts stained and some damage (some folios loose). 72 folios, only those with writing on numbered in modern pencil foliation, viz: fos. numbered [i], 1-12 (followed by 20 blank folios), 12-19 (followed by 9 blank folios), 20-32 (followed by 5 blank folios), 33-34 (followed by 2 blank folios), 35.

PR/MAS.1/4 (Baptisms and Burials 1731-1759; Marriages 1731-1754)
Parchment register, 12½" x 7¾", 50 folios, paginated 1-100.
Inside front cover:
Masham Register Vol: 3
The Content of Masham Church Yard (the Ground that the sd. Church Stands on Included) is:
A.   R.   P.
1:      2:   5
Witness my hand Henry Procter
12ᵗʰ of 8ᵇᵉʳ 1743
N: The above survey was taken by Henry Procter, Gent: Steward to Abstrupus Danby Esq: and deliver'd to me: John Dale, Curate
front paper: This Book was Bought in the Year 1730: William Jackson, Curate, for the use of the Parish of Masham.

PR/MAS.1/5 (Baptisms and Burials 1759-1801; Banns 1779-1800)
Paper register. 460 mm. x 240mm. 240 pages, only those with writing on numbered in modern pencil pagination, viz., pp. numbered i-ii, 1-59 (followed by 113 blank pages), 60-67 (followed by 22 blank pages), 68-106 (followed by 97 blank pages).

PR/MAS.1/10 (Marriages 1754-1812)
Two printed paper marriage registers bound together, the first being the normal 1754 register with four entries per page, 17½ x 11 inches, headed: Marriage Register (*printed*) 'for the Parish of Masham taking place at Lady-Day 1754, Robt Radclyffe, Curate', pp. 100, the last four being blank. It covers marriage entries from 1754 to 1779. Bound with it is a printed register of the same size, pp. 160, but in tabular form with eight printed column headings per page, viz: *When Married / Names of Persons Married / The man's Profession / Title / Age /*

Banns or License / By whom Married / In whose Presence married /. This is the type of register named after Revd William Dade, the deviser of a more detailed system of parish registration while serving as curate of St Helen's, Stonegate, York, a system supported by Archbishop William Markham of York at his primary visitation of 1777.[1] Registration begins at this way in Masham in 1779 for marriages but not until 1801 for baptisms and burials. This register contains marriages 1779 to 1812.

Officiating Clergy

With the exception of Revd Edward Moises, who was vicar of Masham between 1755 and his death in 1790, the other vicars of Masham for this period - Peter Save (1703-32); Goodricke Ingram (1732-55); Richard Kershaw (1790-1) and William Lawson (1791-1833) - are rather shadowy figures as far as the registers are concerned. Most of their work was undertaken by curates, notably Henry Clement who occurs in the 1720s and probably married the widow of a previous curate, Paul Gelly; Francis Storey who is mentioned in 1729; a Mr Shepherd who and William Jackson occur in 1730; John Dale who is found as curate between 1733 and 1749; his successor Robert Radclyffe was curate from the 1750s until his death in 1785; and Joseph Burrill, who served as curate for almost fifty years from 1789. In addition, several officiating ministers are found from time to time on an occasional basis, and there may have been additional curates, since Thomas Dixon and Thomas Greenbank are so styled in 1764-5 and 1766-88 respectively.

The following abbreviations have been used for officiating clergy in the registers:

A.P.	All: Penny	R.H.	Robert Harrington
E.M.	Edward Moises	R.R.	Robert Radclyffe
H.M.	Hugh Moises	T.D.	Thomas Dixon
J.B.	Joseph Burrill	T.G.	Thomas Greenbank
J.L.	J. Lonsdale	T.T.	Thomas Tennant
J.S.	Joseph Stoney	W.L.	William Lonsdale
J.W.	Joseph Wilson	W.P.	William Powley
L.H.	Leonard Howson		

Abbreviations

The following general abbreviations have been used:

b	born	esq	esquire
bach	bachelor	gent	gentleman
bapt	baptised/baptism(s)	lic	(by) licence
bur	buried/burial(s)		
d	daughter (of)/died	marr.	married
dd	daughters (of)	pa.	parish

---

[1] See W.J. Sheils, 'Mobility and registration in the north in the late eighteenth century', *Local Population Studies*, 23 (1979), pp. 41-4.

s	son (of)		wdr	widower
spr	spinster		wid	widow
ss	sons (of)		wf	wife

Acknowledgements

Grateful thanks are due to the Revd David Cleeves, Vicar of Masham, for permission to print the register, and to Mr Michael Ashcroft, former County Archivist, and Mrs Judith Smeaton, for generous assistance with the parish records in their custody, and to the Chairman and Secretary of the Parish Register Section for their encouragement and help.

Parish Register PR/MAS.1/3

[*loose sheet at front of the volume, containing many jottings and 'trial runs' for entries in the main register. The only additional entry not in the register is: John s John Gray bapt 17 June 1731*]

[fo. 1r]
Notes at top of folio:
William s Joseph Pickersgill born 2 Jan. 1708
William Rodwill born 9 Mar. 1707

Baptisms 1716/17

Masham	Mar	5	Miles s John Clayton
Healey		10	Elizabeth d Christopher Smerthit
Ellingstring		30 [*i.e. 1717*]	Leonard Lye's child
Swinton		24	John s John Burnet
Roomer		24	Miriam d Christopher Pickersgill

Baptisms 1717

Masham	Mar	31	Georg s Georg Thornbury
Ellington	Apr	7	Mary d Thomas Wyn
Pickersgill in Moorhead	May	5	Thomas s William Demain
Swinton		3	Mary d Thomas Fall
Masham		19	Isabel d Thomas Hebden
Swinton		23	Hannah d Ann Burneston
Ilton		23	Mary d Thomas Milner
Low Ellington	June	9	Henry s Henry Thompson
Masham		16	Margaret d Thomas Gainforth
Masham		23	Elizabeth d Joseph Pickersgill
Masham	July	7	Barnabas s Thomas Clarkson
Masham		7	John s Robert Banks
Burton Const[ablery]		7	James s James Metcalf
Ellingstring		21	Christopher s John Henley
Moorhead		14	Sarah d Christopher Toller
Swinton		28	Catherine d William Lightfoot
Healey	Aug	11	Thomas s Thomas Lye
Ilton		11	Ann d John Raper
High Ellington		18	Margaret d John Bollon
Healey		25	James Windress

[fo. 1v]

High Mains	Sept	1	Thomas s Thomas Plews

Ilton		22	Margaret d Ralph Horsman
Healey	Oct	6	Frances d Christopher Rud
Arnegil Moorhead		13	Isabel d Peter Burrel
Swinton		13	Christopher s William Pickersgill
Ellingstring		27	Richard s Richard Serjeant
Fearby		30	Annis d Thomas Fauns
Healey	Nov	22	Phyllis d John Walker
Healey		24	Dorothy d Robert Theakston
Roomer		24	William s William Robinson
Masham	Dec	2	Robert s Robert Stavely
Masham		8	Mary d Thomas Wilson
Ilton		29	Hanna d John Atkinson
[blank]		24	Marmaduke s Mr William Beckwith

Baptisms 1717/18

Warthermarske	Jan	5	Mary d Robert Cass
Fearby		12	Jane d John Hodgson
Masham		26	Antony s George Webster
Healey	Feb	2	Bridget d Matthew Place
High Ellington		2	Ann d John Beck
Masham		16	William s Rose Gill
Masham		23	Samuell s John Wrather
Masham		23	Jane d Jonathan Walker
Low Ellington	Mar	9	John s John Wharton
Masham		9	Christopher s John Scurra

[note at the bottom of the folio: Warthermarske Thomas s Thomas Leathley born 11 Ap 1718]
[fo. 2r]

Masham		16	Sarah d Edward Beckwith
Moorhead		16	Mary d John Tolder
High Ellington		16	Christopher s Christopher Coats

Baptisms 1718

Ilton	Mar	30	Ruth d George Shaw
Moorhead		30	Richard s Richard Burrel
Fearby	Apr	13	Mary d John Close
Masham		13	Samuel s Samuel Bows
Masham		15	Sarah d Edward Beckwith
Ellingstring	May	3	Thomas s Richard Pickersgill
Masham		25	Ann d Thomas Hagston
Warthermarske		25	John s John Oliver
Masham	June	8	Benjamin s Benjamin Ellswood
Healey		8	Thomas s Robert Wintersgil

Masham		15	Ann d Richard Rogerson
High Ellington		15	Mary d Thomas Plews
Masham		22	Mary d William Horner
Pickersgill		22	Sarah d Robert Walker
Ellington	July	27	William s Thomas King
Fearby		27	John s Edward Stevenson
Masham	Aug	3	Barbara d Robert Asquith
[*cancelled entry, unfinished:* Breary Banks John s ....]			
Moorhead		10	Ellen d Peter Preston
Masham		10	Thomas s Thomas Banks
Ellingstring		8	John s Robert Fawber

[fo. 2v]

[*blank*]		15	John a child of Matthew Parrot
Ellingstring		24	Thomas s George Wright
Masham		31	Catharine d Francis Horner
Masham	Sept	28	Francis s Robert Wardrop
Ellingstring	Oct	6	Ralph s Richard Thompson
Ellingstring		25	Christopher s Christopher Mason
Roomer		25	Anne d William Beckwith
Masham	Nov	8	William s George Thornbury
Ilton		9	William s Christopher Gerton
Moorhead		9	William s Edward Plews
[*cancelled entry, unfinished:* Masham Christopher s ...]			
Masham		30	Jeffrey s Thomas Clarkson
Masham	Dec	14	Ales d Robert Chewer
Masham		21	Mary d William Thirkil

Baptisms 1718/19

Masham	Jan	11	William s William Hird
Ilton		25	Jane d William Teesdale
Ilton	Feb	22	Mary d William Burnet
Swinton	Jan	31	Christopher s George Imeson
High Mains	Feb	22	Ellen d Thomas Pleweas
Masham	Mar	15	Jane d William Lupton
Masham		15	Elizabeth d John Wardrop
Healey Cote		15	Mary d Christopher Smorthit

Baptisms 1719

High Ellington	Apr	5	Henry s Thomas Thompson
Masham		5	Elizabeth d Thomas Webster
Masham		5	Elizabeth d Thomas Carter

[fo. 3r]

Masham		19	Hanna d John Wright
Fearby	May	3	Elesabeth d Christopher Dason
Ilton		12	Peter s T. Harrison
Ellingstring		31	Thomas s Thomas Jackson
Ellingstring		25	Thomas s Thomas Bell
Masham	June	14	John s John Ganford
Ellingstring		24	Mary d John Henley
Healey	May	24	Doret d Thomas Lye
Fearby	June	28	Elizabeth d John Breary
Masham		28	Edward s William Horner
Masham	July	5	Ann d Leonard Girsam
Masham		25	Christopher s Christopher Nelson
Burton		26	Thomas s James Medcalfe
High Mains		17	Mary d William Asbridge
Crab House	Aug	9	Mary d John Theakston
Fearby		9	John s John Close
Masham		14	Thomas s Mr Thomas Harkasel
Healey	Nov	6	Ester d Edward Smorthit
Swinton	Oct	11	Elizabeth d John How
Healey		11	Elizabeth d Thomas Sager
Masham		25	George s Thomas Gainforth
Swinton	Nov	14	Christopher s Charles Petch
Swinton		15	John s William Lemin
Swinton		21	Thomas s Mr Toby Wolrich
Ilton		28	Isabell d Ralph Horsman
Masham		8	Elizabeth d Robert Plews
Ilton	Dec	6	Anthony s William Taylor
Low Mains		20	Mary d Ralph Stelling

Baptisms 1719/20

Swinton	Jan	3	Mary d William Pickrgill [sic]
Nutwith Cote		14	Elizabeth d William Hall
Masham		17	Mary d Jonathan Brown
Masham		24	Sarah d William Askou

[fo. 3v]

Fearby		30	Mary d Thomas Fawns
Roomer		30	John s John Pickard
Low Ellington		31	John s Christop[h]er Cots
Roomer	Feb	5	Elizabeth d William Beckwith
Fearby	Mar	6	Mary d Daniel Ibison
Masham		6	William s Robert Stanley
Ellington		12	Jane d Thomas King
Ellington		12	John s John Beck

4

Masham		13	Margaret d Richard Imyson

Baptisms 1720

Fearby	Mar	27	Edward s John Wintersgill
Masham	June	14	Robert s Robert Jaques
Masham	July	3	Thomas s Thomas Hebden
Masham	June	28	John s Thomas Banks
Healey Mill	July	24	Fransis d John Vite
Swinton	Aug	28	Dorothy d George Imeson
Burton	Sept	25	Richard s Thomas Ryley
High Ellington	Oct	30	John s Thomas Plews
Masham	Nov	22	Mary d John Scurrow
Healey Cote	Dec	3	Ann d Matthew Jackson

Baptisms 1720/1

Swinton	Jan	11	John s Thomas Fall
Masham		29	Elizabeth d Robert Strodder
Ilton	Feb	4	Mary d Matthew Smelt
Moorhead		11	Matthew s John Towler
Nutwith Cote		11	William s William Hall
Warriner's House		18	Sarah d Matthew Parrot
Low Mains		19	Ann d R. Stelling
[*inserted entry: Ellingstring*			*James s John Williamson born 28 Apr 1720*]
Swinton		25	William s William Imeson
Masham	Mar	8	Elizabeth d Christopher Nelson
Ellingstring		12	Ann d Richard Sergison
Masham		13	Agnes d William Lupton
Masham		19	Edmund s William Herd
Fearby		23	John s Robert Ryder

Baptisms 1721

[fo. 4v]

Healey	Apr	1	Hannah d Joseph Steel
Masham		11	Dorothy d Joseph Pickersgil
High Mains		14	Ann d William Scot
Fearby		29	James s John Close
Fearby	May	6	Edward s Edward Stevenson
Fearby		18	James s John Close (*sic*)
Swinton		31	Charles s Charles Petch
Masham	June	4	Margaret d William Horner

Masham	May [*no day*]		William s Robert Ascough
Fearby	June	10	Ann d Robert Wintersgill
Ilton		10	John s William Teasdale
Masham		10	Sarah d Robert Banks
Breary Banks		25	Jane d Richard Gill
Swinton		25	Elizabeth d Thomas Smith
Masham	July	2	Roger s Robert Wardrop
Masham		13	Thomas s Thomas Willson
Warthermarske		23	William s William Medcalf
Masham	July [*no day*]		Margaret d Thomas Clapham
Ilton		28	Margaret d Christopher Clark
Ellingstring	Aug	20	John s George Wright
Masham		9	Jane d William Thirkill
Roomer		23	Constance d John Pickard
Masham		29	John s Christopher Sturdy
Masham	Sept	3	Robert s Thomas Hagstone
Masham		9	Michael s Samuel Bowes
Fearby		16	Thomas s Thomas Fawnes
Ilton		16	Christopher [*altered from Anthony*] s William Taylor
Moorhead		23	Marmaduke s John Oliver
[*no place*]		26	Mary d Peter Forbis, a stranger
Ilton	Oct	1	Margaret bastard d Ann Atkinson
Masham		15	Mary illeg d Ann Appleby, a stranger
Leighton		28	Mary d John Burral

[fo. 4v]

Swinton	Nov	6	Rebecca d William Burnet
Healey		7	Thomas s Christopher Rid
Healey Cote		12	John s Matthew Jackson
Ilton		12	John s John Place
Sourmire		16	Constance d John Poole
Fearby		25	Ann d Christopher Dawson
Ash Head	Dec	6	Thomasin d Peter Burral
Low Ellington		14	John s John Stelling
Healey		24	Richard bastard s Dorothy Wintersgil

Baptisms 1721/2

Masham	Jan	1	Jane d John Wardrobe
Masham		14	Ann d Robert Plewes
Masham		23	John s Thomas Banks
Masham		31	William s Thomas Gainforth
High Ellington	Feb	11	William s Christopher Coates
Healey Mill		25	John s John Vitty
Moorhead		27	Phillis bastard d Margaret Toulard

6

| Masham | Mar | 16 | Ann d John Jaques |
| Burton Constablery | | 20 | Marmaduke & Elizabeth twin children James Medcalf |

Baptisms 1722

Fearby	Mar	26	Mary d John Breary
Swinton		26	Mary d John Burnet
Ellingstring	Apr	8	Peter s Peter Jackson
Pickersgill		15	Robert s Robert Walker
Ellingstring		22	William s Robert Fawvert
Swinton		26	Mary d John Imeson
Pickersgill		29	Thomas s Thomas Walker
Ilton	May	12	Mary d Ralph Horseman
Fearby		20	Elizabeth d Daniel Ibbison
[no place]			Catherine d Mr Clement, b at Lieth [Leith] near Edinburgh May 26
Arnagill		26	Sarah d Richard Burral
Healey	June	3	George s Thomas Medcalf
Healey	[no date]		George s Thomas Risdeal

[fo. 5r]

Breary Banks		17	Ellin d John Walker
Masham	July	14	Christopher s Anthony Watson
High Mains		16	Elizabeth d William Scot
Masham		22	Jane d Thomas Clerkson
Ilton		22	Margaret d John Watson
Masham		29	Peter s Edward Carter
Masham		29	Ann d William Leeming
Ilton		29	Elizabeth d Thomas Blaids
Sourmire	Sept	5	Peter s Robert Preston
Ellingstring		23	Rebecca d Thomas Bell
Swinton	Oct	11	Hatton s Mr Tobias Woolrich
Ellingstring	Nov	7	Richard s John Williamson
Healey		18	Esther d Matthew Jackson
Masham		27	John s Robert Jaques
Ellington	Dec	27	John s Thomas Jackson
Healey	Dec	1	Ann d Edward Smorthwait
Fearby		2	John s Thomas Bowes
Low Mains		13	Catherine d Ralph Stelling
High Ellington		15	Alice d Thomas King
Masham		16	Mary d John Weighill
Gollinglith Foot		16	Robert s John Walker
Swinton		18	Catherine d George Imeson
Masham		15	Sarah d William Lupton

[fo. 5v]

Healey		25	William s Thomas Medcalf
Healey		29	Matthew illeg s Elizabeth Medcalf

Baptisms 1722/3

Masham	Jan	10	John s Thomas Ryder
Masham		13	Thomas s Thomas Clapham
High Ellington		26	John s Thomas Jackson
Masham		27	Robert Trueman, a person of riper years
Ellingstring		31	Elizabeth d Leonard Lye
Roomer	Feb	4	William s William Harland
Masham		4	Christopher s Christopher Smith
Healey Cote		9	Barbary d John Ascough
Healey		9	Thomas s Christopher Rid
Healey		9	Thomas s Peter Toulard
Warthermarske		11	John s John Ward
Swinton		16	Hannah d William Imeson
Masham		24	Joseph s Thomas Banks
Ellingstring	Mar	10	Christopher s John Henley
Fearby		22	Ann d John Close

Baptisms 1723

Healey	Apr	14	Joseph s Joseph Steel
Ellingstring		14	Thomas s Thomas Norrish

[fo. 6r]

Masham		30	Robert s Michael Rylah
High Ellington	May	19	Elizabeth d Thomas Plewes
Healey		30	William s William Hodgson
Masham	June	18	Thomas s Thomas Banks
Fearby		18	Solomon s Thomas Fawnes
Masham		23	George s Thomas Hebdon
Agill		[ ]	John s Anthony Barker
Moorhead	July	7	Elizabeth d Christopher Toulard
Ellingstring		28	Mary d Moses Jackson
Fearby	Aug	18	Maudlin d John Burnet
Masham		25	Mary d Thomas Kay
Swinton	Sept	22	Alice d Charles Petch
Masham	[	]	James s James Saunderson had private bapt. administred
Healey	Oct	5	Henry s Henry Craggs
Masham		6	Charles s Mr Clement b Oct 1 and bapt
Masham		10	Anthony s Anthony Watson
Burton Mill		12	John s Richard Geldart

Masham		18	Anthony s Christopher Sturdy
Arnagill	Nov	6	John s Richard Burral

[fo. 6v]

Ellingstring	Dec	1	Jane d Peter Jackson
Fearby		1	Robert s Robert Ryder
High Ellington		14	Faith d Thomas Towlard
Ilton		18	John s John Watson
Masham		20	John s John Banks
Ilton		27	James s Matthew Smelt
High Ellington		28	Richard s Richard Wetherelt

Baptisms 1723/4

Ilton	Jan	18	John s John Watson
Masham		26	John s William Herd
Masham	Feb	9	Elizabeth d Thomas Hagstone
Ilton		9	John s William Taylor
Low Burton		14	Jane d George Fleeming
Healey		15	Mary d Thomas Medcalf
Ilton		15	Elizabeth d Ralph Horsman
Low Ellington		18	Isabel d John Stelling
Masham		22	Rebecca d Thomas Godsalve
Healey		22	Thomas s Matthew Jackson
[ ]	Mar	7	Mary d John Wrather
Ellingstring		8	Matthew s Thomas Jackson
Masham		10	Ann d John Robinson
Masham		12	John s John Jaques
Masham		13	Jane d Edward Imeson
High Ellington		21	Edith d John Beck
Fearby		21	Margaret d Christopher Dawson

Baptisms 1724

[fo. 7r]

Ellingstring	Mar	29	Catherine d Robert Norrish
High Ash Head	Apr	7	Charles s Peter Burral
Masham	May	3	Mary d Robert Plewes
Masham		28	John s Tom Wilson
Healey Cote	June	6	Elizabeth d John Asquith
Pickersgill		13	Elizabeth d Thomas Wintersgill
Leighton		13	John s John Burral
Masham		16	Thomas s William Lupton
Masham		20	Mary d Sarah Carter
Masham		21	John s Robert Wardropp

Masham	July	4	John s William Thirkill
Roomer		7	Mary d Marmaduke Milner
Masham		11	Laurence s Joseph Pickersgill
Fairthorn		14	Sarah d Henry Scaife
Warthermarske	Aug	9	[ ] d Richard Cass
Masham		16	Elizabeth d Thomas Banks
Ellingstring		23	George s George Wright
Burton Constablery		23	John s James Metcalf
Masham	Sept	6	John <William> s Thomas Clapham
Burton Mill		13	William s William Stevenson
Fearby		27	[ ] s William Langstaff

[fo. 7v]

Warthermarske	Oct	13	George s William Metcalf
Ellingstring		18	Martha d Richard Sergison
Swinton		20	Thomas s Francis Leaf
Masham		27	Prudence d William Horner
Fearby	Nov	9	John s John Burnet
Masham		20	Prudence d William Horner (*sic*)
Healey		22	Michael s Michael Vitti
Masham	Dec	29	Robert s Ralph Stelling
Masham		30	Margaret d T. Clarson

Baptisms 1724/5

Fearby	Jan	15	Sarah d John Close
Masham		22	John s John Wihil
High Ellington	Feb	6	Elizabeth d R. Wetheril
Masham		6	George s Anthony Watson
Masham		9	Charles s Mr T. Hardcastle
Fearby		14	Mary d Edward Stevenson
Moorhead		21	Thomas s John Theakston
Warthermarske	Mar	2	Margaret d William Oliver
Swinton		13	William s John Burnet
Healey		21	Dorothy d Christopher Rud
Ellingstring		4	Margaret d John Williamson [*after Ibbeson entry Apr 25*]

Baptisms 1725

Swinton	Apr	29	Jane d John Imeson
Fearby		25	William s Daniel Ibbeson
Masham		25	William s Susan Burgess
Healey	May	14	Francis s Will Paine
Moorhead		16	Elizabeth d Peter Towler

10

BAPTISMS

[fo. 8r]

Fearby		26	Thomas Fawnes
Masham	June	1	Henry s Michael Raley
Warthermarske	Mar	25	Hester d John Ward
Masham	June	6	Ann d Catherine Brandforth
Roomer		6	Hanna d William Harland
Warthermarske Head		8	Jane d William Burnit
High Mains	Aug	1	John s Thomas Pattison
Fearby		1	Beatrice d John Place
Masham		2	William s William Leeming
Masham		13	Mary d Thomas Banks
Healey		19	Hannah d Edward Smorthit
Masham		29	Christopher s John Gainforth
Masham	Sept	4	Mary d Mr Thomas Wrather
Moorhead	Nov	18	Elizabeth Preston
Healey		27	Matthew s Matthew Jackson
Masham	Dec	17	Margaret d Christopher Sturdy
Masham		27	Mary d Thomas Gill

Baptisms 1725/6

Masham	Jan	22	Jane d Anthony Watson
Ellingstring		26	Leonard s Leonard Lye
[Masham	Jan	30	Dorothy wf/d T. Hebden *cancelled entry, see burials under this date*]
Masham	Feb	4	Margaret d John Banks
Masham		8	Henry s Robert Hebden

[fo. 8v]

[Moorhead	Mar	12	Elizabeth d Christopher Preston *cancelled entry*]
Fearby	Mar	5	Sarah d Thomas Carter
Masham		5	Georg s William Hird

Baptisms 1726

Masham	Mar	27	Michael s Robert Jaques
Masham		29	Ann d Joseph Pickersgil
Burton	Apr	10	Thomas s Thomas Gainforth
Masham		12	John s John Robinson
Masham		16	William s Thomas Banks
Fearby		16	Thimaty [*sic*] s Robert [*corrected from Thomas*] Rider
Swinton		30	Thomas s Thomas Smith
Aldburgh	May	7	Rachel d Christopher Collier
Masham	June	5	Elizabeth d George Kay

11

Masham		7	Thomas s John Jaques
Ilton		19	Richard s William Tayler
Healey Cote		22	Thomas s John Ascough
Healey	July	2	Michael s Thomas Metcalf
Fearby		16	Elizabeth Langstaff
Pickersgill		17	Margaret Gill

[fo. 9r]
at the top of the folio:

James s Thomas Toller, b. 19 Sept 1719
Abraham s Thomas Toller, b. 3 May 1721
Faithe d Thomas Toller, b. 18 Nov. 1723
Sara d Thomas Toller, b. 8 Feb. 1725[/6]

Baptisms 1726 (contd)

Swinton	Sept	2	Jane d John Wriglesworth
Masham		8	Margaret d John Body
Ellingstring	Oct	16	Mary d William Bottomley
High Ellington	Nov	15	Henery s John Beck
Swinton		20	Christopher & Elizabeth twin s & d Thomas Burneston
Roomer		20	Marmaduke Milner

Baptisms 1726/7

Masham	Mar	10	Ralph Wilson
Warthermarske		12	Richard s Richard Cass
Healey		14	Dorothy d John Vitty

Baptisms 1727

Masham	Apr	6	William s William Johnson
Masham	May	23	Thomas s Pars Metcalf
Healey		30	Henry s William Hodgson
Masham		31	Elizabeth d Mr Thomas Wrather
Masham	June	23	Robert s Robert Plews
Masham		23	George s William Thirkill
Swinton	July	1	Ann d John Imeson
Masham		2	Margaret d Robert Wardrop
Fearby	Aug	10	Peter s Daniel Ibbeson
Warthermarske	Sept	30	Hanay d Thomas Leadly
Warthermarske	Nov	22	Will[iam] s Will[iam] Burnit

[fo. 9v]

Ellingstring	July	9	Elizabeth d Thomas Jackson
Fearby		15	Diana d Thomas Fawns
Low Ellington	Oct	21	Thomas s Thomas Howson

BAPTISMS

Masham		27	Margaret d Michael Raley
Masham		30	James s Joseph Calvert
Sutton Penn	Nov	15	William s Christopher Whorlton
Healey	Dec	26	Christopher s Thomas Pattison
Ilton		26	Hester d Hesther Gerton

Baptisms 1727/8

Masham	Jan	9	Christopher s Christopher Sturdy
Masham		1	Ann d Frans [sic] Brig
Healey	Feb	2	Elisabeth d Matthew Jackson
Masham		23	Thomas s Will[iam] Lemin
Masham		11	Ann d Robeart Hebin [sic]
Masham	Mar	1	Ann d Thomas Harland
Swinton		8	Elizabeth & Margaret children John Ward
Kirkby		8	Samuel s Simon Wrather of Beggar Bush
Healey		8	Phillis d Peter Toller
Masham		10	Thomas s Peter Hall
Warthermarske		16	Elizabeth d William Oler
Aldburgh		17	Mary d Peter Brown

Baptisms 1728

Swinton	Apr	15	Ann Hauxwell

[*There are included here two burial entries for Apr. 1728 - see Burials below*]

[fo. 10r]

Aldburgh			Jane d Mr John Kirkby born 12 Jan 1728/9, bapt 11 Feb 1728/9
Burton Constablery	Sept	1	Jane d James Medcalf
Masham		1	James s William Herd
[*no place*]		3	Joshuah s Joseph Pickersgill
Nutwith Cote		7	William s William Wrangham
Fearby	Oct	13	Grace d Robert Burnet
Masham	Nov	17	Thomas s Edward Croft
Ellingstring		24	James s Joseph Steel
Ellingstring		24	Anne d Joseph Steel
Masham		8	Mary d William Banks
Masham	Dec	17	William s John Robinson
Swinton	Oct	29	Isabel d John Oliver jnr, mason
Masham	Dec	15	Thomas and Margrit s & d Thomas Banks jnr
Masham		25	Eles[abeth] d John Huntan

13

Baptisms 1728/9

Roomer	Feb	9	Marmad: s Marmad: Milner
Fearby	Mar	1	Christopher s Christopher Dauson [*placed after Nov 8 entry above*]

Baptisms 1729

Masham	Mar	27	Mary d M. Harrison
Summerside	Apr	8	Margaret d John Wintersgill
Ellington		8	Jane d Christopher Coats
[fo. 10v]			
Swinton	Feb	23	Batina d Abstrupus Danby esq.
Fearby	May	22	Jane d Robert Rider
Low Wood	June	21	Elizabeth d Ralph Ballen
Swinton Green	July	6	Mary d Thomas Smith
Swinton		12	Ursela d William Imison
Healey		20	Trothy d Christopher Rudd
Warthermarske	Aug	28	Mary d Thomas Leadly
Burton Constablery	Nov	9	John s Thomas Gill
[fo. 11r]			
Swinton	Oct	25	Mary d Joshua Taylor
Aldburgh	Nov	2	Jane d Peter Brown
Ellingstring		15	Ann d John Ascough
Fearby		22	Tabitha d Thomas Fawnes
Fearby	Dec	4	Mary d Robert Blackburn
Moorsides		21	Christopher s Mary Towlard, wid

Baptisms 1729/30

Masham	Jan	17	Margaret d Joseph Calvert
Ellington		17	Isaack s Thomas Towler
Warthermarske	Feb	27	Katherine d William Glew

Baptisms 1730

Masham	Mar	28	Ellin d John Bodye
	Apr	5	Mary d Joseph Betfield
Ellingstring	[*no date*]		Matthew s Thomas Raggs

[*There follow three burial entries for 1730 - see Burials section below*]

[fo. 11v *blank*]

[fo. 12r]

Heading at top of folio: Christians Registred now dated in the Revd Mr Shepherd now present Curate 1730 [*sic*]

Swinton	June	26	Ann d William Robinson
Healey Pasture Gate		27	Mary d John Walker
Masham		30	Thomas s William Thurkeld
Warthermarske	July	4	Eliz(abeth) d William Medcalf
[*no place*]		10	William s John Wreather
[*no place*]	May	31	Christopher s Thomas Banks
Ilton	July	5	Anne d William Leetham
Masham	Dec	14	Francis s Christopher Sturdy
[*no place*]	Aug	15	William s Robert Smith born
[*no place*]	Dec	5	Ann d Richard Horsman
[*no place*]		6	Thomas s William Harland
[*no place*]		6	Mary d Thomas Lye
Healey		20	Peter s Peter Toulerton
[*no place*]		26	Elizabeth d Jo: Imeson
[*no place*]		26	Mary d Jo: Askew
Ellingstring	Aug	5	Elinger d Jo: Wiliamson

[fo. 12v *blank*]

[fo. 13r]

> Ann Jackson bapt 3 Dec 1720
> Easter Jackson bapt 28 Nov 1722
> Thomas Jackson bapt 22 Feb 1723/4
> Matthew Jackson bapt 27 Nov 1725
> Elizabeth Jackson bapt 2 Feb 1727/8

[fo. 13v *blank*]

[fo. 14r]

Marriages 1719

Nov	17	Matthew Jackson of Healey Cote and Mary Carter of Healey
	29	Francis Greathead of East Witton and Elizabeth Riley otp, banns
Dec	26	Robert Cundall of Kirkby Malzeard and Cordelia Fothergill of Bedale, lic

Marriages 1719/20

Feb	16	William Imyson and Mary Dawson btp, banns
	24	Robert Fryer of Kirkby Malzeard and Ellen Grange otp, lic
Mar	1	William Ianson of Finghall and Mary Maw, banns

Marriages 1720

Apr	18	Thomas Metcalf and Mary Askwith btp, banns
Nov	13	Thomas Banks and Barbary Motherset btp, banns
	15	Christopher Sturdy and Sarah Wood btp, lic

Marriages 1721

Apr	11	John Watson and Ann Pickersgil btp, banns
	18	Mr George Jefferson of Bedale and Mrs Mary Johnson of Low Burton, lic
	19	Richard Horner and Ellin Williamson both of Low Ellington, banns
	23	Anthony Watson otp and Margaret Fleeming of Gebdykes, pa. Well, lic
	27	Mr Clement, curate of Masham, and Mrs Gelly otp, lic
July	13	Robert Preston otp and Elizabeth Thompson of Wath, lic
Oct	7	Thomas Wintersgill and Hannah Walker btp, banns
[fo. 14v]		
Oct	29	Edward Raper and Ann Walker both of Masham, banns
Nov	29	Thomas Bowes of Fearby and Mary Watson of Leighton, banns

Marriage 1721/2

| Jan | 31 | Thomas Loftus of East Witton and Alice Burral otp, banns |

Marriages 1722

Apr	2	Peter Jackson and Margaret Bell btp, banns
	24	Michael Rylah and Ann Reynard btp, banns
May	3	Thomas Blaids and Ann Atkinson btp, banns
	3	John Ward and Elizabeth Barker btp, banns
	3	Thomas Norrish and Elizabeth Pouter btp, banns (Ascension Day)
	13	William Harland and Jane Imeson btp, banns (Whitsunday)
	15	Anthony Barker and Margaret Oliver btp, banns
	17	Moses Jackson and Mary Thompson btp, lic
Nov	12	John Norrish of Bedale and Margaret Beckwith of Masham, banns
	14	John Banks and Mary Carter both of Masham, lic
[fo. 15r]		
Nov	27	Richard Geldart and Barbary Greenwood btp, banns

Marriages 1722/3

| Jan | 9 | Christopher Reynard of Kirkby Malzeard and Elizabeth Thorpe otp, banns |
| | 8 | John Clement and Ann Watson |

Feb	5	Enoch Ragg and Ann Appleby both of Masham, banns

Marriages 1723

Apr	15	John Simpson of Pateley Bridge and Ann Pickersgil of Ilton, banns
	17	Thomas Girsham of Jervaulx, pa. East Witton (Gervice) and Margaret Thwaites otp, banns
	23	Charles Pickersgil and Ann Fawcet both of Masham, banns
Jun	24	Leonard Pybus of Ilton and Sythe Horner of Masham, banns. The Woman, to prevent the Creditors coming on her new-married Husband for the Debts contracted by her former Husband, had nothing to cover her Nakedness during the solemnizing of the Wedding, but her Shirt
Oct	4	William Sharp of Thornbrough, pa. Tanfield and Elizabeth Beckwith of Masham, banns

[fo. 15v]

Dec	3	Richard Sugget of Whitby and Grace Trueman of Masham, banns

Marriages 1723/4

Jan	12	William Clapham and Elizabeth Metcalf btp, banns
	27	Francis Windrass and Mary Imeson, banns
Feb	5	Thomas Burneston and Mary Rawlinson btp, lic
	13	Thomas Atkinson of Hampsthwaite and Eleanor Dowgill of Kirkby Malzeard, lic, mar at Kirkby by the curate of Masham
	26	Parcivil Medcalf and Millifred Foss btp, banns

Marriages 1724

Apr	8	Henry Hodgson and Jane Horner of Kirkby Malzeard, banns, mar at Kirkby by the curate of Masham
	13	Thomas Gill and Margaret Plewes btp, banns
May	3	William Oliver and Elizabeth Imeson btp, banns
	25	Abraham Smith and Margaret Johnson of Kirkby, banns, mar at Kirkby by the curate of Masham

[fo. 16r]

Aug	4	Mr Thomas Wrather and Mrs Dorothy Atkinson both of Masham, lic

Marriages 1725
[No dates given]

Christopher Preston of Masham and Elizabeth Serjenson of K[irkby] M[alzeard]

Christopher Long and Sarah Long of Winsloe

Ralph Peirson of Rip[on] and Elizabeth Hutchinson of K[irkby] M[alzeard]
John Anniken and Ann Anniken of K[irkby] P[arish]
Francis Smith and Deborah Ripley of K.P.
Robert Raper and Sarah Haw of K.P.
Dew Bell of Pocklington and Margaret Pickersgill of K.P.
Robert Smith and Beatrice Grange of K.P.
John Auton of K.P. and Lucy Tailforth of Thirsk
Thomas Freer and Catherine Botchby of K.P.
William Bramley and Ellen Smirk of K.P.
Thomas Brown of Rip[on] and Susan Johnson of Masham
Robert Hebden and Dorothy Calvert of Masham
John Stephenson and Ann Harrison Pd fees Pap.
Stephen Slee and Ann Atkinson of Masham P[arish]
Peter Hutchinson and Isabel Darby of Masham P.

[fo. 16v]

Marriages 1725/6

Christopher Wharlton and Ann Ienson of Masham P.

Nov   26   Thomas Clapham and Elizabeth Jackson
John Slee and Ann Towler
William Wood and Mary Thwaits
John Mallabie and Jane Bennet
Thomas Bows and Jane Walker
Joseph Calvert and Ellen Ripley

Marriages 1726

William Atkinson of Ripon and Elizabeth Geldert
William Watson and Jane Watson L[icence]
Richard Hanley and Mary Wharton of Mas[ham] L.
John Plummer and Grace Clayton L.
Marmaduke Metcalf and Jane Lambert L.
John Robinson and Dorothy Metcalf

Aug   30   Thomas Leadly and Elizabeth Blackburn
William Wrangham and Mary Dodsworth

Aug   22   Thomas Harland and Mary Turnbull
Dec   4   John Brown and Mary Bell

[fo. 17r]   **Marriages 1727**

May   1   Simon Wrather and Mary Sutton of K.P.
       1   Peter Hall and Ann Cowart

MARRIAGES

	1	Wilks Metcalf of Cundall P[arish] and Martha Dixon of K.P.
	2	John Stot and Mary Wilkinson
[*no date*]		Henry Hinman and Ann Metcalf of K.P.
June	13	William Lightfoot of Masham and Ann Terry of Ripon
May	[ ]	Peter Brown and Mary Place
Jun	15	Jonathan Bartram of Masham Parish and Elizabeth Oliver of Swinton
Jul	4	Robert Smith of K.P. and Jane Skurra of M[asham] P[arish]
Aug	2	Robert Wrather and Mary Lancaster

Marriages 1728

July	20	Rolland Hutchinson and Dorothy Wintersgil of Masham
	24	Antony King and Margaret Hardcastle of Kirkby

Marriages 1729

Apr	20	John Peatoft and Hannah Lynn both of Ripon
May	25	Anthony Whaits and Martha Harling both of Masham
Dec	23	Thomas Jackson of Low Ellington and Ursula Dawson of Sutton, btp

Marriages 1730

Nov	19	William Imeison and Mary Brown btp, banns
	22	Matthew Gains and Susanah Pickersgil, banns
	29	Benjamin Banks and Mary Robison btp, banns

[fos. 17v, 18r-v *blank*]

[fo. 19r]   Francis Storey Curate 25 June 1729

[fos. 19v, 20r *blank*]

[fo. 20v]   Death's dark Shades
Seem, as we journey on, to lose their horror
At near approach, the Monster form'sd by fear
Are vanisht all, and leave the Prospect clear:
Amidst the Gloomy Vale, a Pleasing Scene
With Flowers adorn'd, and never fading Green,
Inviting stand to take the wretched in.
No Wars, no Wrongs, no Tyrants, no Despair
Disturb the Quiet of a Place so fair,
But injur'd Mortals find Elizium there

Row's Tamer

None know what Death is but the Dead   Pomfret

Death ends our Woe
And the kind Grave shuts up the mournful Scene

Dicique beatus
Ante obitum nemo supremaque funera debet

[fo. 21r]   **Burials 1716/17**

Healey	Jan	23	Elizabeth d Robert Theakston
Ellington		27	Robert Stockdale, aged 105
Roomer	Feb	4	Elizabeth d John Lonsdayl
Fearby		6	Elizabeth wf Robert Mankin
Roomer		23	Margaret d Thomas Nicolson
Ilton		26	Christopher s John Atkinson

Burials 1717

Masham	Mar	26	Mary d Henry Robinson
[*no place*]	Apr	15	Marey wf Peter Burgess
Ellingstring		17	Mary Brown, wid
Ellingstring		27	Mary d George Wright
Masham	May	1	Ann d Benjamin Ellwood
Swinton		7	Mary d Richard Imeson
Fearby		12	Elizabeth wf John Nicolson
High Ellington		24	Dorothy wf Marmaduke Archer
High Ellington	Jun	3	Jane d Thomas Thwaits
Low Ellington		16	Henry Thompson
Fearby		26	Christopher Walker
High Ellington		28	Henry Thwaites
High Ellington	Jul	6	Henry s John Beck
Ellingstring		23	Christopher s John Henley
Swinton Green	Aug	6	Margaret wf Francis Freer
Ilton		13	Elizabeth d George Wood
Ellington		15	Ann Gill
Masham		18	William s Ralph Horner
Ellingstring		25	Thomas Renelside
Ellingstring	Sept	22	Samuel s Mary Williamson
Moorhead		27	Peter s Peter Preston
Masham	Oct	22	John s William Clayton

[fo. 21v]

Low Mains	Nov	15	Matthew Dawson
Masham	Dec	6	Thomas Banks
Swinton		12	Elizabeth wf Marmaduke Ward
Ellingstring		24	Christopher Serjeant

Burials 1717/18

Warthermarske	Jan	3	John Oliver, jun.
Moorhead		22	Matthew Hamilton
Moorhead		25	John Pickersgill
Ellingstring		28	Ellen Williamson
Masham		31	Matthew Waneman
Moorhead	Feb	5	John Smith
Masham		7	Elizabeth d William Lupton
Warthermarske		21	Mary d Richard Cass
Fearby		27	Isabel wf John Hodgson
Ilton	Mar	12	George s George Wood
Fearby		24	Mary Blackburn

Burials 1718

Low Ellington	Mar	26	Ann d George Wane
Masham		27	Susanna d Mr William Beckwith
Masham	Apr	6	Thomas s Thomas Gainforth
Masham		7	Thomas Jaques
Moorhead		20	Francis Freer
Moorhead	May	9	Ann wf George Burrel
High Ellington	Jun	11	Christopher s Christopher Coats
Healey		15	Thomas s Thomas Lye

[fo. 22r]

Healey		22	George Whitfeild
Masham		28	Thomas s Harry Stevenson
Ellingstring	Jul	6	Henry Hebden
Masham		12	Robert s Robert Body
Fearby		13	Mary d John Close
Swinton		13	Elizabeth Aumond
Low Ellington		20	John s John Wharton
Low Ellington		20	Margaret d John Wharton
Ellingstring		22	Ann wf Thomas Williamson
Breary Banks	Aug	5	John s John Walker
[Moorhead			Ellen d Peter *unfinished entry*]
Fearby	Sept	4	Mary d Peter Wrigglesworth
Swinton		12	Christopher Beckwith
Masham	Nov	21	Christopher s John Scurra

Warthermarske		23	Sarah wf Thomas Leadley
Fearby	Dec	23	Markeras Longstaffe
Masham		23	William Glew
Fearby		23	Margaret Langstaff [see two entries above]
Ellingstring		13	Christopher s Christopher Mason

Burials 1718/19

Warthermarske	Jan	27	Margaret wf John Oliver
Masham	Feb	7	Mr William Beckwith
Masham		12	Mary d Mr Thomas Hardcastle
Masham		18	Margaret Fothergill
Swinton	Mar	12	Ellen d William Lightfoot

Burials 1719

Ellingstring	Apr	9	Georg Ward
[fo. 22v]			
Warthermarske		14	Isack s John Olever
Masham		24	Elizabeth d Thomas Walker
High Ellington		29	Sarah Bedford
Healey	Jun	21	Mary Gill
Fearby	Jul	2	Mary wf John Hodgson
Masham	Aug	15	Anthony Thwaits
Swinton	Sept	1	Mr William Lightfoot
[no place]	Aug	18	Elizabeth d William Beckwith
Masham	Oct	5	Sarah d Edward Beckwith
Masham	Nov	9	Alice wf Christopher Smith
[no place]		13	Mrs Moon
Masham		14	Elizabeth wf Thomas Banks
High Ellington	Dec	20	Mary wf Peter Jackson
Masham		23	Jane Bland, wid
Healey		24	Jane Wintersgill
Ilton		24	Marmaduke Lodge
Masham		26	Henry Body

Burials 1719/20

Swinton	Jan	6	Christopher Peik (?)
Ilton		6	John Atkson [sic]
High Ellington		10	Christopher Jackson
Fearby		18	Thomas Bous
Breary Banks	Feb	16	Helen Arnett

Fearby	Mar	12	Edith Pickersgill
Swinton		20	William Burnett

Burials 1720

Swinton	Mar	31	Mary d Mr Gregg
Wardinhow	Apr	19	Thomas Benit
Healey	Jun	14	Esther wf Thomas Thorp
Low Ellington	Aug	20	Gorg [sic] s John Stelin
Masham		21	Samuell Pindar
Masham		28	Jonathan Walker
Low Ellington	Sept	22	Antony Wilimson
Swinton		24	Mary wf John Barnett
[fo. 23r]			
Masham	Oct [no day]		Ruth Ragg
Swinton Mill		30	Margaret Harland
High Ellington	Nov	20	Elizabeth Place
Moorhead		24	Ruth Sagar
High Ellington	Dec	6	Simon Body
Burton Const[ablery]		7	Richard Ripley
Low Ellington		22	Christopher Jackson & Elizabeth his wf

Burials 1720/1

Swinton	Jan	3	John Lambart
Healey		22	Catherine Smorthwaite
Nutwith Cote	Feb	3	Elizabeth d William Hall
High Ellington		11	Elizabeth Williamson
Fearby		15	Richard Carter
Swinton Green		19	Thomas Walker
Low Ellington		19	Elizabeth Williamson
Masham		27	Richard Imeson
Masham		28	Thomas Beckwith
High Ellington	Mar	5	Jane d Thomas King
Masham		13	Ann wf Henry Stevenson

Burials 1721

Masham	Mar	25	Agnes d William Lupton
Masham		29	Sarah Bramley
Swinton	Apr	7	William s William Imeson
High Mains		16	Ann d William Scot
Masham	May	6	Ann Wardrop

Roomer		12	Thomas Bateman
Masham		20	William s William Horner
Masham		27	Miles Clayton
Masham		28	George s Thomas Hebdon
Masham	Jun	1	Henry Hawkeswell
Masham		12	Mary d Jonathan Brown
Swinton		28	Jane wf John Hove
[fo. 23v]			
Ilton	Jul	12	Bettrice d John Place
Masham		19	A child of Thomas Wilson's
Swinton	Aug	9	Robert Burnet
Pickersgill		14	John Bennet
Swinton		17	Henry Jackson
High Ellington		29	Christopher Durham
Masham	Sept	4	Ann d John Robinson
Masham		8	A child of Samuel Bowes
Masham		15	Ann wf John Robinson
Low Ellington	Oct	4	John s William Williamson
Masham		10	Jane wf John Banks
Ellingstring		17	Richard Thompson
Moorhead		22	Elizabeth Bawtry
Ellingstring	Nov	8	William King
Healey Cote		22	John s Matthew Jackson
Masham		24	Ralph Horner
Low Ellington	Dec	1	Samuel Williamson
Swinton		2	Frances wf John Smith
Masham		8	Thomas Wilson
Masham		11	Peter Harland
Healey		16	Thomas a child of Christopher Rid
Masham		28	Ellin wf John Body

Burials 1721/2

Masham	Jan	15	Elizabeth wf Leonard Girsham
Masham		20	Jane Banks
Ilton		28	Francis s Ralph Horseman
Masham		29	John Boddy
Burton Constablery	Feb	3	Ann wf Thomas Gainforth
Ilton		19	Simon Hanley
Ellingstring	Mar	13	Francis Hebdon
[fo. 24r]			
Masham		20	Ann Pickersgill
Healey		23	Robart Smorthwait

BURIALS

Burials 1722

Masham	Mar	31	Ann Wardropp
Masham	Apr	11	William s Samuel Bowes
Masham		28	John Beckwith the sexton
Masham		29	John Pickersgil
Thorp	May	1	Dorothy Auton
Masham		3	Mary wf William Lewis
High Ellington		6	John Thompson
Ellingstring		9	Thomas Brown
Ellingstring		24	Jane King, wid
Sourmire		26	Peter Preston
Healey	Jun	10	Thomas Atkinson
Masham		27	John s Thomas Banks
Masham	Jul	6	Joseph s Jonathan Banks
Burton Constablery	Aug	17	Elizabeth a child of James Medcalf's
Masham		23	Anthony Medcalf
Ilton	Sept	13	Luce Milner
Low Ellington		16	Crispin s Thomas Winn
Swinton		25	Frances Richmond
Breary Banks		27	Jane child of Richard Gill's
Masham	Oct	2	Joseph s Joseph Pickersgil
Masham	Nov	8	Joseph s Mr William Horner
[fo. 24v]			
Ellingstring		20	Matthias s Richard Serginson
Masham	Dec	2	Elizabeth Jaques
Swinton		[ ]	Ellin d Marmaduke Smith
Masham		22	Sarah an infant of William Lupton's
Ellingstring		29	Mary d Thomas Williamson

Burials 1722/3

Masham	Jan	7	Ann Thompson
Burton Constablery		7	Marmaduke s James Medcalf
Masham		11	Jane d Joseph Pickersgil
Masham		11	Frances d Jonathan Banks
Burton Constablery		13	William a child of Thomas Gainforth
Masham		14	Joseph an infant of Thomas Godsalve's
Fearby		16	John Hodgson
Masham		20	Christopher s Thomas Clerkson
High Ellington		23	William s Henry Parker
Masham		24	Cicily an infant of John Pickersgil's
Masham	Feb	9	Christopher an infant of Christopher Smith's
Low Burton		10	Reverend Mr Thomas Johnson

Masham		11	Susan wf Jonathan Brown
Masham		12	Francis s Cicily Staveley
Masham		14	Ann d Robert Plewes
Masham		15	Ann d Richard Roginson
Masham		19	Robert s Thomas Hagstone
Masham		25	Jane Walker
Masham		27	Mary d John Scurrah
[fo. 25r]			
Masham	Mar	17	Elizabeth Beckwith
Masham		18	Thomas a child of Thomas Clapham's
Gollinglith Foot		18	Margaret d John Walker

Burials 1723

Pickersgill	Mar	25	Robert Walker
Masham		31	Margaret d Thomas Clapham
Ilton	Apr	7	Anthony Ryder
Ellingstring		7	Mary d Robert Plewes
Pickersgill		28	Robert s Richard Gill
Nutwith Cote	May	15	Jane Watson
Fearby		19	Mary wf Thomas Bowes
Low Ellington		24	Mary Allen
Fearby		30	William Ripley
Agill in the Moorhead	Jun	3	Richard King
Ellingstring		6	Francis Greathead
Healey		16	Christopher s Christopher Rid
Healey		28	Mary d Thomas Lye
[fo. 25v]			
High Ellington	Jul	5	Thomas Plewes snr
Ellingstring		[ ]	Mary Ascough, wid, bur. in East Witton church
Fearby		27	William s John Place
Fearby	Aug	3	Elizabeth Dawson
Ilton		23	Margaret d Ann Atkinson
High Ellington	Sept	11	Ann Durham
Healey Mill		16	Henry Ridd
Well		20	Thomas Walker formerly an inhabitant of this town
Masham		22	Troath wf William Smith
Fearby	Oct	3	Margaret d Richard Mankin
Stone Fold		6	John Horseman
Masham		6	Mr Thomas Ryder, grocer
Angram Cote		20	Richard Pickersgil in the parish of Witton
Fearby		21	Robert s Robert Ryder

Ellingstring		27	John Bennington
Masham		27	Grace Auton
Fearby	Nov	15	Ellen d William Pickersgill
Fearby	Dec	3	Maudlin d John Burnet
Masham		13	Jane Gray
Moorhead		15	Jane Wade
Masham		30	Grace Ward

[fo. 26r]   **Burials 1723/4**

Pickersgill	Jan	27	Ailce d Elizabeth Walker
High Ellington		27	Richard a child of Richard Wetherell
Fearby	Feb	7	Robert s Robert Dawson
Ilton		7	Ann Teasdale
Swinton		7	Susans [sic] Burnet
Masham		10	Edward Carter
Ilton		11	Christopher Kearton
Gollinglith Foot		14	Ester d John Walker
Masham		19	Jane Smith
Low Ellington		28	Ann d Thomas Winn
High Ellington		29	Dorothy Thompson
Masham	Mar	4	Margaret Thompson
Masham		8	Christopher a child of Ant. Watson's
High Ellington		9	Marmaduke Archer
High Ellington		9	Dorothy Plewes
Stotfold in Moorhead		19	Constance Burral

Burials 1724

Healey	Mar	25	Ann Glew
Healey		29	Ann d Edward Smorthwait
Fearby	Apr	2	Ann d Christopher Dawson
Ilton		2	Thomas s Robert Watson
Healey		9	Ozwald Medcalf
Healey		12	Mary Frank grand-daughter to Thomas Thorp
[fo. 26v]			
Masham		12	John Robinson snr
Healey		15	John s Henry Cragg
Masham		18	John Smith
Masham	May	22	Elizabeth d Thomas Hagstone
Fearby		25	John French
Masham	Jun	12	Jane d Edward Imeson
Masham		15	Mary Lupton

Masham		25	Charles s Henry Clement, curate of Masham, d. June 24
Toulerton or Sourmire	Jun	26	John s John Touler
Mickley		26	Mr Thomas Johnson formerly of Low Burton bur. here
Fearby	Jul	3	John s William Pickersgil
Masham	Aug	2	William Bancks snr
Masham		9	Ann d William Leeming
Ilton		13	Ann wf Richard Handley
Healey Cote		30	Ann wf John Walker
Ellingstring	Sept	18	George a child of George Wright's
High Ellington		22	Peter Jackson
Masham		22	Margaret Banks
Ellingstring		27	Elizabeth Norriss
Fearby	Oct	24	Grace Carter

[fo. 27r]

Masham		27	Edward Beckwith jnr
Ilton	Nov	8	Elizabeth wf William Mawer
Masham		15	Elizabeth Pindar
Masham		8	Edward s Edward Beckwith
Healey Cote		28	Ann Auton
[blank]	Dec	13	Catharine Haw
Ilton		21	William Teasdale
Ilton		8	James Teasdale

Burials 1724/5

Ilton	Feb	10	Christopher Lightfoot
Thornton Steward		12	Jane Castellane
Moorhead		25	Elizabeth wf Thomas Walker
Ellingstring	Mar	1	Margaret Jackson
Breary Banks		4	Thomas Walker
Low Mains		19	Jennet Rose

Burials 1725

Masham	Mar	29	William Lewis
Healey	Apr	3	Francis Smorthit
High Ellington		12	Mary wf Christopher Coats
Healey		16	Robert Wilson
Fearby		17	Edward Williamson
Fearby		25	Mary Tailor
High Ellington		29	Elizabeth Jackson

Moorhead	May	25	Peter Burrell [*altered from Burgess*]

[fo. 27v]

Burton	Jun	6	John s James Metcalf
Masham		27	Elizabeth d Thomas Banks
Warthermarske	Jul	6	George s William Metcalf
Fearby	Aug	1	Jane d John Hodgson
Fearby		2	Thomas s Richard Robinson
Healey		11	Elizabeth King
Masham		29	Ann Gainforth
Masham	Sept	16	John Gainforth
Ellington	Oct	17	Henry Parker
Moorhead	Nov	3	Elizabeth Wintersgil
Ilton		11	Cathrine Latimoore
Moorhead		18	Elizabeth Preston
Crab House		20	Ann Baker
Fearby	Dec	19	Elizabeth Williamson
Masham		21	Enoch Raggs
Fearby		24	Ann Hutchinson
Masham		25	Elizabeth Wardrop

Burials 1725/6

Grewelthorpe	Jan	2	Paul Crompton
Masham		30	Dorothy wf Thomas Hebden

[fo. 28r]

Ilton Low Side		31	Martha Walker
High Burton	Feb	9	Mr Samuel Beckwith
Moorhead	Mar	12	Elizabeth d Christopher Preston
Ellingstring		17	Margaret Williamson
Masham		19	Margaret Renard

Burials 1726

Masham	Apr	16	Troth Webster
Ilton		27	Mary Freer
Masham		20	Ann d John Jaques
Masham	May	31	Elizabeth Dale
Fearby	Jun	14	Robert Wintersgill
Fearby		26	Ann wf Marmaduke Wintersgill
Healey	Jul	7	Jane Metcalf
Breary Banks		8	William Walker
Ellington		10	Isabel Jackson
Healey		25	Dorothy Lye
Ilton	Aug	2	William Beckwith

Ellington		8	William s Thomas Bell
Masham		11	John Scurra
Swinton		26	Jane wf William Holliday
Swinton	Dec	13	Christopher s John Wrigglesworth
[fo. 28v]			
Sutton Penn	Sept	14	Francis Wharlton
Swinton		30	Thomas s Thomas Leathley
Warthermarske	Nov	24	Mary Leathley, wid
Swinton		27	Jane Imison, wid
High Ellington	Dec	1	Mary Parker
Masham		30	Henry Thompson

Burials 1726/7

Masham	Jan	1	Robert s Robert Jaques
Healey		14	Frances Windress
Fearby		25	Mary wf Henry Thwaits
Masham	Feb	11	Joseph Scurra
Swinton		19	Christopher Imison
Masham		22	Robert s Thomas Clapham
Fearby		27	Jane Smorthet, wid

Burials 1727

Masham	Apr	7	Michael Jaques
Masham	May	2	Thomas Gainforth
Ellingstring		4	Thomas Williamson
Masham		9	Thomas Banks
Fearby		26	Joan d John Wintersgill
Masham	Jun	15	Robert Asquith
Masham		10	Ann Metcalf
[fo. 29r]			
Ilton		10	John s John Watson
Fearby	Aug	10	William s Thomas Burneston
Masham		17	Thomas s Gorg [sic] Metcalf
Low Mains		23	Thomas Rose
Fearby	Sept	5	Marmaduke Wintersgill
Fearby		8	Dorothy Moses
Low Ellington		11	George Waine
Swinton		19	Dorothy Burneston
Fearby	Oct	7	Margaret Mankin
Healey Cote		26	Christopher Preston
Ellingstring		29	Ann wf John Jeff
Low Ellington	Nov	17	Henery Wilimson

BURIALS

[*blank*]		16	A poor man died in this Const[ablery], bur by overs[eers]
Ellingstring	Dec	16	Christopher Norwich

Burials 1727/8

Masham	Feb	2	Ann d Fransis Brigs
Masham	Jan	14	Richard Brown
Fearby		24	John Breary snr
Healey		[ ]	Jan Clag
Ellingstring		29	Mary Wite
Ellington	Feb	20	John Watson
Ellington		25	Ann Pickersgill
Healey		27	Frances Rud
High Ellington		29	Thomas Pickersgill
[fo. 29v]			
Swinton	Mar	1	Margaret Burnet
Moorhead		2	John s John Wintrgill [*sic*]
Low Ellington		3	Mary Hanley

Burials 1728

Masham	Apr	9	Grase Smothit
Fearby		17	Catharin Dawson
Swinton		23	Hanna Burnet

[*two entries taken from fo. 9v among the baptisms, but which should be here:*

[*blank*]	Apr	25	Abstrupus a child of Mrs Elizabeth Danby's died travalling toward Masham
Ellingstring		25	Elizabeth Chambers]
[*blank*]		26	A poor passenger called Margaret Toller
Moorhead Pott		29	Sara Scaif a child
Healey	May	3	Robert Plews
Low Ellington		19	Thomas Greg
Low Ellington		20	Reuben s William Williamson
High Ellington	Jun	19	Ann Hodgson
Masham		22	George Gainforth
Ilton	Jul	14	William Bell
Angram Cote (pa. East Witton)		24	Ann Watson, wid
Masham	Aug	10	Sarah Smith
Low Mains		23	Thomas Hudson
Kerby		24	Ann Pickersgill
Fearby		24	Richard Robinson
Swinton	Sept	10	William Imeson
Fairthorn		18	Mary wf Henry Skafe

31

Ellingstring		21	Richard Manking
High Ellington	Oct	13	Ann West, wid
Masham		14	John Jacques
Warthermarske		21	Thomas Medcalf

[fo. 30r]

Leighton	Nov	10	Mary Hanley
Low Ellington		23	John s Richard Hanley
High Ellington		24	Ellin Place
Swinton	Dec	3	Ann Burnet
Masham		8	Joshuah s Joseph Pickersgill
Healey		24	Margaret d Francis Glew

Burials 1728/9

Ilton	Jan	11	William Moiser
Low Mains		12	Thomas s John Beck
Fearby		30	Elizabeth wf John Blackburn
Ellingstring	Feb	9	Henry Tireman
Ellingstring		11	Thomas Willimson
[blank]		17	Wilfrey Dallow, stranger
Moorhead		26	Christopher Toler
Ilton		26	Leonard Pybus
Moorhead		26	Thomas Burill
Healey		26	Thomas Wilimson
Masham		28	Anne Gibson
Masham	Mar	1	Anne wf William Plughs
North Cote		3	Thomas s John Robinson

Burials 1729

Michel-how	Mar	28	Mary d William Burnett
Summerside		30	George Burrell
Low Ellington	Apr	1	Jane Atkinson

[fo. 30v]

High Ellington		15	Dorothy Parker
Moorhead		17	Christopher Tollard
Roomer		27	John Cowper
Ellingstring		28	Robert Walker
Ellingstring		29	Elizabeth Norish
Healey		30	Margaret Theeckston
Masham	May	1	Magdalen Gill
Moorhead		12	Richard Burell
Ilton		13	[blank]
Roomer		14	William Harland

Healey		22	William Johnson
Fearby		23	Mary Hodgson
[*blank*]	Aug	29	Ann d William King

[fo. 31r]

Swinton	May	24	Batina d Abstrupus Danby, esq.
High Ellington	June	2	George Pickersgill
Warthermarske		3	Elizabeth d William Metcalf
Ellingstring		6	Margaret Smorthet
Masham		6	Grace Plues
Warren House		14	Christopher s Rowland Hutchison
Warthermarske		15	Elizabeth Bennet
Pickersgill	Aug	8	Elizabeth wf John Smith
Masham Town		9	Ann wf John Gray
Swinton Green		10	John s Thomas Smith

[fo. 31v]

Warthermarske	Sept	2	Sarah Hanlah
Grewelthorpe		7	Thomas Galbert
Ilton		23	William s William Leedom
Fearby	Nov	6	John Hodgson
Aldburgh		23	John Johnson
Healey		25	Mary Glew
Fearby		30	William s William Pickersgil
Healey		30	Thomas Theakston
Masham	Dec	6	Jane wf John Thwaites
Ellington		10	Jane Parker
Low Wood		17	Marjary Ballan
Masham		17	Robert Jefferson
Masham		24	Anthony s James Sanderson

Burials 1729/30

Masham	Jan	1	George s William Hurd
Masham		2	William s William Johnson
Warthermarske		4	Elizabeth Trufit
Low Burton Park		8	Jane d James Metcalf
Swinton		11	Dorothy Burnett
Swinton		15	Mary Burnett, wid
Swinton		31	Ann d John Imison
Ellington	Feb	17	Thomas West
Masham	Mar	13	Susan wf Thomas Bramley
Masham		17	Elizabeth Horner, wid
Masham		20	John s John Weighell
Ilton		21	Ann Pickersgil, wid

Burials 1730

Low Wood	Mar	31	Ralph Ballan
Masham	Apr	3	William Smith
Masham		10	John Body
Masham		19	Robert Plews
Ellington		23	Thomas Wyn (Winn *in repeat entry on fo. 11r*]

[*The next two entries appear among the Baptisms on fo. 11r:*

Healey		24	Peter Carter, butcher
[*no place*]	June	16	Mary Horseman, wid]
Swinton		11	Frances Burnet

[fo. 32r]

Fearby		28	Ann Bowes
Fearby	Jul	24	Jane d William Pickersgill
Roomer	Oct	30	Peter Skaiffe

[fo. 32v *blank*]

[fo. 33r]

June 14 1730	Collected for the poor	Tho: Wrather	0. 3. 4
July 12 173[0]	Collected for the poor	Tho: Inman	0. 5. 0
Nov 29 1730	Collected for the poor	Tho: Wrather	0. 5. 0
Dec 27 1730	Collected for the poor	Tho: Wrather	0. 10. 0
Feb 7 1730[/1]	Collected for the poor	Tho: Wrather	0. 3. 6
Apr 11 1731	Collected for the poor	Tho: Wrather	0. 6. 0

[fos. 33v, 34r *blank*]

[fo. 34v   *cancelled entry:*

Collected at Whitsuntide at the Communion

May 24 1729	6s. 0d.	
July 6 1729	Collected at the Monthly Communion	6s. 6d.
Aug 3	Collected at the Communion	9s. 0d.
Aug 31	Collected at the Communion	4s. 0d.
Nov 2	Collected at the Communion	8s. 6d.
Dec 7	Collected at the Communion	2s. 6d.
Dec 25	Collected at the Communion	4s. 10d.
[1729/30]		
Jan 4	Collected at the Communion	3s. 8d.
Feb		5s. 6d
Mar		3s. 6d.

Mar 25	Collected at the Communion	1s. 6d.
Mar 27	Collected at the Communion	11s. 0d.
Mar 29	Collected at the Communion	8s. 0d.
May 10		7s. 2d.

[fo. 35r *blank*]
[fo. 35v]
Breifs Collected from Dec 6 1724

A Breif for Neath church collected	0. 3. 7.
A Breif for Michael & Grimston	0. 6. 2.
A Breif for Camps Hill	0. 4. 3.
A Breif for Wirksworth Church	0. 3. 5½.
A Breif for Market Lavington	0. 6. 5.
Breif for Cricklade	0. 5. 2.

Aug 22 Thomas Harlan was mared with Saray Tornboll
Aug 6   Rob. Hebin was mared with Dority Calurd

[*inside back cover:*   Fran: Storey hujus Ecclesiae Curate 12 Maij Anno Domini 1729]

[*End of Register*]

[Parish Register PR/MAS.1/4]

[*In PR/MAS.1/4 the curate signed the bottom of each page, on the majority of occasions in the middle of a year rather than at a year-end. Revd John Dale signs as curate until 1749 and was then succeeded in that capacity by Revd Robert Radclyffe. Between 1733 and 1751 some of the churchwardens of Masham also signed. The following churchwardens sign:*]

1733-4	*Tho: Clarkson; Robert Plews*	1743-4	*Peter Young; Marma: Ascough*
1734-5	*John Wighill; Tho. Cundall*	1744-5	*Jno. Bolland; Marmaduke Ascough*
1735-6	*Wm. Horner; Christopher Sturdy*	1745-6	*Robert Jaques; Willm. Renard*
1736	*John Wrather, John Rogerson*	1746-7	*Robert Blackburn; Thomas Banks*
1737	*no wardens sign*	1747-8)	*John Robinson; Richard Hanley*
1738-9	*Robert Rider; Wm. Holiday*	1748-9)	*John Robinson; Richard Hanley*
1739-40	*Thomas Wrather; Charles Hird*	1749	*Thomas Metcalf*
1741	*no wardens sign*	1749-50	*Joseph Calvert; Thomas Metcalf*
1742-3	*Moses Jackson; Matt. Jackson*	1750-1	*Robert Rider; Ralph Edon]*

[p. 1]   **Baptisms 1730/1**

| Masham | Jan | 17 | John s Jo: Gray |
| Breary Banks | | 31 | Sarah d Steven Smith |

Moorhead		31	Mary d Jo: Barker
Masham	Feb	5	James s Thomas Firbank
Healey		6	Ann d Jo: Carter
Healey		20	Mary d Christopher Reed
Healey		20	Edward s Jo: Nicholson
High Ellington	Mar	13	Elizabeth d Aron Jackson
[after Toulerton entry Mar. 27]			
Swinton	Mar	2	Ann d Abstrupus Danby esq. born & bapt.

Baptisms 1731

Warthermarske	Mar	27	Eliner d William Steel
Healey		27	Peter s Matthew Jackson
Ellingstring		27	Thomas s Joseph Steel
Toulerton	Apr	10	Mark s Mark Toulerton
Masham		13	Thomas s Peter Robinson
Ellingstring	May	30	William s Christopher Fawbert
Aldburgh	June	2	Eliner d Jo: Kirkby
Sutton Penn		8	John s Christopher Wharleton
Healey		7	Richard s William Hodshon

[p. 2]

Masham	Aug	22	Joseph s Benjamin Banks
Masham	Oct	5	Elizabeth d Thomas Clarkson
Masham		8	Anthony s Benjamin Metcalf
Masham		10	Mary d William Tomson
Ellington		24	Jacob s Thomas Touler
Ellington		30	Christopher s Thomas Jackson
Fearby	Nov	4	Robert s Robert Blackburn
Masham		12	Edward s Edward Crofts
Warthermarske		20	George s Thomas Leadley

[p. 3]

Healey	Dec	5	Thomas Crag
Ellington		14	Elizabeth d Wintergill [*sic*]
Ellington		27	Ann d Christopher Coats
Ilton		28	Matthew s William Taylor

Baptisms 1731/2

Ilton	Jan	16	Isabel d Jo: Watson
Ellingstring		22	Mannuel s Leonard Lye
Masham	Feb	12	Michael s Michael Raley
Moorhead		22	Elizabeth d Jo: Bennet
[blank]		26	George s George Metcalf

Masham	Mar	5	Ann d Thomas Gill
Masham		13	Hesleington s Jo: Robinson

note: Visitation at Masham April the 19 1732

Baptisms 1732

Warthermarske	Apr	22	William s William Glew
Healey		23	Edward s Edward Smethwait

[p. 4]

Fearby		22	Thomas Beckwith
Swinton		25	Mary d William Imeson
Healey	May	14	Robert s Christopher Smothet
Ellington		27	Aron s Aron Jackson
Warthermarske	June	16	William s William Glew
Swinton		16	Thomas s Matthew Imeson
Moorhead	July	8	Ann d Richard King
Swinton		8	Thomas s William Imeson
[*blank*]		9	John s Christopher Wharleton
Masham	Aug	2	John s John Body
Swinton		20	William s William Kirby
Masham	Sept	27	Jane d Mr Thomas Wrather
Aldburgh	Oct	7	Phillis d Jo: Kirby
Ilton		21	Ralph s Ralph Horsman
Fearby	Nov	8	Robert s Christopher Dawson
Masham		9	Jo: s Marmaduke Smith
[*blank*]		12	Jane d Jo: Whates
Moorhead		18	John s Jo: Malleby
[*blank*]		18	Ann d Mary Towler
Healey	Dec	2	Christopher s Christopher Rudd

[p. 5]

Baptisms 1732/3

Ilton	Jan	1	Mary d George Press
Healey		2	Robert s Matthew Jackson
Masham		6	Joseph s Matthew Gaines
Healey		13	John s Thomas Lye
Fearby		15	John s Nicholas Wade
Masham		21	Richard s Christopher Sturdy
Warthermarske		30	Thomas s William Metcalf
Masham	Feb	1	Mary d Henry Askew
Masham		22	Jane d Thomas Firbank
Moorhead	Mar	11	William s John Barker

Moorhead		17	William s Mark Towler
Moorhead		18	Stephen s Stephen Smith

Baptisms 1733

Moorhead	Mar	28	Jane d Thomas Plews
Masham	Apr	6	Elizabeth d Robert Smith
Ashfoot		7	Sarah d Henry Skeif
High Ellington		16	Elizabeth d Thomas Beckwith
Ellingstring		27	John s John Williamson
Fearby	May	10	Elizabeth d Edward Haukswell
Healey		13	Elizabeth d Robert Wintersgill
Round Hill		19	Thomasin d Peter Burrell
Masham		22	Isabella d Edward Ripley
Sourmire		27	Mary d William Hudson

[p. 6]

High Roomer	June	9	Chr[istopher] s John Oliver
Masham		17	Robert s Robert Wardropp
Body Close		23	Grace d John Walker
Ilton		30	Marmaduke s William Teasdale
Pott Hall	July	4	Mary d Phillip Rucroft
Masham		6	Christopher s William Thirkill
Healey		15	Matthew s Thomas Metcalf
Fearby		22	Thomas s John Nicholson
Fearby	Aug	5	Hannah d Edward Stephenson
Pott Moor		8	Elizabeth d William Jeff
Fearby		26	Ann d John Burnet
Fearby	Sept	1	John s Thomas Horsman
Masham		14	Frances d George Kay
Masham		16	William s Will: Rodwell
Ilton		22	Alice d Will: Blackburn
Ilton	Oct	3	William s Mark Hutchinson
Ellingstring		17	Christopher s Elizabeth Faubert, wid
Moorhead		31	Mary d John Bennet
Fearby	Nov	4	Mary d William Langstaff
Ilton		11	Eleanor d John Slee
Ellingstring		15	Luke s John Ascough

Baptisms 1733/4

Masham	Jan	3	Hannah illeg d John Wardrop jnr and Mary Ascough

[p. 7]

Masham		9	Mary illeg d Margaret Inman and Henry Procter jnr of Swinton
Masham		16	Joseph s Joseph Raily
Ilton		28	John s John Wells
Low Ellington		31	George s William Ashton
Ilton	Feb	2	Margaret d Anthony Barker
Ilton		2	John s William Walliss
Pickersgill		9	Ann d Simon Watson
Ilton	Mar	9	Elizabeth d George Foss
Grimes Gill[1]		9	William s George Metcalf
Masham		16	Elizabeth d Matthew Wardrop

Baptisms 1734

Masham	Mar	27	Mary d. Benj[amin] Banks
Healey Pasture End		30	Esther d Tho[mas] Graham
Masham	Apr	10	Isabella d Michael Raleigh
Swinton[2]		21	William s Thomas Harland
Healey		27	Peter s John Carter
Healey		27	Eleanor d Peter Toler
Sutton	May	5	Ann d Christopher Whorleton
Ilton		9	James and George twin ss Thomas Blades
Healey Cote		15	Barbara d John Ascough
Healey	June	1	Thomas s Thomas Craggs
Warren House		1	Elizabeth d George Kendall
Ilton		8	Ann d Peter Huthinson [sic]
Ilton		15	Mary d Christopher Miller
High Ellington		15	James s Abraham Illingworth
Low Ellington		20	Robert s Chr[istopher] Jackson
Swinton[3]		20	John s William King
Masham		23	Catharine d Robert Jaques
Masham		28	Joseph s John Robinson

[p. 8]

Masham	July	7	Matthias s Matthias Allen
Sourmire		21	Ann d George Barker
Aldburgh		21	Dorothy d Peter Brown
Ilton		29	George s George Press
Masham	Aug	4	Thomas s Michael Beckwith

---

1   *altered from* Pott Moor

2   *altered from* Ilton

3   *altered from* Masham

Masham		4	Margaret d Thomas Gill
Masham		6	Jane d Robert Hebden
Swinton	Sept	3	Faith d William Kerby
Masham		8	Margaret d Anthony Thwaites
Masham		15	John s Joseph Gibbons, a traveller
Masham		22	Matthew s Mathew Gaines
High Roomer		22	Elizabeth d Edward Scafe
Masham		27	Robert s William Herd
Masham		29	Marmaduke s Marmaduke Smith
Masham		30	Deborah d Peter Robinson
Lamb Hill	Oct	2	Dorothy d Mr William Beckwith
Masham		4	Ann d John Boddy
High Ellington[4]		6	Gillin d Aaron Jackson
Fearby		30	Prudence d Nicholas Wade
Healey	Nov	16	Ann d Edward Smothwait
High Ellington		17	Thomas s John Wilkinson
Swinton	Dec	1	Matthew s Matthew Imeson
Masham		6	Elizabeth d Joseph Calvert
Warthermarske		6	Thomas s John Watson
Masham		10	Robert s Robert Wardrop

[p. 9]

Baptisms 1734/5

Masham	Jan	3	Sarah illeg d Gabriel Kay and Ann Hagston
Masham		6	Francis s Thomas Firbank
Swinton		11	Hannah d Joseph Iminson
Masham		22	Jonas s Thomas Metcalf
Swinton Mill	Feb	9	John s Henry Buckle
Masham		13	Mary d William Johnson
Sourmire		16	Rachel d John Barker
High Ellington		22	Christopher s Christopher Coates
Leighton		23	Edward s Matthew Jackson
Masham		25	Mary d George Robinson
Masham	Mar	3	Ann d Henry Kendrew
Masham		9	William s John Banks
Masham		15	Mary d William Rodwell

Baptisms 1735

Ilton	Mar	25	John s Mark Hutchinson
Healey		27	Edward s William Metcalf

---

[4]   *altered from* Masham

40

Masham	Apr	7	Robert s William Plews
Moorhead		28	John s William Jeff
Masham	May	13	Jane d Thomas Clapham
Moorhead		18	Henry s Henry Scafe
Warren House		31	Ann d Peter Burrel
Swinton	June	7	John s William Robinson
Pickersgill		28	Jane d John Mallaby

[p. 10]

Masham	July	11	Thomas s Christopher Sturdy
High Ellington	Aug	9	Thomas s Thomas Beckwith
Masham		13	William s Charles Herd
Masham		23	John s John Musgrave
High Ellington		28	Thomas s John Robinson
Ellingstring		30	Eleanor d George Ascough
Fearby	Sept	14	Eleanor d Thomas Horsman
Masham	Oct	4	Elizabeth d George Hagstone
Sourmire		11	John s Thomas Barker
Masham		12	Matthew s Matthew Wardrop
Ilton		19	Ann d George Press
Howe	Nov	4	Margaret d James Robinson
High Ellington		6	Sarah d Abraham Illingworth
High Roomer		15	Elizabeth d John Oliver
Masham	Dec	8	Isabella d Thomas Hagstone
Low Ellington		11	Ann d William Ashton
Fearby		20	William s George Jackson
Towler Hill		21	Jane d William Hotson
Warthermarske		30	Mary d William Metcalf

Baptisms 1735/6

Masham	Jan	8	Dorothy d Matthias Allen
Ellingstring		10	Leonard s Leon: Lye

[p. 11]

Masham		18	Margaret d George Kay
Healey		18	Hannah d Thomas Metcalf
Warthermarske	Feb	21	Elizabeth d Anthony Barker
Masham		25	John s Henry Kendrew
Grimes Gill	Mar	6	Jane d George Metcalf
Healey		12	John s Thomas Craggs
Masham		21	William s Matthew Gains

Baptisms 1736

Nutwith Cote	Mar	25	Jane Thompson of riper years, a Quaker
Ellingstring	Apr	29	Brian s John Ascough
High Ellington	May	8	Mary d Chr[istopher] Coates
Masham		17	Esther d Benjamin Metcalf
Swinton		23	Rosamond d William Kirby
High Ellington	June	3	John illeg s John Hawxwell of Well and Eleanor Thompson
Sutton		4	Frances d Christopher Whorleton
Healey		20	Robert s Robert Wintersgill
Masham	July	2	Elizabeth d William Thirkil
Swinton		19	John s John Imeson
Lamb Hill	Aug	1	Mary d Mr William Beckwith
Masham		4	Margaret d Edward Ripley

[p. 12]

Swinton		20	Joseph s Joseph Imeson
Ilton		29	David s Edward Blackburn
Masham	Sept	3	Joseph s Peter Robinson
Healey		5	William s Christopher Rudd
Masham		14	William s William Beckwith
Fearby		21	Elizabeth and Margaret twin dd John Nicholson
Fearby		21	Rebeccah d John Burnet
Fearby		26	William s William Beckwith
Leighton	Oct	3	Edmund s Matthew Jackson
Gollinglith		16	John s John Bennet
High Ellington	Nov	3	Lydia d Christopher Jackson
Swinton	Dec	31	Matthew s William Robinson

Baptisms 1736/7

Masham	Jan	14	Judith d William Boddy
High Ellington		30	Ruth illeg d Henry Williamson of Low Ellington and Mary Bell
Masham	Feb	1	Anna d William Rodwell
Masham		4	Ann d Thomas Jew
Swinton		20	Elizabeth d Marmaduke Smith
Swinton		20	Margaret d Thomas Harland
High Ellington	Mar	6	Isabella d William Bradley
Towler Hill		13	William s William Hotson

[p. 13]

Ilton		19	William s Chr[istopher] Milner
Fearby		19	Thomas s George Jackson
Masham		19	Thomas s George Hagston

BAPTISMS

Baptisms 1737

Sourmire	Mar	26	George s George Barker
Masham	Apr	3	Elizabeth d Anthony Thwaites
Masham		14	Dorothy d Thomas Metcalf
High Ellington		16	George s Aaron Jackson
Summerside	May	14	Elizabeth d Richard King
Pickersgill		19	Nancy d Simon Watson
Healey		21	Esther d John Carter
Masham	June	9	Thomas s Charles Herd
Masham		11	Margaret d Mr Matthias Allen
Masham		18	Joseph s Henry Kendrew
Healey		21	Reuben s Peter Toler
Masham		29	Peter s Robert Smith
Warren House	July	10	William s Peter Burrel
Sourmire		10	Thomas s John Barker
Ilton		17	James s William Taylor
Masham		18	Mary d Joseph Calvert
Gollinglith		27	Christopher s Chr[istopher] Metcalf
High Ellington	Sept	8	John s John Robinson
Breary Banks	Oct	26	Matthew s Thomas Gill
Burton		28	Thomas s Joseph Norriss
Masham	Nov	13	Elizabeth d Thomas Gill
Swinton Mill		19	Thomas s Henry Buckle
Masham		26	Elizabeth d John Farrah

[p. 14]

Masham	Dec	7	Thomas s William Johnson
Fearby		10	Thomas s Thomas Horseman
Masham		11	Ann d Thomas Norriss
Low Ellington		29	John s Thomas Wintersgill

Baptisms 1737/8

Masham	Jan	6	Ann d Matthew Gaines
Healey		6	Ann d Thomas Craggs
Warthermarske		12	Peter s Edward Scafe
Healey		15	Rachel d William Metcalf
Howe		28	Eleanor d James Robinson
Ilton	Feb	3	George s George Press
Breary Banks		11	Stephen s Stephen Smith
Warthermarske		11	William s Anthony Barker
Masham		22	John s Mr John Lonsdale
Masham	Mar	24	George s Robert Hebden

43

Baptisms 1738

Sourmire	Mar	25	Joseph s Thomas Barker
Aldburgh	Apr	2	Richard s Peter Brown
York Gate in Wath pa.		3	Mary d John Wilks
Pickersgill		8	Joseph s John Mallaby
Swinton		8	Robert s Matthew Imeson
Masham		9	Dorothy d Matthew Wardrop
Lamb Hill		14	Catharine d Mr William Beckwith
Sutton		22	Christopher s Christopher Whorleton
Warthermarske		28	James s William Metcalf
Fearby	May	13	Robert s Robert Blackburn
Ilton		20	George s Edward Blackburn
High Ellington		27	Isaac s Abraham Illingworth
High Roomer	June	3	Henretta-Maria d John Oliver

[p. 15]

Fearby	July	2	William illeg s Elizabeth Williamson
Masham		8	Thomas s Peter Robinson
Swinton		9	Thomas s William Robinson
Ilton	Aug	6	Elizabeth d Peter Huthinson [sic]
Masham		13	George s George Kay
Warthermarske	Sept	2	Thomas s Thomas Jackson
Healey		3	Agnes d Thomas Metcalf
Masham		15	John s Thomas Thwaites
Low Ellington	Oct	21	William s William Ashton
Gollinglith		21	Esther d John Bennet
Swinton		23	Frances d Henry Smith
Masham		24	Mary d Henry Kendrew
Sutton in pa. Kirklington		26	Christopher s Christopher Firbank (son of Mr Thomas Firbank late of Sutton in Kirklington pa.) and Dorothy his wf, d Christopher Dale late of Pickhill, born & bapt at Masham
Healey		28	Catharine d Ralph Norriss
Masham	Nov	6	Anthony s Edward Croft
Masham		12	Jane d Thomas Ryder
Ellingstring		14	Dorothy d John Ascough
Ellingstring		23	George s Leonard Lye
Swinton	Dec	9	Christopher s Joseph Imeson
Swinton		22	Margaret d John Imeson

Baptisms 1738/9

Fearby	Jan	8	Samuel s William Beckwith

High Ellington		20	Leonard s John Wilkinson
Low Ellington		26	Thomas s Thomas Jackson

[p. 16]

Masham	Feb	8	Mary d Robert Wardrop
Masham		10	John s John Scurrah
Ilton	Mar	17	Martha d Richard Bain

Baptisms 1739

Ellingstring	Mar	25	George s George Ascough
Fearby		25	George s George Jackson
Masham	Apr	6	John s Thomas Norriss
Low Ellington		12	Thomas and Jane twins Christopher Jackson
High Ellington		14	Hannah d Aaron Jackson
Masham		17	Elizabeth d Charles Herd
Swinton		29	Ann d Marmaduke Smith
Healey		29	William s William Metcalf
Ilton	May	9	Jane d Christopher Hanly
Swinton		21	Dorothy illeg d Christopher Imeson and Margaret Walker
Healey		21	James s James Richardson
Masham		26	Eleanor d Robert Hodgson
Ellingstring	June	2	Richard s Richard Pickersgill
Masham		7	Ann d Mr William Beckwith
Masham		22	Charles s William Thirkill
Swinton	July	28	Frances d Thomas Harland
Masham	Aug	4	John s Michael Beckwith
Masham		26	Richard s Matthias Allen
Masham		26	Matthew s Thomas Hagston
Masham		26	Frances d George Hagston
Healey	Sept	23	Diana illeg d Ann Kendall,[5] wid
Low Mains		27	Frances illeg d Frances Margely
High Burton		27	Robert s Thomas Pickersgill
Masham		30	Dorothy d David Bell
Fearby		30	Joseph s Thomas Burneston

[p. 17]

Sourmire	Oct	13	Frances d John Barker
Masham		21	Mary d Anthony Thwaites
Low Ellington	Nov	1	Ann d Thomas Wintersgill
Summerside		6	Richard s Richard King
Low Ellington		13	Thomas s Thomas Wynn

---

[5]   *altered from* Wintersgill

Masham		20	Elizabeth d Henry Kendrew
Sutton	Dec	23	Francis s Christopher Whorleton

Baptisms 1739/40

Healey	Jan	2	Mary d Thomas Craggs
Healey		3	Mary d Thomas Gill
Towler Hill		12	Mary d William Hodgson
Swinton		18	Elizabeth d Jonathan Elsworth
Healey		26	Mary d Robert Wintersgill
Masham		27	Joseph s Joseph Calvert
Masham	Feb	16	Thomas s John Banks
Fearby		16	Jane d Edward Doughsy
Kell Bank		22	Mary d Peter Toler
Swinton	Mar	21	George s William Robinson
Sourmire		22	Esther d Thomas Barker

Baptisms 1740

Masham	Mar	30	Mary d William Frear
Masham	Apr	7	Susanna d Matthew Gaines
Marton cum Grafton		9	Ann d John Kay born at Brock Ridding
Ilton	May	11	Rebeccah d George Press
Masham		20	Thomas s Thomas Thwaites
Ilton	June	1	Edward s Edward Blackburn
Low Ellington		15	Sarah d Smythson Wynn
High Ellington		18	Ann d Abraham Illingworth
Masham		21	Thomas s Thomas Court
Healey	July	20	David s Thomas Metcalf
Low Ellington		24	Elizabeth d Thomas Jackson
Healey Pasture End	Aug	11	Christopher s John Walker
Pickersgill	Aug	16	David s Simon Watson
Fearby		21	Mary d Robert Blackburn
Aldburgh		23	Eleanor d Thomas Becroft
Masham	Sept	21	Mary d Christopher Kerton
Swinton		21	Ann d William Kerby
Fearby		28	Sarah d Thomas Horseman
Ilton	Oct	12	Hannah d William Walliss
Gollinglith		21	Mark and George ss John Bennet
Lamb Hill	Nov	28	Elizabeth d Mr William Beckwith
Masham	Dec	2	Peter s Peter Young

[p. 18]

| Masham | | 4 | Elizabeth d David Broderick |
| Pickersgill | | 6 | Jane d John Gill |

Baptisms 1740/1

Masham	Jan	6	William s Richard Thirkill
High Roomer		31	Mary d John Oliver
Howe		31	Esther d James Robinson
Masham	Feb	19	John s Matthew Wardrop
Ellingstring		26	George s George Kendrew
Masham	Mar	9	Thomas s Thomas Ryder
Ellingstring		15	Margaret d Thomas Faubert

Baptisms 1741

Low Ellington	Mar	28	Jane d Christopher Jackson
Masham	Apr	12	William s Thomas Beckwith
Burton Constablery		16	Dorothy illeg d Ann Cass
High Burton		16	Mary d Thomas Pickersgill
Healey		20	Thomas s Edward Thorp
Swinton		5	Mary d John Robinson
Masham		28	John s Robert Hodgson

[p. 19]

Masham	May	9	William s Mr John Bolland
Masham		11	Peter and Jane twin s & d Peter Robinson
Fearby		29	Matthew s William Beckwith
Swinton	June	4	Stephen s Joseph Imeson
Fearby		14	John s Marmaduke Wintersgill
Masham		21	Martha d Anthony Thwaites
Masham		26	Ann d Christopher Sturdy born 9 Nov. last
Fearby		29	Mary d George Jackson
High Ellington	July	26	Mary d Aaron Jackson
Masham	Aug	2	Thomas s George Kay
Low Ellington		18	William s Thomas Thwaites
High Ellington		25	Christopher s John Durham
Pickersgill	Sept	19	Sarah d John Mallaby
Masham		27	Ruth d Henry Kendrew
Masham		27	Mary d George Wilson
Ilton	Oct	2	Ann d Richard Pickersgill
High Ellington		23	Dorothy d William Broadley
Masham	Nov	11	John s John Atkinson
Ilton		18	Ann d William Walliss
Ilton		23	James s George Press

Breary Banks[6]	Dec	1	Eleanor d John Walker
Gollinglith		12	Eden d Christopher Metcalf
Masham		13	Timothy s Thomas Court
Masham		26	Elizabeth d John Scurraah
Masham		31	Thomas s David Bell

Baptisms 1741/2

Masham	Jan	7	Edward s Mr William Beckwith
Ellingstring		14	Elizabeth d John Ascough
Masham		24	Margaret d Thomas Norriss
Masham		31	Elizabeth d William Simpson
Fearby	Feb	14	Robert illeg s Eleanor Stephenson
Masham		26	Ann d Mr John Bolland
Healey		28	Margaret d Thomas Craggs
Sourmire		28	John s John Barker

Baptisms 1742

Swinton	Apr	3	Sarah d Ann Harland
Healey		17	Esther d Thomas Smothwaite
Masham		24	Mary d George Hagston
High Mains		25	George s George Mason

[p. 20]

Masham	May	3	Ann d William Hunter
Sutton		9	Dorothy d Christopher Whorleton
Masham		16	John s Thomas **Ryder**
Swinton		23	Jane d Matthew Imeson
Masham		29	Dorothy d Christopher Sturdy
Masham		29	Margaret d Thomas Thwaites
High Ellington	June	4	John illeg s Alice King
Masham		6	Mary d Matthew Gaines
Healey		13	Benjamin s Thomas Metcalf
Warthermarske		22	Francis s William Glew
Swinton		27	Edward s William Robinson, tailor
Healey	July	11	Ann d William Metcalf
Healey		17	Thomas s John Carter
Masham	Aug	8	Sarah d Thomas Gill
Ilton		21	Ann d Richard Bain
Ilton		22	Mary d Edward Blackburn

---

[6]   *altered from* Pickersgill

Masham	Sept	17	Robert s Clement Harrison
Sourmire	Oct	2	Chr[istopher] s Thomas Barker
Fearby		26	Thomas s Robert Blackburn, wright
Fearby	Nov	12	Ann d Thomas Dawson
Masham		21	William s Michael Beckwith
Fearby	Dec	26	Sarah d Edward Hauxwell

Baptisms 1742/3

Ilton	Jan	1	Dorothy d Richard Pickersgill
Masham		9	Thomas s Thomas Thirsby
Gatenby, pa. Burneston		29	Henry s Robert Dinsdale, born at Fearby
Masham	Feb	4	Mary d Henry Kendrew, barber
Masham		7	John s Mr John Bolland, grocer
Fearby		20	John illeg s Elizabeth Williamson
High Burton		21	Edward s Thomas Pickersgill
Swinton Mill		24	Jane d Henry Buckle
Healey		24	John s Edward Thorp
Healey		24	William illeg s Elizabeth Atkinson
Ellingstring	Mar	3	Christopher s George Ascough
Masham		16	Christopher s Edward Croft

[p. 21]

Baptisms 1743

Masham	Mar	29	Dorothy d Matthew Wardrop
High Ellington		30	Jane illeg d Mary Bell (born, as affirm'd by 3 women present at her birth, the 14 day of April 1740)
Swinton		30	Elizabeth d Joseph Imeson
Fearby	Apr	10	Francis s Thomas Horseman
Low Wood		12	William s William Horseman
Masham		21	Mary d John Chapman
High Ellington		27	Jane d Abraham Illingworth
Low Ellington	May	22	Joseph s Smythson Wynn
Masham	June	3	Margaret d Peter Robinson
Masham		5	Elizabeth d George Wilson
Healey Cote		19	Anna d Thomas Smorthwaite
Healey		19	Prudence d Robert Wilson
Healey		19	Mary d (Ralph Norriss if living and) Martha Norriss
Masham		26	Mathew s Thomas Ryder
Ilton	July	9	William s William Atkinson

Masham		10	Mary d Thomas Hutchinson, weaver
Masham	Aug	6	Mary d Lawrence Carter, shoemaker
Ellingstring		14	Jane d Benjamin Todd, weaver
Low Ellington		17	Thomas s Thomas Jackson
Masham	Sept	3	Charles s Peter Young
Lamb Hill		24	Dorothy d Mr William Beckwith (the second of that name)
Healey		25	Edmund s Thomas Metcalf, blacksmith
Masham	Oct	7	Elizabeth d John Atkinson
Fearby Cross Lanes	Nov	1	Robert s George Jackson
Masham		1	William s George Park of Burrill, pa. Bedale, born at Masham
Masham		4	Elizabeth d William Robinson
Ilton		6	Anthony s George Press
Healey		13	Mary d William Metcalf
Ellingstring		20	Mary d Thomas Faubert

[p. 22]

High Ellington	Dec	1	Christopher s Christopher Jackson
Nutwith Cote		19	John s Mr Thomas Ascough, born & bapt
Masham		25	Mary d Thomas Court

Baptisms 1743/4

Masham	Feb	7	Ann d David Bell
Masham		12	Joseph s Thomas Metcalf
Fairthorn		17	Hannah illeg d Eleanor Scafe
High Ellington	Mar	2	Elizabeth d John Durham
Masham		4	Christopher s Thomas Norriss
Gollinglith		10	Esther d Christopher Metcalf
Fearby		23	Sarah d Thomas Dawson

Baptisms 1744

Masham	Mar	30	Elizabeth d William Pickersgill, glazier
Ilton	Apr	1	Rebeccah d Richard Baine
Fearby		11	Thomas s John Cundal
Ilton		12	Peter s Peter Hutchinson
Healey		13	John s Robert Wintersgill
High Ellington		14	Moses s Aaron Jackson
Masham		15	Margaret d Richard Hanly
Masham		29	Hannah d William Simpson
Masham	May	24	Dorothy d Revd Mr John Dale, Curate of Masham, born May 22

Low Ellington		25	Elizabeth d Thomas Thwaites
High Burton		31	James s Thomas Pickersgill
Masham	June	3	David s Jane Broderick, wid
Sourmire		3	Elizabeth d John Barker
Masham		15	Jane illeg d Ann Boddy
Fearby		27	Sarah d Robert Blackburn, wright
Masham	July	1	Mary d John Scurrah, cooper
High Ellington		22	Margaret d William Broadly
Healey		22	Christopher s Thomas Craggs
Sutton		26	Barbara d Christopher Whorleton
Pott Hall	Aug	4	Edmund s George Barker
Stone Fold		11	John s John Blackburn
Low Wood		13	William s William Horseman
Gollinglith		23	Mary d John Walker

[p. 23]

Fearby	Oct	13	Jane d Marmaduke Wintersgill
Swinton		14	Ann d William Whitelock
Swinton		21	Elizabeth d Matthew Imeson
Warthermarske		23	Matthew s Thomas Jackson
Ilton		27	Jacob s Edward Blackburn
Fearby	Nov	16	James s James Williamson
Nutwith Cote		19	Samuel s Marmaduke Ascough
Masham		23	Jonathan s Peter Robinson, blacksmith
Masham	Dec	1	William s John Blews [*sic*]

Baptisms 1744/5

Ilton	Jan	5	Ralph s George Press
Nutwith Cote		6	Thomas s Mr Thomas Ascough, born Jan 5
Masham		7	Margaret d Thomas Huthinson [*sic*] junr
Masham	Feb	8	Frances d Clement Harrison
Pickersgill		16	Mary d John Gill
Sourmire		23	Mark s Thomas Barker
Masham	Mar	17	Alice d Thomas Theasby
Ilton		24	Richard s William Blackburn

Baptisms 1745

High Ellington	Apr	1	William s Edward Plews jnr
Masham		8	Henry s Henry Kendrew
Sourmire		20	Mark s Mark Barker
Masham	May	5	Jane d Mr John Bolland, grocer
Masham		27	Frances d John Shepherd

Masham		31	George and Frances s & d George Wilson
Masham	June	9	Isabel d George Hagston
Swinton Mill		16	Jane d Robert Hodgson
Healey		19	Sarah illeg d Mary Toler
Low Ellington		20	Ellen d William Ashton
Swinton	July	5	Isabel d Joseph Imeson
Ilton		21	John s Richard Pickersgill

[p. 24]

Swinton	Aug	9	William s John Robinson
High Ellington		31	Elizabeth d John Beck jnr
Masham	Sept	14	William s Thomas Court
Fearby		24	Robert s John Ryder
Stotfold		28	Elizabeth d Immanuel Teal
Masham	Oct	1	Elizabeth d Thomas Metcaff
Masham		7	Dorothy d John Thompson, wright
Low Ellington		8	Ann d Thomas Jackson
Healey		19	Edward s Edward Thorp
Masham		28	William s Robert Wardrop
Swinton	Nov	1	William s William Whitelock
Masham		3	Edward s Michael Beckwith
Ellingstring		28	Jane d John Ascough
Masham	Dec	9	Jane d Thomas Thwaites
Ellingstring		26	Jane d Thomas Fawbert

[p. 25]   **Baptisms 1745/6**

Masham	Jan	11	Thomas s John Atkinson
Masham		24	John s John Plews
Fearby Cross Lanes	Feb	22	Esther d George Jackson
Ellingstring		27	Jane d Robert Fawbert
Swinton		27	Mary d Thomas Metcalf
Masham	Mar	8	Thomas s Thomas Ryder
Masham		8	John s Abraham Illingworth
Masham		11	Mary d Revd Mr John Dale, Curate of Masham, born Mar 3
Masham		13	William s Thomas Theasby
Quarry House		23	William s William Lightfoot

Baptisms 1746

Ilton	Mar	28	Richard s Richard Bain
Summerside	Apr	14	Sarah d Richard King
High Ellington		20	Moses s Aaron Jackson

Healey		24	Frances d George Metcalf
Masham	May	16	Ann d John Shepherd
High Ellington		22	Mary d Christopher Jackson
Sourmire		31	David s John Bennet
Masham	June	5	John s Laurence Carter
Masham		8	Ann d John Scurrah
Agill		15	Debora d Richard Hanley
Masham		20	Susanna d Richard Hanley
Masham		29	John s Peter Young
Masham	July	4	Jane d Jeffry Clarkson
Healey		5	William s William Hodgson
Sourmire		6	Ellen d John Barker
Masham		27	Elizabeth d Thomas Norriss
Swinton	Aug	6	Thomas s Thomas Terry
Pickersgill		30	Isabel d John Mallaby
Masham	Sept	7	Thomas illeg s Esther Hanley
Ellingstring		14	Benjamin s Benjamin Todd
Ellingstring		17	Christopher s Christopher Hinly
Ellingstring		17	John s George Ascough
High Burton		26	Elizabeth d Thomas Pickersgill
Masham	Oct	5	Mary d William Robinson, tailor
Healey Cote		11	Thomas s Thomas Smothwaite

[p. 26]

Healey		12	George s Robert Wintersgill
Masham		21	John s Samuel Bowes
Fearby		25	Elizabeth d Robert Blackburn, wright
Fearby		25	Dorothy d John Cundal
High Ellington		30	Mary illeg d Alice King
Sutton	Nov	5	Jacob s Christopher Whorleton
Swinton		29	Mary d Thomas Dawson
Masham	Dec	21	Thomas s Matthew Wardrop
Nutwith Cote		21	Mary d Marmaduke Ascough
Low Ellington		26	George s George Williamson

Baptisms 1746/7

Masham	Jan	9	John s John Chapman
Gollinglith		12	John s John Walker
Masham	Feb	6	Charles s James Hird
Ilton		14	Ann d Edward Blackburn
High Ellington		17	Thomas s William King
Masham		22	James s Mr John Bolland
Masham		14	Richard s Clement Harrison
Swinton		28	Richard s William Whitelock

Swinton	Mar	10	Henry s Henry Smith
High Roomer		18	David s David Walker
High Ellington		21	Edith d John Durham
Masham		24	Christopher and George twin ss John Gill

[p. 27]   **Baptisms 1747**

High Ellington	Mar	29	Edward s Edward Plews
Healey	Apr	2	George s George Metcalf
Sourmire		24	Thomas s Thomas Barker
Sourmire	June	4	Ann d Mark Barker
Masham	July	7	John s John Atkinson
Swinton		14	Ann illeg d Susanna Breary
Masham	Aug	1	William illeg s Elizabeth Bearpark
Masham		1	Margaret d John Harrison
Masham	Sept	17	Margaret d Thomas Court
Healey		20	Esther d Edward Thorp
Masham		25	Mary d William Pickersgill
High Ellington		30	Ann d John Beck
Masham	Oct	1	Matthew s John Thompson
Masham		9	William s Thomas Lupton
Masham		11	Frances d John Shepherd
Breary Banks		27	Elizabeth d Thomas Ascough
Fearby	Nov	7	Edward s Marmaduke Wintersgill
Low Ellington		12	William s William Broadley
[p. 28]			
Ilton	Dec	11	Mary d Richard Pickersgill
Masham		11	Elizabeth d Samuel Bowes
Masham		12	Mary d Abraham Illingworth
Masham		18	Thomas s Thomas Thwaites
Ellingstring		29	George s John Ascough

Baptisms 1747/8

Masham	Jan	1	Richard s Richard Hanly
Quarry House		12	Elizabeth d William Lightfoot
Laddah Hole		21	Ann d Thomas Plews
Masham		21	John s Ralph Alderson
Ellingstring		22	Ann d Thomas Plews
Masham		24	Christiana d George Wilson
Ilton		28	Mark s Peter Hutchinson
Gollinglith	Feb	11	Jane d Christopher Metcalf
Masham		14	Hannah d Thomas Metcalf

Healey Cote		14	Agnes d William Hodgson
Ilton		20	Dinah d William Blackburn
Masham		22	Elizabeth d Ann Hunter, wid
Masham		23	Ann d Revd Mr John Dale, Curate of Masham, born Feb 22
High Roomer		29	John s John Houseman

[p. 29]

Masham	Mar	1	Joseph s John Atkinson
Low Ellington		3	Ursula d William Ashton
Ellingstring		18	Dorothy d Robert Fawbert

Baptisms 1748

Masham	Mar	25	Thomas s Thomas Hutchinson
Low Ellington	Apr	2	Abigail d George Williamson
Healey		16	Esther d Thomas Craggs
Ellingstring	May	15	Thomas s Thomas Fawbert
Masham		20	Joseph s John Gill
Low Wood	June	13	Margaret d William Horseman
Fearby		14	Elizabeth d John Cundal
Masham		15	Elizabeth and Mary twin dd Geffrey Clarkson
Ellingstring		16	Thomas s George Ascough
Swinton		27	John s William Whitelock
Sourmire	July	10	Phebe d John Barker
Stone Fold		10	Ann d John Blackburn
Summerside		12	Ralph s Ralph Eden
Masham		16	James s John Lupton
Gollinglith		24	Mary d Robert Walker
Fearby	Aug	5	Hannah d John Ryder
Healey		19	Ann d George Metcalf
Warthermarske		20	Mary d William Glew
Masham		21	William s John Scurrah

[p. 30]

Masham	Sept	1	Richard s Thomas Rogerson
Masham		11	Richard s Henry Thompson
Masham		18	Jane d William Rodwell
High Ellington		27	Christopher s Aaron Jackson
Masham		30	Isaac s John Robinson
Swinton	Oct	19	Susanna d Thomas Terry
Swinton Mill		25	Robert s Robert Hodgson
Masham		30	Thomas s John Clarkson
Ilton		30	Elizabeth d George Press
Masham	Nov	1	William s Thomas Ryder
Fearby Cross Lanes		15	Matthew s George Jackson

Masham	Dec	14	Eleanor d Charles Hird
Swinton		19	Thomas s Thomas Dawson
Masham		22	Margaret illeg d Ann Boddy
Masham		28	Margaret d Mr John Bolland

[p. 31]   **Baptisms 1748/9**

High Burton	Jan	1	Thomas Carter s Thomas Pickersgil
Swinton		11	Esther d Christopher Pickersgil
Masham		18	Ann d William Terry
Ellingstring	Feb	7	Christopher s Timothy Court
Masham		12	George s George Hagstone
Masham		17	Alice d William Banks
Low Roomer		18	William s Richard Batty
Masham		19	Mary d Thomas Banks
Swinton	Mar	13	Mary d William Danby of Swinton in Mashamshire, esq., born Mar 12

[p. 32]   **Baptisms 1749**

Masham	Mar	25	Isabel d Laurence Carter
		31	Rebeccah d Ann Jackson, a traveller
Gebdykes pa. Well	Apr	7	Thomas s John Banks
Masham		9	Dorothy d Thomas Norriss
Masham		11	John s John Wardel
Sourmire		16	Ruth d Mark Barker
Masham		23	William s William Thornton
Swinton	May	7	Jane d Peter Trees
Swinton		10	Matthew s Thomas Metcalf
Body Close House		26	David s William Walker
Masham	June	4	Sarah d Henry Kendrew
Ilton		5	Ann d Jonathan Lobly
Masham		10	Ann d Mr John Wrather, grocer
Masham		22	Thomas s Thomas Lupton
Stotfold		23	Ann d Luke Jefferson
Ellingstring	July	2	Ann d Thomas Emmerson
Ilton		9	Esther d Edward Blackburn
[p. 33]			
Stotfold		13	Robert and Mary twins Robert Ruecroft
Sourmire	Aug	11	James s Thomas Barker
Low Ellington		14	Ann d Henry Thompson
Masham		20	Esther d Thomas Court
		20	William s Nicholas Glave of Token House Yard in

			the pa. of Lothbury, London
Fearby		26	Mary d John Cundall
Masham	Sept	10	James s James Hird
Masham		17	Thomas s John Chapman
Summerside	Oct	14	George s Immanuel Teal
High Ellington		19	Mary d William King
Masham		29	Simon s John Shepherd
Gollinglith	Nov	8	Esther d Robert Walker
Masham		19	Mary d Ralph Alderson
Towler Hill	Dec	9	Mary d Christopher Mallaby
High Ellington		24	Elizabeth d Christopher Jackson
Ellingstring		24	Thomas s Thomas Plews
Fearby		25	John s John Ryder

[p. 34]

Baptisms 1749/50

Masham	Jan	3	Ellen d Thomas Theasby
Quarry House		11	Mary d William Lightfoot
Masham		30	Elizabeth d Thomas Todd
High Ellington	Feb	3	Esther d John Beck
Masham		5	Thomas s William Terry
Swinton		6	Marjery d Mark Ryder
Swinton		10	Margaret d Joseph Imeson
Masham		13	Margaret d John Gill
High Ellington	Mar	7	Mary d John Durham
Ilton		16	Agnes d John Richmond
Ilton		16	John s Jonathan Lobley
Masham		16	Ann d Richard Hanley

[p. 35]

Fearby		17	Jane illeg d Elizabeth Burneston

Baptisms 1750

Swinton	Mar	25	William s John Wood
Masham		26	George s John Robinson
Pickersgill		26	Isabel d Thomas Gill
Masham		27	John s John Brunton
Masham	Apr	1	Mary d Samuel Bowes
Masham		5	Troth d John Harrison
Low Ellington		7	Elizabeth d William Ashton
Healey		17	Elizabeth d Edward Thorp
Ilton		25	Robert s George Press
High Roomer	May	17	Ann d John Ouzeman

Healey Cote	June	24	Mary d William Hodgson
High Ellington	July	1	Jane d Edward Plews
Pickersgill		7	Hannah d John Mallaby
Fearby		29	Elizabeth d Aaron Alderson
Healey		29	Dorothy d Robert Wintersgill

[p. 36]

Fearby	Aug	9	Jane d John Wintersgill
Swinton		11	Hannah d Hugh Robinson
Ellingstring		14	George s Christopher Hinley
Healey		19	Hannah d Thomas Craggs
Ilton		20	Elizabeth d William Atkinson
Masham		21	Thomas s William Hardcastle, gent, born Aug 20
Masham		22	John s John Porter, wool-comber
Masham		22	Margaret d Thomas Banks
Masham	Sept	4	Margaret d Francis Thompson
Healey		24	Christopher s Robert Smorthwaite
Masham	Nov	4	Henry s Mr John Bolland born & bapt
Ellingstring		5	Mary d George Ascough

[p. 37]

Masham		8	James s Henry Kendrew
Masham		16	Mary d John Thompson
Swinton		27	Richard s Thomas Terry
Masham	Dec	1	Hannah d John Clarkson
Healey		1	Edward bastard s Mary Rudd
Ilton		9	Hannah d William Blackburn
Masham		15	Robert s William Banks
Masham		21	Henry s Geffrey Clarkson
Masham		23	Ann d Peter Young
Masham		26	Esther d George Wilson
Fearby		27	Peter s George Jackson

Baptisms 1750/1

Masham	Jan	20	Christina d John Atkinson
Masham		20	Ann bastard d Elizabeth Brown

[p. 38]

Masham		27	Thomas s Henry Thompson
Breary Banks	Feb	4	Thomas s Thomas Ascough
Masham		8	Mary d Mr John Wrather, grocer
Sutton Penn		11	Abraham s Ralph Eden
High Ellington		15	Thomas s John Jackson
Masham		18	Joseph s John Scurrah
Sourmire		23	Matthew s Mark Barker
Ilton		27	Jonathan s Jonathan Lobley

Roomer	Mar	2	Ann d Robert Bellerby
Masham		2	Mary d Thomas Thwaites
Gebdykes		10	Mary d John Banks

Baptisms 1751

Masham	Apr	8	Robert s Thomas Rider
Ellingstring		12	Robert s Robert Fawbert
Sourmire		21	Jacob s John Barker
Ellingstring		23	Sarah d Thomas Fawbert
Gollinglith	May	22	Eden d Christopher Metcalfe
Fearby	June	20	John s John Cundall
Body Close		20	John s William Walker
Masham		22	Stephen s Timewell Quick
Swinton Mill	July	3	Christopher s Robert Hodgson
Healey		3	Thomas s George Metcalfe
Low Ellington		14	John s William Bradley
Summerside		14	Ralph s John Walker
Masham		30	Elizabeth d William Terry
Masham		31	James posthumous s John Robinson
Masham	Aug	8	James s John Atkinson
High Burton		18	Edward s Thomas Pickersgill
Masham		25	Thomas s John Burnit
Masham		25	John s William Wildman
Masham		25	Elizabeth d Laurence Carter
Masham		26	Charles s Charles Hird
Swinton	Sept	1	Christopher s Thomas Dawson
[p. 39]			
Masham		15	William s William Hardcastle, gent, born Sept 14
Ellingstring	Oct	5	Jane d Thomas Plews
Ellingstring		5	Thomas s John Jackson
Masham		7	Thomas s Thomas Rogerson
Fearby		8	Thomas s John Rider
Masham		20	William s Timothy Court
Ellingstring		20	John s Austin Mullinder
Low Ellington		23	Robert s George Williamson
Gollinglith	Nov	2	John s Robert Walker
Masham		4	Anne d Michael Beckwith jnr
Ilton		9	Elizabeth d John Richmond
Ellingstring		13	Joseph bastard s Anne Steel
Masham		24	Peter s Thomas Theaseby
Low Ellington	Dec	13	Henry s Henry Thompson
Fearby		21	Mary d John Wintersgill

Baptisms 1752

Swinton	Jan	1	Elizabeth d Peter Trees
Masham		6	William s John Porter
Fairthorn		17	Jane bastard d Ellen Scaife
Ilton		18	Joseph s Edward Blackburn
Masham	Feb	14	Joseph s Joseph Atkinson
Masham		25	Ann d Thomas Croft
Masham		26	Jeffrey s Jeffrey Clarkson
Ellingstring	Mar	28	Troth d Robert Fawbert
Pickersgill	Apr	12	Robert s Marmaduke Hammond
Quarry House		26	Thomas s William Lightfoot
Masham	May	18	Ellen d William Rodwell
[blank]		19	[blank] Bell
Aldburgh		23	Thomas s Francis Metcalfe
Swinton		25	John s John Wood
Millstone Bank		25	Thomas s John Bellerby
Masham		29	Jane d Richard Hanley
Masham	June	11	Richard s John Brunton
Masham		21	Jane d John Burn
Low Ellington		25	Henry s John Beck
Breary Banks	July	22	Elizabeth d Robert Ruecroft

[p. 40]

Masham	Aug	16	Mary d William Hardcastle, gent
Low Ellington		16	David s William Ashton
High Ellington		24	Ellen d Christopher Jackson
Masham	Sept	17	Margaret d Ralph Alderson
Masham		24	Henry s Thomas Lupton
Masham	Oct	1	Sarah bastard d Ann Robinson
Masham		5	Mary d William Metcalfe
Healey Mill		9	John s John Vitty
High Roomer		19	Thomas s Robert Bellerby
Healey Cote		29	Richard s William Hodgson
Masham	Dec	2	Thomas s Mr John Bolland, grocer
Warthermarske		19	Elizabeth d John Ward

Baptisms 1753

Masham	Jan	2	Elizabeth d Thomas Hartley
Swinton		3	William s Christopher Pickersgill
Healey		15	Anna d Robert Smorthwaite
Healey		21	Elizabeth d Jonathan Lobley
North Cote		25	Jane d Thomas Metcalfe
Masham	Feb	18	Ann d John Atkinson

Fearby		18	Joseph s John Rider
Masham		25	Ellis d John Thompson
Masham		28	Esther d John Scurrah
Masham	Mar	11	Joseph s Michael Beckwith

[p. 41]

Ellingstring		22	John s Christopher Hinley
Swinton		26	Jane d Thomas Terry
Sourmire	Apr	8	Margaret d Mark Barker
Sutton Penn		9	Frances d Ralph Eden
High Roomer		15	Mary d John Ouzeman
High Ellington	June	2	Thomas s John Mainman
Sourmire		3	Prudence d John Barker

Huc Ex. per E.P. C:

Ilton		9	Frances d George Prest
Swinton		10	Stephen s Mark Rider
Warren House		16	George s John Kendall
Ellingstring		16	William s Austin Mullinder
Masham		20	Brian s Charles Hird
Masham	July	20	Ann d Thomas Thwaites
Masham		20	Elizabeth d John Wrather jnr
Masham		20	Frances d William Terry
Swinton Mill		26	John s Robert Hodgson
Masham	Aug	5	Hannah d John Banks
Masham		12	Thomas s Thomas Banks
Masham		21	Elizabeth d Thomas Halfpenny
Masham		26	Thomas s James Robinson
Masham	Sept	16	Frederick s Thomas Theaseby
Masham		16	John s Thomas James
Fearby		28	William s George Jackson
Swinton	Oct	1	Robert s Thomas Dawson
Masham		6	John s William Hardcastle, gent
Masham		16	Edward s Thomas Croft
Masham		17	Elizabeth d Henry Thompson
Ellingstring		20	Moses s Thomas Plews
Fearby		22	William s John Cundall
Ilton	Nov	19	Rachel d Edward Blackburn
Masham		23	Mary d George Wilson
Healey	Dec	6	Christopher s Robert Smorthwaite
Masham		11	William s Peter Young
Millstone Bank		21	William s John Bellerby

[p. 42]

Baptisms 1754

High Ellington	Jan	24	Benjamin s Christopher Jackson

61

Masham			Frances and Elizabeth twin dd Josiah Shepherd, bapt Jan 25 and bur Jan 27
Pickersgill		26	Nancy d John Mallaby
Pickersgill		26	Hannah d Thomas Gill
Masham	Feb	12	Christopher s John Atkinson
Masham		17	Ann d Thomas Court
Masham		22	Anthony s Francis Sturdy
Body Close	Mar	2	William s William Walker
Masham		6	Ruth d Michael Beckwith
Pickersgill		30	Esther d John Wilson
Fearby		31	Stephen s Robert Blackburn
Fearby	Apr	2	Ann d John Wintersgill
Masham		7	Thomas s William Metcalfe
Ash Head		18	Aaron s William Bradly
Masham		19	Ann posthumous d Thomas Rider

Huc usque Exam. per E.P. C:

Masham	May	14	Nancy d Robert Fleeming
Swinton		24	Hannah d Benjamin Akers
Masham	June	4	Francis s Francis Thompson
Ellingstring		7	Harry s George Jackson
Masham		10	John s Thomas Rogerson
Masham	July	14	William s Lawrence Carter
Ellingstring		21	Mary d John Lye
Body Close	Aug	4	John s James Strother
Swinton		25	Elizabeth d Thomas Terry
Fearby		30	William s John Rider
Healey		30	Marmaduke s Marmaduke Hammond
Masham	Sept	8	George s George Fletcher
Masham		8	Elizabeth d John Atkinson
Healey		15	William s Thomas Thorp
Masham		22	Thomas s Hugh Robinson
Ilton	Oct	6	Joseph s William Atkinson
Masham		6	Jane d Timewell Quick

[p. 43]

Ellington		10	Margaret bastard d Ellis Fennick
Breary Banks		13	James s Robert Ruecroft
Fearby		19	Isabel d Samuel Smithson
High Ellington	Nov	8	John s John Beck
Masham		10	Matthew s Jeffrey Clarkson
Low Ellington		14	Esther d Christopher Jackson
Swinton		16	Mary d Humphrey Wood
Masham		22	Ann d Richard Hanley
Healey		30	Catherine d George Metcalfe
Healey	Dec	7	Robert s Robert Smorthwaite
Swinton		8	Margaret d Thomas Dawson

Masham	29	Elizabeth d William Hardcastle, gent, born Dec 28
Masham	31	William s William Smith

Baptisms 1755

Stotfold	Feb	17	William s Thomas Ascough
Warthermarske		18	Ann d John Ward
Quarry House		18	John s William Lightfoot
High Ellington		21	Robert s John Wilkinson
Ellingstring		21	Jane d Austin Mullinder
Warren House		21	Elizabeth d John Kendall
Ilton		28	Ann d John Lodge
Ellingstring	Mar	3	Betty d John Tempest
Masham		12	Thomas s Thomas Clarkson
Masham		14	Elizabeth d George Pickersgill
Masham		19	William s Mr John Bolland, grocer, born Feb 7
Gollinglith		31	Hannah d John Mallaby
Healey Cote	Apr	27	Anna d William Hodgson
Low Ellington	May	4	Mary d Henry Thompson
Healey Mill		9	Ann d John Vitty
Fearby		9	John s John London
Ilton		10	Rachel d Edward Blackburn
Masham		22	Elizabeth d George Medley
Masham	June	5	Matthew s William Imeson
Masham		6	Elizabeth d Thomas Thwaites
Fearby		18	Jane d Humphrey Blackburn
Masham		22	John s Francis Sturdy
Masham	July	6	John s John Atkinson
Masham		13	Ann d Ralph Alderson
Ellingstring	Aug	11	Mary d Thomas Plews

[p. 44]

High Roomer		31	Thomas s William Deighton
Healey	Sept	14	Dorothy d Jonathan Lobley
Masham		14	William s Thomas Hartley
Masham	Oct	3	Isabel posthumous d John Wrather, grocer
Ilton		5	James s James Toler
Masham		18	John s Thomas Langdale
Masham		19	Joseph s John Jackson
Ellingstring		19	Mary d Jeremy Metcalf
Masham		26	George s Thomas Theasby
Ellingstring		27	Robert s Robert Bellerby
Low Ellington	Dec	18	Thomas s William Ashton
High Ellington		26	Abigail d John Durham

Baptisms 1756

Masham	Jan	1	Christopher s Jeffrey Clarkson
Masham		2	Ursula d Thomas Croft
Swinton Mill		25	Miriam d Robert Hodgson
Millstone Bank		30	James s John Bellerby
Masham		30	Catharine d John Mainman
Fearby	Feb	20	Betty d John Wintersgill
Fearby		20	Mary d Samuel Smithson
Fearby		27	Hannah d George Jackson
Healey		27	Betty bastard d Ann Towler
High Ellington		29	Nancy d Thomas King
Masham	Mar	7	Richard s William Hardcastle, gent, born Feb 23
Masham		19	William s William Britton
Swinton		21	Jane d John Wood
Swinton		22	Hannah d Mark Rider
Masham	Apr	11	Dinah d Thomas Ripley
Masham		12	Margaret d John Clarkson
Sourmire		14	Hannah d Mark Barker
Masham		20	Robert s Robert Webster, schoolmaster
Ellingstring	May	9	Lenny s John Lye
Ellingstring		9	Jane d Christopher Hinley
Fearby		15	William s Thomas Nelson
High Ellington		16	Alice d of a vagrant woman (name unknown) born at High Ellington
Masham		21	John s William Smith
Breary Banks		26	Elizabeth d Thomas Wintersgill

[Baptisms continued after Marriages section]

[p. 45]

Marriages 1730/1

Feb	23	Thomas Wintersgill and Ann Jackson, Ellington
	23	Samuel Veraty and Eliner Burral, Moorhead

Marriages 1731

Oct	2	Marmaduke Smith and Eliner Wardrop, Masham
	5	Peter Burril and Ann Atkinson, Moorhead
Nov	2	George Press and Elizabeth Wiliamson, Ilton
	10	Christopher Jackson and Jane Siver, Ellington

MARRIAGES

Marriages 1732

May	18	John Wilkinson and Ann Thompson, Ellington, banns
	18	Mark Hutchetson and Cathrina Walker, banns
June	29	Edward Ripley and Jane Body, Low Burton
Nov	5	William Strickland and Ann Skeif, Roomer, banns
	9	William Jeff and Mary Scot, Moorhead, banns
	11	William Horsman and Mary Tompson, Fearby, banns
	15	William Blackburn and Elcey Pibus, Ilton, banns
	23	Michael Cundall and Jane Hodshon, Masham, banns
[p. 46]		
	28	Jo: Hutchetson and Elizabeth Morland, Masham, banns
	30	William Atkinson and Margaret Smorthw[ai]t, Healey, banns

Marriages 1732/3

Jan	6	Christopher Chapman and Mary Place, Fearby, banns
	30	William Johnson and Ann Wharton, Masham, banns

Marriages 1733

Apr	26	Thomas Grime and Mary Walker, Moorside, banns
July	15	George Barker of Sourmire and Ann Blackburn of Ellingstring, banns
Aug	12	John Wilson and Ann West of High Ellington, banns
Oct	6	James Robinson of Howe and Esther Hodgson of Fearby, banns
Nov	27	Joseph Imynson of Swinton and Elizabeth Smythies of Ilton, banns
Dec	20	Mr Thomas Beckwith of Masham and Mrs Mary Wynn of Nosterfield, pa. Well, lic

Marriages 1733/4

Feb	21	Thomas Barker of Sourmire and Ann Horner of Ludge, pa. Kirkby Malzeard, banns
	26	William Metcalf of Healey and Eleanor Place of Fearby, banns
Mar	24	Henry Buckle and Mary Taylor of Swinton Mill, lic

Marriages 1734

[p. 47]

Apr	16	William Plews and Elizabeth Beckwith, Masham, banns
May	4	William Nicholson of High West Field, pa. Kirkby Malzeard and Elizabeth Pickard of Ilton, banns

	7	Henry Procter and Dorothy Pickersgill of Nutwith Cote, lic
Sept	26	George Ascough of Ellingstring and Eleanor Smothwait of Healey Cote, banns
Nov	10	Philip Kirton of Winksley Banks, pa. Kirkby Malzeard and Mary Burrill of Arnagill
	11	John Robinson of Langwith, pa. Well and Thomasin Parker of High Ellington
	12	Thomas Hagstone and Dorothy Mood of Masham
	12	William Boddy and Judith Udder both of Masham

Marriages 1734/5

Jan	6	George Almond of Exelby, pa. Burneston and Margaret Hutchinson of Masham
Feb	17	Roger Lofthouse of Arkleside, pa. Coverham and Margaret Plews of Ellingstring

[p. 48]

Marriages 1735

May	13	Mr William Beckwith and Mrs Hannah Faucet, Masham
Oct	8	John Imeson and Mary Ripley, Swinton
Nov	21	William Frear of Low Burton and Elizabeth Bell of Clifton, pa. [Thornton] Watlass
Dec	28	Edward Blackburn and Mary Croft, Ilton

Marriage 1735/6

Mar	21	George Burrell of Ash Head and Cicely Atkinson of Ilton, banns

Marriages 1736

Apr	27	William Broadly and Margaret Jackson, High Ellington
Nov	30	Matthew Wynn and Mary Glew, Ilton

Marriages 1736/7

Jan	9	William Spence of Azerley and Elizabeth Ballan of Masham
Feb	24	Thomas Gill of Pickersgill and Jane Place of Healey

MARRIAGES

Marriages 1737

Nov	7	David Broderick and Jane Sympson, Masham
	21	Thomas Thwaites and Grace Fothergill, Masham

Marriages 1737/8

Jan	2	John Wilks of Wath and Mary Wintersgill of Fearby
	26	Thomas Jackson and Elizabeth Leadly, Warthermarske

Marriages 1738

May	8	John Wardrop and Dorothy Thompson, Masham
	14	James Richardson of Kiplin, pa. Catterick and Ann Windrass of Healey
June	15	Gabriel Kay and Elizabeth Johnson, Masham
	24	John Burton and Ann Bointon, Ellingstring
July	16	Richard Pickersgill and Elizabeth Ascough, Ellingstring
Aug	24	John Graham of Birks, pa. East Witton and Mary Lye of Ellingstring

Marriages 1738/9

Jan	1	David Bell of Swinton and Mary Banks of Masham
	6	Thomas Wynn and Rosamund Miller, Low Ellington
Mar	6	John Stephenson of Hammer, pa. East Witton and Esther Smothwaite of Healey
	6	John Pratt of Swinton and Jane Pybus of Ilton

[p. 49]

Marriages 1739

July	21	Peter Young and Ann Hardcastle, Masham
	26	Walter North of Tanfield and Margaret Shepherd of Mickley
Nov	10	William Farmery of Middleton, pa. Wath and Elizabeth Pickersgill of Masham
	13	Richard Hanley of Kirkby Malzeard and Ann Wrather of Masham
Dec	2	George Graham of Birks, pa. East Witton and Ann Walker of Healey Pasture

Marriages 1739/40

Feb	2	James Hammond of Preston, pa. Wensley and Frances Vitty of Healey Mill

	21	Christopher Sturdy and Mary Hardcastle, Masham

Marriages 1740

Apr	10	William Johnson of Bedale and Mary Hamleton of Swinton
	13	Henry Walton of Masham and Ann Clarkson of Well
	16	George Kendrew and Ann Grason, High Burton
May	13	Christopher Kerton and Ann Dennison, Masham
	24	Christopher Place and Ann Fowens, Fearby
	26	Christopher Ripley of Fearby and Sarah Dawson of Quarry House
June	9	William Atkinson of Ilton and Catharine Hutchinson of Healey Cote
Sept	16	James Calvert of Mickley, pa. Kirkby Malzeard and Margaret Ripley of Masham
Oct	8	John Atkinson of Masham and Margaret Bolton of High Ellington
	23	John Durham and Ann Beck of High Ellington
Nov	11	William Morland of Ilton and Ann Plews of Ellingstring
	14	Matthew Metcalf of Grimes Gill and Margaret Skothorp of Swinton
	26	George Wilson and Frances Kay, High Burton

Marriages 1741

Aug	10	Richard Walker of Healey Pasture End and Isabel Pratt of Colsterdale
[p. 50]		
Sept	27	William Hunter of Masham and Margaret Pickard of Lamb Hill
	30	William Watson and Elizabeth Wilson of Dallowgill
Oct	10	The Revd Mr John Dale, Curate of Masham and Mrs Mary Denison of [Thornton] Watlass

Marriages 1741/2

Feb	6	Robert Blackburn and Hannah Maslah of Fearby
	16	Thomas Thirsby of Sleningford, pa. Ripon and Catharine Lightfoot of Ilton
	20	Henry Raper of East Witton and Mary Smothwait of Healey Cote

Marriages 1742

Apr	22	Edward Duffield of Kirby Hill by Boroughbridge and Jane Walker of Ellingstring
June	27	John Brown of Eavestone, pa. Ripon and Sarah Dribble of Ringbeck, pa. Kirkby Malzeard
July	18	Richard Langstaff and Margaret Theakstone of Low Ellington

Aug	12	William Hotson, widower, and Ann Kendall, widow, both of Healey
	14	Benjamin Todd and Elizabeth Faubert of Ellingstring
	16	Thomas Hutchinson, weaver, and Catharine Imeson of Masham
Nov	25	William Bateman and Mary Allinson of Kirkby Malzeard
Dec	7	Laurence Carter and Elizabeth Steel of Swinton

Marriages 1742/3

Feb	3	John Hanley and Jane Braithwaite, Stone Fold
	4	William Rymer of Bondgate, pa. Ripon and Jane Mitchel of Masham

Marriages 1743

May	24	John Blackburn of Fearby and Ann Walker of Lobley Hole
	30	William Elsworth of Newfield, pa. Kirkby Malzeard and Ann Batty of Low Roomer
June	23	John Cundall and Elizabeth Dawson of Fearby
Nov	10	James Slinger of Newstead, pa. East Witton and Elizabeth Gill of Swinton
Dec	28	William Garbert of Ripon and Dorothy Hinly of Ellingstring

[p. 51]

Marriages 1743/4

Jan	12	William Whitelock jnr and Esther Burrel of Swinton
	24	William Imeson of Swinton, weaver, and Elizabeth Walker of Lobley Hole

Marriages 1744

Apr	1	Mark Barker of Sourmire jnr and Margaret Horner of Angram, pa. Kirkby Malzeard
July	29	Edward Plews and Patience Walker of High Ellington
Sept	30	Thomas Ballan of High Mains and Mary Horner of Masham
Oct	18	John Beck of High Ellington jnr and Esther Ward of Warthermarske
Nov	12	Henry Thompson and Mary Whorleton of Low Ellington
	13	John Thompson, wright, and Dorothy Place of Masham
	15	George Williamson of Low Ellington and Mary Durham of High Ellington
	28	John Ryder of Low Mains and Mary Metcalf of Healey

Marriages 1744/5

Jan	1	James Hird and Mary Lupton of Masham

	1	Major Haw jnr of Laverton, pa. Kirkby Malzeard and Ann Hebden of Masham
	2	Evan Caunce of Rufford, pa. Croston, co. Lancs. and Mrs Ann Plumb of Masham
Feb	11	Charles Burrel of Ash Head and Ann Berry of Quarry House
Mar	7	Thomas Plews and Mary Jackson of Ellingstring

[p. 52]

Marriages 1745

May	29	Robert Fawbert of Ellingstring and Jane Rudd of Healey
June	4	John Cass of Well and Mary Ascough of Masham
	11	William Lightfoot of Quarry House and Hannah Stoney of Bracken Ridge, pa. Kirkby Malzeard
July	8	Jonathan Dovenar of Middlesmoor, pa. Kirkby Malzeard and Mary Robinson of Cover Head, pa. Coverham
	15	George Metcalf, blacksmith, and Jane Metcalf of Healey
	26	Christopher Pickersgill and Esther Clapham of Howe
Aug	4	Samuel Bowes and Ann Thompson of Nutwith Cote
	10	John Harrison and Ann Ianson of Masham
Sept	4	John Watson of Larton, pa. Kirkby Malzeard and Mary Scaife of Fairthorn
Oct	30	Thomas Metcalf, blacksmith, and Elizabeth Windrass both of Healey
Nov	10	Thomas Walker and Mary Thwaites of Masham
Dec	2	Matthew Metcalf of Healey and Faith Toler of High Ellington

Marriages 1745/6

Jan	12	George Tanfield of Aysgarth and Mary Wilson of Pickersgill
Feb	4	William Bucton of Spennithorne and Ann Thompson of Masham
[p. 53]		
	9	Thomas Nelson of Aldburgh and Christiana Smith of Breary Banks
	17	Mr John Plumb of Masham, officer of excise, and Mrs Hannah Beckwith of Masham, wid
	18	Thomas Plews of Healey and Elizabeth Clapham of Howe
Mar	2	William Hodgson and Margaret Imeson of Healey

Marriages 1746

Apr	1	William Stavely, carpenter, and Elizabeth Elsworth, wid, both of Swinton
	6	Mr John Gilbertson of Ripon and Mrs Mary Plumb of Masham
	22	William Thompson of West Scrafton, pa. Coverham and Elizabeth Ruecroft of Leighton
May	1	Thomas Rogerson and Mary Jeff of Masham

June	24	Thomas Lupton of Helm Ing, pa. Thornton Watlass and Dorothy Thompson of High Ellington
Dec	3	Joseph Atkinson of Masham and Dorothy Robinson of Fearby
[p. 54]		
	16	Ralph Alderson and Mary Kay of Masham

Marriages 1746/7

Jan	1	John Banks of Masham and Elizabeth Lambert of Fearby
	12	Matthew Wood of Warsel and Dorothy Vitty of Healey Mill
	14	John Wilkinson and Ann Lofthouse of High Ellington
Mar	2	George Caudbeck and Alice King of High Ellington

Marriages 1747

Aug	13	Charles Hird and Jane Lupton of Masham
	25	Thomas Banks and Elizabeth Plews of Masham
	29	Robert Walker of Healey Pasture End and Dorothy Lye of Healey
Sept	29	Henry Thompson and Elizabeth Strodder of Masham
Nov	10	William Dobby and Catharine Horner of Masham
	12	John Robinson of Masham and Mary Taylor of Swinton
[p. 55]		
	22	William Banks of Ilton, weaver, and Mary Plews of Sowden Beck House, pa. East Witton
Dec	22	Thomas Gill of Healey and Frances Margely of Fearby
	29	John Clarkson of Masham and Margaret Oliver of Swinton

Marriages 1747/8

Feb	2	William Imeson of Swinton and Hannah Kiplin of Masham
	16	Luke Jefferson of Spennithorne and Elizabeth Hanley of Lamb Hill
	16	John Jackson and Elizabeth Jackson of Ellingstring
	21	Peter Trees of Quarry House and Elizabeth Oliver of Swinton
Mar	7	Robert Smorthit and Ann Ianson of Healey

Marriages 1748

Apr	5	Richard Ackers of Melmerby, pa. Wath and Jane Healah of Swinton
	12	Edward Thompson of Scruton and Ann Walker of Ellingstring
June	28	William Terry of Swinton and Ann Scott of Masham
July	23	William Walker and Elizabeth Lawson of Body Close

[p. 56]

	25	Richard Sergeant of Ellingstring and Ann Ryder of Ilton
Aug	18	Thomas Scott and Ann Wells of Masham
Oct	17	John Brunton and Mary Hunter of Swinton
Nov	3	Mr John Wrather, grocer, and Mrs Elizabeth Brown, both of Masham
	10	Jonathan Lobly of Healey Cote and Elizabeth Wintersgill of Healey
	14	Matthew Place of Healey and Rebeccah Wilson of Masham
	15	Francis Thomson and Margaret Clarkson, both of Masham
	15	Robert Ruecroft of Leighton and Judith Braithwaite of Summerside

Marriage 1748/9

Feb	2	Christopher Imeson and Jane Burneston of Fearby

[p. 57]   **Marriages 1749**

June	12	Christopher Robinson of Brompton upon Swale, pa. Easby and Jane Mason of Nutwith Cote
Aug	21	Thomas Beckwith of Low Ellington and Ann Carter of Fearby
Oct	16	Luke Hutchinson of Leyburn, pa. Wensley and Rachel Procter of Masham
	23	John Porter and Ann Thornberry, both of Masham
Nov	20	John Freer of Grewelthorpe, pa. Kirkby Malzeard and Jane Greathead of Roomer

Marriage 1749/50

Feb	20	Charles Walker of Tanfield and Elizabeth Buck of Swinton

Marriages 1750

May	5	William Pickard of Melmerby, pa. Coverham and Jane Ryder of Low Mains
	8	Francis Metcalfe and Jane Wilson of Aldburgh
	21	Hugh Robinson and Ann Meek, both of Swinton, banns
	22	John Jackson and Ann Thwaites, both of Low Ellington, banns
[p. 58]		
Aug	2	John Johnson of Well and Elizabeth Barker of Healey, banns cert. by Richard Thistlewaite, Vicar of Well
Sept	29	John Mallaby and Hannah Wintersgill, btp, banns
Nov	6	John Burnitt, labourer, and Ann Hunter, both of Masham, banns
	8	James Metcalfe, labourer, and Elizabeth Robinson, both of Masham, banns
	12	John Strange, wool comber, and Isabell Gill, both of Masham, banns

| Dec | 5 | Austin Mulinder and Hannah Steel, both of Ellingstring, banns |

Marriages 1750/1

| Jan | 21 | Edwin Harrison of [Thornton] Watlass and Sarah Walker otp, banns cert. by Mr J. Stapylton, Rector of [Thornton] Watlass |
| Feb | 4 | Michael Beckwith and Ruth Whitton both of Masham, banns |

Marriages 1751

May	4	John Vitty of Healey Mill and Ann Ascough of Ellingstring, banns
	18	Timewill Quick and Jane Hagstone both of Masham, lic
June	1	John Bellerby of Millstone Bank and Mary Hinley of Ellingstring, banns
[p. 59]		
Aug	28	George Thirkell and Elizabeth Walker both of Masham, banns
Sept	16	Joseph Atkinson and Ann Hammond both of Masham, banns
Oct	12	Humphrey Blackburn and Anne Dawson both of Fearby, banns
	28	David Briggs and Mary Buckle btp, banns
Nov	11	Jeremy Metcalfe of East Witton and Mary Downham otp, banns cert. by Leonard Howson, Curate of East Witton
	12	Thomas Metcalfe and Jane Plews btp, lic
	30	John Burn of Kirklington and Mary Gill of Masham, banns cert. by R. Eller, curate of Kirklington
Dec	3	Thomas Hartley and Mary Imeson both of Masham, banns
	26	Robert Tempest and Jane Watson both of Masham, banns

Marriages 1752

Jan	6	Francis Glew and Deborah Dodgson both of Healey, lic
Feb	6	John Earl of Kirkby Malzeard and Margaret Dawson otp, banns cert. by Goodricke Ingram, Vicar of Kirkby
Mar	10	John Lye and Ann Steel both of Ellingstring, banns
	16	Marmaduke Hammond and Elizabeth Gill btp, banns
May	5	John Ouzeman and Hannah Harland btp, banns
Aug	4	Mark Plews and Ann Dovenor both of Body Close, banns
[p. 60]		
Nov	22	Francis Coates of Wensley and Mary Smith otp, banns cert. by J. Buchanan, Curate of Wensley
	23	John Tempest of Skipton and Dorothy Greathead otp, banns cert. by Walter Priest, Vicar of Skipton
Dec	12	Christopher Mankin of South Stainley and Ellen Williamson otp, banns cert. by W. Craggs, Curate of South Stainley

24   William Bretton of Topcliffe and Jane Hodgson of Kirkby Malzeard, lic

Marriages 1753

Jan	28	John Mallaby and Dorothy Walker btp, lic
Apr	23	John Wilson and Ann Carter, btp, banns
Aug	4	George Fletcher and Frances Kay both of Masham, banns
	25	Benjamin Akers and Hannah Raper btp, banns
Sept	2	William Smith and Margaret Calvert both of Masham, lic
Nov	19	William Plant and Rachel Barker btp, banns
Oct	22	Francis Sturdy and Sarah Longstaff both of Masham, banns
Nov	21	Christopher Ascough and Alice Wallis btp, banns

Marriages 1754

Jan	9	Christopher Jackson and Easter Jackson btp, banns
	10	Samuel Smithson and Mary Burniston btp, banns
Feb	18	Nathaniel Clissold of Reading and Jane Kirby of Aldburgh, lic
	25	James Strother and Grace Walker btp, banns

[p. 61]   **Baptisms 1756** [*continued*]

Warthermarske	June	2	Judy d Robert Ruecroft
Masham		8	Anne d John Porter
Swinton		19	Joseph s Benjamin Akers
Masham		20	Mary d William Terry
Masham		27	Mary d George Medley
Fearby	July	18	Mary d Thomas Holmes

Huc usque Ex. per Ed. Place Comm[missarium]

Masham	Aug	1	Mary d John Kidd
Fearby		8	Christopher s John Cundall
Ellingstring		8	James s Thomas Moor
Ash Head		11	Jane d William Bradley
Masham		15	Elizabeth d John Banks
Masham		18	Thomas s George Fletcher
Body Close		18	Elizabeth d William Walker
Masham	Oct	4	Michael bastard s Jane Hird
Masham		10	Margaret d John Baines
Healey		16	Hannah d George Metcalfe
Masham		16	Robert s Henry Thompson

Ilton	Nov	13	Elizabeth d John Hutchinson
Ilton		13	Nancy bastard d Catharine Stephenson
Swinton		22	Matthew s Peter Hammond
Masham	Dec	5	Mary d John Gill
Fearby		9	Ann d John London
Sutton		10	Margaret d Anthony Ballan
Masham		19	Roger s Mr John Bolland

Baptisms 1757

Masham	Jan	23	Ann d George Wilson
Pickersgill		29	John s John Wilson
Ellingstring	Feb	13	George s Robert Fawbert
Masham		13	Margaret d John Atkinson
Fearby		15	Timothy s John Rider
Masham		20	John s Michael Beckwith
Ash Head		20	Isabel d Thomas Atkinson
Masham		27	Francis s Adam Barnes
Fearby	Mar	5	Sarah and Jane twin dd Samuel Smithson

[p. 62]

Ellingstring		17	Margaret d Thomas Plews
Masham		23	Ann d William Joy
Masham	Apr	6	John bastard s Ann Walker
Healey		9	Mary d Edward Thorp
Low Ellington		16	Matthew s Matthew Craggs
Low Ellington	May	21	James s Henry Thompson
Warthermarkse	June	12	Mary d John Ward
Ilton		12	Alice d Thomas Casling
Burton		17	John s William Leeming
Healey		18	Robert s Christopher Walker
Swinton		19	Peter s Peter Trees
Swinton Mill	Aug	7	James s Robert Hodgson
Masham		14	Isabel d Thomas Thwaites
Masham	Sept	2	Jane d Peter Young
Masham		2	Thomas s George Medley
High Roomer	Oct	6	Jane and Catherine twin dd John Ouzeman
Swinton		20	Mary d George Morrel
Masham		21	John s Richard Hanley
Masham	Nov	7	Sarah d Francis Sturdy
Masham	Dec	4	William s Henry Hodgson
Breary Banks		12	Thomas s Thomas Wintersgill
Low Ellington		16	Thomas s John Beck
Masham		20	John s Edward Nicholson
Masham		20	William s William Towler

Healey		20	Ann d Mark Towler jnr

Baptisms 1758

Quarry House	Jan	11	Hannah d William Lightfoot
Healey		28	John s Marmaduke Hammond
Sutton		28	Mary d Anthony Ballan
Masham		29	William s John Baines, grocer
Gollinglith	Feb	1	Michael s William Walker
Masham		1	William and Elizabeth twins George Thirkill

[p. 63]

Ellingstring		25	Elizabeth d Robert Bellerby
Healey		25	Elizabeth d Jonathan Lobley
Healey Cote	Mar	5	Henry s William Hodgson
Fearby	Apr	2	Mary d George Holmes
Breary Banks		21	John s Robert Theackstone
Masham	May	14	Mary d William Imeson
Masham		18	Jane d Revd Mr Robert Radclyffe, Curate of Masham, born and bapt
Masham	June	22	Jane d William Hardcastle
Masham		30	Betty d William Smith
Masham	July	9	Ellen d Henry Storry
Masham		16	Edward s John Porter
Masham		16	Thomas s Adam Barns

[p. 64]

Masham	Aug	5	Frances d George Thornberry[7]
Low Roomer		6	Thomas s Robert Stoney
Low Ellington		6	Denis d Henry Thompson
Ellingstring		7	Betty d John Ascough jnr
Masham		27	George s Ralph Alderson
Low Ellington		27	Mary d Matthew Craggs
Fearby	Sept	8	Mary d Thomas Nelson
Millstone Bank		10	John s John Bellerby
Masham		10	John s John Richmond
Masham		17	Jane d John Crofts
Ilton		26	Nancy d John Taylor
Swinton	Oct	1	Benjamin s Benjamin Akers

[p. 65]

Round Hill		1	Thomas s Thomas Atkinson
Masham		6	Anthony s Anthony Sturdy

---

[7] *This entry is repeated under Aug 27 but with the note:* 'The 1ˢᵗ is right this being her admission'.

Swinton		7	Henry s Thomas Halfpenny
Masham		13	Joseph s Joseph Miller
Gollinglith		14	Jane d John Mallaby jnr
Round Hill		26	Mary d Robert Jackson
Masham	Nov	2	Mary and Barbary twin dd John Banks jnr
Ellingstring		2	Dorothy d Thomas Plews
High Ellington		18	John s John Durham
Ellingstring		18	Ann d Robert Tempest
Masham	Dec	3	Catherine d Richard Dobby
Masham		5	Elizabeth d George Fletcher
Masham		7	Nancy d Thomas Bradberry

[p. 66]

Low Ellington		9	Ann d William Ashton
Masham		11	Isabel d John Banks
Fearby		15	George s John Rider
Healey		30	Christopher s Christopher Walker

Baptisms 1759

Ilton	Jan	5	William s Thomas Jackson
Warthermarske		10	Palley d Thomas Theakstone
Healey Mill		10	Jane d John Vitty
Masham		14	Ann d Thomas Hartley
High Ellington		18	George s John Wilkinson
Ellingstring		18	George s Thomas Woburn

[p. 67]

Swinton		21	Mary d John Wood
Fearby	Feb	4	Mary d John London
Masham		7	Thomas s James Hamilton
Masham		14	Christopher s William Towler
Ellingstring		23	Reuben and Prudence twins John Lye
Masham		25	Thomas s John Bolland, grocer
	Mar	7	Peter s Thomas Hall (a serjeant in the 52 Regiment of Foot now in North America)
Ilton	Apr	2	Thomas s Thomas Casling
Masham	June	10	William s Lawrence Carter
Towler Hill		17	William s John Smith

[p. 68 *blank*]

[p. 69]

Burials 1730/1

Pickersgill	Feb	9	John Wiliamson

[blank]		23	Magdalene Wiliamson
High Ellington		27	Elizabeth Jackson
Fearby	Mar	2	Mary Stephenson
Ilton		8	Dorothy Horsman
Birks		10	Mary Walker
Masham		10	Andrew Cundall
Warthermarske		21	Thomas Garbet

Burials 1731

Moorhead	Apr	5	Richard Gill
Masham		17	Ann Beckwith
Masham	June	30	Edward Banks
Ellington	July	2	Jo: Whates
Healey		10	Thomas s Robert Wintersgil
Fearby		25	Mary Robison
Sutton Penn	Aug	12	Jo: Wharleton
High Ellington		29	Mary Jackson
Fearby	Sept	17	Austin Hodshon
Ellington	Oct	4	Henry s Jo: Beck
Masham	Nov	3	Ann Scott
Howe		10	Elsey d Nicholas Ward
Masham		22	Dorothy wf Simon Langdale

Burials 1731/2

Breary Banks	Jan	4	Ann Hudd
Ellington		11	John Atkinson

[p. 70]

Burials 1732

Warthermarske	Apr	8	Thomas Leadley
[blank]		11	Isabel Ward
Fearby		19	Hannah wf William Blackburn
Masham	July	6	Thomas Ovington
[blank]		17	Robert Ballan
[blank]		22	Ralph Ballan
Ilton	Aug	7	William Leetham
[blank]		27	Hannah Winn
Healey	Oct	25	Jane Metcalf, wid
Swinton	Dec	10	John Smith
[blank]		17	Robert Clepam

BURIALS

Burials 1732/3

Breary Banks	Feb	7	Stephen s Stephen Smith
Masham		8	John s John Body
Masham		9	Anthony Sturdey
Moorhead		9	John Theackstone
Ellington		14	Elinger Win
Masham		26	Ann Smith
Ellingstring		28	Christopher Farebert

Burials 1733

Healey	Mar	27	Thomas Sadler
Swinton	Apr	29	William [*altered from* Robert] s Robert Rippley
Masham	June	7	Elizabeth Glew
Low Ellington		10	Thomas Bell
Masham	July	20	Elizabeth d Elizabeth Ballan, wid
Fearby	Aug	24	Hannah d Edward Stephenson
Grewelthope	Sept	1	Margaret wf William Atkinson

[p. 71]

Masham		20	Barbara wf Thomas Banks
Masham		20	Will: s William Rodwell
Masham		27	Richard Rogerson
Ellingstring	Oct	15	Matthew s Thomas Jackson
Low Burton		20	Deborah Hanly
Healey	Nov	1	Elizabeth Williamson
Ellingstring		17	Christopher s Elizabeth Faubert
Masham		19	Eleanor Thwaites
Masham		29	Robert s Robert Wardrop
Ellingstring	Dec	28	Leonard [*altered from* Edward] s Leonard Lye

Burials 1733/4

Masham	Jan	22	Edward Beckwith
Masham	Feb	18	Ruth Hodgson
Ilton	Mar	2	Jane Toler
Masham		19	Elizabeth d Matthew Wardrop
Masham		19	William Kipling

Burials 1734

Ilton	Apr	5	Thomas Horsman
Laverton in Kirkby Malzeard pa.		12	Mary wf William Johnson
Grimes Gill	June	2	Isabella d George Metcalf
Fearby		4	Thomas Lambert
Swinton		21	Elizabeth wf William King
Swinton		22	John s William King
Ellingstring		22	Ann Brown
Ilton		24	George s Thomas Blades
Fearby		29	Mary d Ann Lambert

[p. 72]

Low Roomer	Aug	23	Percival Metcalf
Ilton		30	James s Thomas Blades
Ilton		31	William s Mark Hutchinson
Ilton	Sept	12	George s George Press
Fearby	Oct	31	Elizabeth wf Thomas Fawns
Fearby	Nov	6	Thomas Blackburn
Ellingstring		11	Mary wf John Williamson
Fearby		12	Susanna wf John Wardrop
North Cote	Dec	1	Ann wf William Leeming
Swinton		8	Ann wf William Whitelock
Masham		21	Peter Burgiss
High Ellington		30	Thomas Ascough

Burials 1734/5

Leighton	Feb	25	Edward s Matthew Jackson
Healey	Mar	9	Jane Metcalf
Masham		17	Christopher Smith

Burials 1735

Masham	Mar	27	William Watson
Healey	Apr	9	Mrs Isabella Atkinson, wid
Kell Bank		12	Thomas King
Masham		21	John Gainforth
Fearby		23	Thomas Ripley
Masham		29	Benjamin Banks

[p. 73]

Masham	May	14	Jane d Thomas Clapham
High Ellington		22	Eden d John Beck

Ellingstring		24	Elizabeth wf Matthew Scargan
Ellingstring	June	30	Mary wf John Bucton
Healey	July	10	Eleanor Johnson
Masham		16	Catharine Wardrop
Masham		21	Elizabeth wf Samuel Bows
Fearby		28	John Wardrop
Fearby	Sept	5	Thomas Ripley
Sourmire		14	Margaret wf John Toler
Masham		23	Joseph s John Robinson
Masham	Oct	5	Elizabeth Gainforth
High Ellington		13	Philip Buckton
High Roomer	Nov	3	Elizabeth Cooper
Ilton		8	Elizabeth wf Francis Dodsworth
Masham	Dec	8	Sarah wf Chr[istopher] Sturdy
Towler Hill		23	Jane d William Hotson
Healey		25	Robert Johnson

Burials 1735/6

Ellingstring	Jan	6	Dorothy d George Ascough
Healey		19	Francis Glew
Masham		25	Elizabeth d George Hagstone
[p. 74]			
Healey	Feb	16	Hannah d Edward Smorthwhait
Fearby		26	Elizabeth Breary
Ilton		29	Richard Watson
Masham	Mar	1	Michael Raleigh

Burials 1736

Masham	Apr	26	Mrs Mary Beckwith
Grimes Gill	May	27	George Metcalf
Masham	June	1	Jane wf Peter Wriglesworth
Fearby		5	Elizabeth d Thomas Fawnes
Warthermarske		7	William Burnet
Masham		20	Thomas Jaques
Masham	July	15	Elizabeth wf James Williamson
Fearby	Aug	3	John Wintersgill
High Ellington		18	Christopher Sivver
Masham		29	Mary d Robert Plews
Masham	Sept	13	John Beckwith
Low Mains		21	Jane Settle
Masham		29	Robert Topham

Masham	Oct	3	Edward Bearpark
Sutton		27	Daniel Ianson
Low Ellington		28	Thomas s George Boide, a traveler

[p. 75]

Masham	Nov	20	Marmaduke Beckwith
Masham	Dec	5	Ann Bradly
Masham		7	Thomas Banks

Burials 1736/7

Masham	Jan	14	Judith wf William Boddy
Masham		19	William s John Banks
Fearby		30	John Langstaff
Masham	Feb	8	Mary Horner
Pickersgill		15	Ann d Simon Watson
Healey		28	William s Christopher Rudd
Healey Mill	Mar	5	John Rudd
High Ellington		5	Thomas Gill
Healey		9	Ann Carter
Towler Hill		16	William s William Hotson
Masham		21	John s Michael Beckwith
Thornton Steward		22	John s Thomas Pattenson

Burials 1737

Healey	Mar	31	John s Thomas Craggs
Masham		31	Ann d Thomas Jew
Masham	Apr	21	Joseph s Mary Banks
Warthermarske		24	Henry Butler
Bedale	May	17	John s William Thompson
Gebdykes		29	Peter Ballan
Ellingstring	June	8	William s Elizabeth Faubert
Ellingstring		9	Joseph s Joseph Steel
Healey		13	Mary Metcalf
Healey		22	Reuben s Peter Toler
Masham	July	1	Rahab wf John Holmes
Ellingstring		6	Ann d Thomas Brown
Ellingstring		6	Catharine d Robert Norriss

[p. 76]

Ellingstring	Aug	8	Leonard s Leonard Lye
Body Close	Sept	4	Eleanor Walker
Healey		12	Ann Morland
Warren House		28	William s Peter Burrel

BURIALS

Place	Month	Day	Name
Ripon		30	Alice d Matthew Beckwith
Masham	Oct	18	Jane d Robert Banks
Ilton	Nov	26	John Hauxwell
Masham	Dec	6	Thomas Wright
Begger Bush		19	Mrs Margaret Robinson

Burials 1737/8

Place	Month	Day	Name
Masham	Jan	14	Thomas Robinson
Healey		18	Rachel d William Metcalf
Masham		25	Thomas s Peter Robinson
Fearby	Feb	12	Mary d Robert Blackburn
Swinton Mill		17	Anthony Watson
Healey		19	Elizabeth wf Thomas Lye
Ilton	Mar	6	Jane wf Richard Lightfoot
Well		23	Mrs Isabella Beckwith d Mr Edward Beckwith late of Nutwith Cote deceased

Burials 1738

Place	Month	Day	Name
Warren House	Apr	1	Peter Burrel
York Gate in Wath		3	Mary wf John Wilks
Masham		5	Mary d William Johnson
Warthermarske		10	William s Anthony Barker
Fearby		17	Thomas s Thomas Fowens
Fearby		17	Sarah Horseman
Masham	June	27	Dorothy Beckwith

[p. 77]

Place	Month	Day	Name
Healey	July	2	Ann wf Edward Smothwaite
Leighton	Aug	1	Philip Scyll
Arnagill	Sept	11	Ann Burrell
Healey Pasture End		21	John Walker
Swinton	Oct	19	Jane Imeson
Sutton in Kirklington pa.		31	Chr[istopher] s Chr[istopher] Firbank
Norton in Wath pa.	Nov	20	Stephen s William James
Ilton	Dec	24	Elizabeth Atkinson

Burials 1738/9

Place	Month	Day	Name
Healey	Jan	3	Thomas Smothwaite
Masham	Feb	13	Margaret Hanley

Masham		15	Joseph s Matthew Gaines
Masham	Mar	4	Thomas Hardcastle, gent
Ilton		7	Alice wf William Blackburn
High Ellington		9	Robert Williamson
Masham		10	Ann d John Boddy
Norton in Wath pa.		13	Eleanor d William James

Burials 1739

Masham	Mar	28	Benjamin Metcalf
Low Ellington	Apr	1	Thomas s Thomas Jackson
High Ellington		22	Elizabeth Pickersgill
Masham	May	1	Eleanor wf Charles Herd
[p. 78]			
Swinton		16	Robert Imeson
Masham	Aug	27	Frances d George Hagston
Swinton		28	Elizabeth wf [*altered from* d] Marmaduke Smith
Masham	Sept	22	Mary wf Mr John Lonsdale
Ilton	Oct	7	Jane d William Taylor
Warthermarske		12	William s Mary Burnet
Broughton by Foxly		18	Susanna d Carr English, a traveler
Masham		23	Margaret Sadler
Healey	Nov	3	Henry Craggs
Swinton		16	Dorothy d Margaret Walker
Grimes Gill		19	Grace Metcalf
Lamb Hill		25	Dorothy d Mr William Beckwith
High Ellington	Dec	4	Ann wf John Wilkinson
Sutton		23	William Whorleton
Pickersgill		31	Richard Gill

Burials 1739/40

Healey	Jan	4	James s James Richardson
Healey		5	Ann Theakstone
Masham		7	George s George Kay
Burton		8	Thomas s Joseph Norriss
Masham		12	Anthony s Edward Croft
Low Ellington		13	Thomas s Christopher Jackson
Masham		15	Simon Langdale
Breary Banks		16	Peter s John Mallaby
Masham	Feb	27	Anthony s Elizabeth Metcalf, wid
[p. 79]			

Masham	Mar	8	Mr Thomas Beckwith

Burials 1740

Masham	Apr	18	Elizabeth wf John Atkinson
Ilton		30	Ann d John Pickard
Ilton	May	11	Ann Farnel
Low Mains		18	Frances d Frances Margely
Masham		20	Martha Beckwith
Low Ellington		20	Jane d Christopher Jackson
Fearby	June	10	Elizabeth wf Edward Williamson
Masham		22	Mary d Mr John Lonsdale
Grewelthorpe	July	20	Henry Askew
Low Ellington	Aug	6	Elizabeth d Thomas Jackson
Masham		8	Thomas s Mr John Wrather
Masham		9	Mary Bramly
Fearby		9	Edward s Edward Stephenson
High Ellington		10	Alice Bolton
Fearby		18	William Pickersgill
Well		18	Frances wf Edmund Brockel
Ellingstring	Sept	6	Brian s John Ascough
Masham		14	Thomas Jew
Swinton Green		22	Christopher Burnet
Pickersgill		23	Jane Gill
Fearby		26	Ann wf John Place
Masham	Oct	25	Robert Hebden
Ilton	Nov	2	Dorothy wf Robert Watson
Crakehall		5	Thomas s James Robinson
Masham		22	Mary d Mary Brown, wid
[blank]		22	Mary d Thomas Brown, a traveller
Masham	Dec	4	Mary Brown, wid
Ilton		5	George and Margaret s & d George Press
Warthermarske		10	John Ward
Masham		13	William Thirkill
Ilton		13	Mary d George Press
Low Mains		20	Robert s Robert Ryder
Ash Head		29	Samuel Verity

[p. 80]

Burials 1740/1

Masham	Jan	8	Elizabeth d George Kay
Fearby		9	Mary d Robert Blackburn
Masham		10	Samuel Bowes

Masham		14	Jane Ashman
Healey		18	John Windrass
Swinton		26	Sarah wf John Imeson
Masham		27	Ann d George Kay
Masham		31	Alice d George Kay
Towler Hill	Feb	2	John Toler
Fearby		20	Mary wf James Ibbotson
Low Ellington	Mar	4	William Clapham

Burials 1741

Ilton	Mar	29	George Darby
Fearby	Apr	2	Dorothy wf Robert Blackburn
Ilton		5	Christopher Horner
Masham		10	Peter s Robert Smith
High Ellington		14	Ann wf William King
Masham		15	William Smith
Ilton		15	Robert Batty
Fearby		15	Margaret Hodgson
Masham		23	Elizabeth d Robert Smith
Burton Constablery		29	Dorothy illeg d Ann Cass
Masham	May	10	William s Mr John Bolland
Healey		13	Thomas Thorp
Masham		16	Ann wf Christopher Kerton
Masham		18	John s Robert Hodgson
Masham		24	Charles s Charles Hird
Masham		29	Thomas s Thomas Ryder
Fearby		31	Matthew s William Beckwith
Masham	June	26	Eleanor wf John Boddy
Masham	July	19	Thomas s Thomas Thwaites
Ilton		22	Sarah d Peter Hutchinson
Ash Head		27	Thomas Burrell
Ash Head	Aug	15	Eleanor Verity
Fearby		19	James Williamson
Mickley	Sept	14	Thomas s James Calvert
Ellingstring		22	Robert Fawbert
Healey		25	Eleanor Windrass
Low Ellington		29	William s Thomas Thwaites
Masham	Oct	1	Dorothy d Matthew Wardrop
Ilton		4	Martha d Richard Baine
Masham		17	Mary d Henry Kendrew
Swinton		18	Frances d Thomas Harland
Healey		25	William Gill

[p. 81]

86

Ilton	Nov	29	Ann d Richard Pickersgill
Blew Cragg	Dec	13	Margaret wf Christopher Frear
Healey		18	Mary Williamson
Masham		20	Sarah d John Plews
Low Ellington		26	Mary Wynn

Burials 1741/2

Masham	Jan	2	Ann Plews
Swinton		3	Thomas Harland
Healey		3	Beatrix d John Place
Ilton		4	Mary Watson
Masham		4	Elizabeth wf Benjamin Elwood
Masham		9	Edward s Mr William Beckwith
Swinton		11	Thomas Bennet
High Roomer		14	John Oliver snr
Ash Head		15	John s Mary Burrel
Pickersgill		16	Jane wf Thomas Gill
Healey		21	Lucy Smorthwait
Fearby		23	Ann d Christopher Dawson
Ellingstring		24	Alice wf James Milner
Fearby		25	John s Thomas Bowes
Fearby		26	Jane Watson
Masham	Feb	4	William Ianson
Howe House		8	David Clapham
Swinton		10	Sarah wf John Turnbull
Stone Fold		17	Marmaduke Ward
Masham		28	Ann d Mr John Bolland
Pickersgill	Mar	21	Elizabeth Walker
Swinton		22	Elizabeth Gregg

Burials 1742

Healey	Mar	25	William Hodgson
Ellingstring	Apr	3	Eleanor Thompson
Swinton		9	Mary wf John Imeson jnr
Healey		18	Mary wf William Hotson
High Ellington		26	Ann Thompson
[p. 82]			
Quarry House	May	17	Eleanor Lightfoot, wid
Ilton		20	William Pickersgill
Mickley		20	John Plews
High Ellington	June	6	William s Christopher Coates

Masham		12	Mary Metcalf, wid
Masham		24	Stephen Smithyes, struck dead in an Instant with Lightning June 22
Masham	July	16	Ann Thwaites
Masham		17	John s Thomas Ryder
Low Ellington		22	Thomas Wynn
Healey		27	Ann d William Metcalf
Ilton	Aug	5	Jane Braithet
Healey		20	Mary d Robert Wintersgill
Swinton		25	Jonathan Elseworth
Masham	Sept	3	Elizabeth wf Thomas Kay
Skelton Close		10	Eleanor wf Martin Thwaites
Masham		11	Thomas Beckwith
Masham		16	John Holmes
High Ellington		17	Hannah Cooper
Healey		24	Bridget d Mathew Place
Fearby		28	Ann wf Robert Clayton
Ilton		29	William Kerton
Stone Fold	Oct	2	John Ward
Azerley, pa. Kirkby Malzeard		5	Christopher West
Ilton		10	John Prat, weaver
Aldburgh		11	Eleanor d Thomas Becroft
Healey		14	Benjamin s Thomas Metcalf
Masham		14	Thomas s Mr William Johnson
Masham		23	Jane d Peter Robinson
Masham	Nov	22	Ann Jew, wid
Moorhead		24	Isabel d Peter Burrel
High Ellington		30	Thomas King
Masham	Dec	5	Matthew s Matthew Wardrop
Swinton		7	Elizabeth Clark
Adderton pa. Birstall		9	Thomas Brooks, a traveler dy'd at Lamb Hill
Low Ellington		19	Mary Inman d Margaret wf Smithson Wynn

[p. 83]

| Gollinglith | | 26 | Eden d Chr[istopher] Metcalf |
| Healey | | 30 | Mary Craggs |

Burials 1742/3

Masham	Jan	2	John s Matthew Wardropp
Fearby		21	Thomas s Robert Blackburn, wright
Ilton		28	Mary d Mary Kerton, wid

Masham	Feb	4	Mr William Beckwith, grocer
North Stainley pa.		20	Christopher Mankin
Ripon			
Low Wood		23	Margaret d William Horseman

Burials 1743

Healey	Mar	26	Catharine Glew, wid
Ilton		27	Elizabeth Bell
Low Wood	Apr	17	William s William Horseman
Healey		28	Catharine wf Robert Jackson
Masham	May	2	Elizabeth wf James Hird
High Ellington		5	John s Alice King
Ellingstring		7	Matthew Sergeant
High Ellington		16	Ann wf Edward Plews
Aldburgh		18	Sir Roger Beckwith, Bart.
Masham		25	Mary wf Christopher Sturdy
Masham		27	Elizabeth Boddy
North Cote		30	Francis Metcalf
High Ellington	June	1	Mary Gill
Healey	July	31	Mary d Ralph Norriss
Crab House	Aug	11	Mary Theakston, wid
Ilton		21	Alice Walliss
Masham		27	Joseph Pickersgill, glazier
Masham		28	Mary Milner
Masham	Sept	16	Mary d Matthew Gaines
Masham	Oct	3	Christopher s Edward Croft
Masham		7	Margaret d Peter Robinson
Masham		12	Mary d Thomas Hutchinson
Summerside		14	Ann wf Humphrey King
Masham		19	Mary d George Wilson

[p. 84]

Quarry House	Nov	13	Margaret wf William Lightfoot
Low Ellington		16	Hannah wf George Williamson
Swinton		21	John Imeson jnr, weaver
Swinton	Dec	6	Jane d Matthew Imeson

Burials 1743/4

Ilton	Jan	22	Anthony s George Press
Masham		23	Mary d John Chapman
Masham		26	Christopher Jeff
Low Ellington	Feb	3	Joseph Swainston

Ellingstring		10	Jane Fawbert, wid
Ilton		12	Mary d William Blackburn
Masham		18	Mary Thwaites
Masham		24	John Thwaites
Healey		27	Alice Craggs, wid
Swinton		28	John Imeson, weaver
Masham	Mar	5	Ann Wardrop
Healey		8	Phillis Toler
Masham		20	David Broderick
Masham		20	Ann d William Robinson 2dus [*i.e. Secundus*]
Swinton Mill		21	Henry Buckle

Burials 1744

Ilton	Mar	25	Richard Lightfoot, mason
Masham		27	John Mudd
Masham		27	Margaret d George Kay
Howe		28	Francis Robinson
Masham		29	William s William Robinson 3tius [*i.e Tertius*]
Body Close House	Apr	4	David s John Walker
Masham		5	William Banks
Masham		5	William Imeson, wright
Masham		6	Joseph s Thomas Metcaff
Masham		9	George Thornbury
High Ellington		15	Moses s Aaron Jackson
Fearby		18	Thomas Fawnes
Masham		20	Thomas Gill
Swinton		22	Miss Judith Danby d Hon. Abstrupus Danby of Swinton in Mashamshire esq.
Masham		25	Matthew Gaines
Masham		29	Dorothy Ragg
[p. 85]			
Masham	May	1	Dorothy Glew
Healey		2	Thomas Horseman
Healey		7	John s Robert Wintersgill
Low Ellington	June	1	Thomas Wintersgill
High Ellington	Aug	1	Mary Bell
Masham		18	Jane wf John Robinson, blacksmith
Fairthorn	Sept	8	Henry Scafe
Masham		23	Thomas Bramly
High Ellington		23	Mary wf George Caldbeck
Healey	Oct	4	Mary Wintersgill

Fearby		29	Ann d Richard Cass
Ilton	Nov	24	James Bell
Healey		28	Judith wf Thomas Sayer
Fearby		29	Hannah d Robert Blackburn, wright
Sourmire	Dec	10	Mark Barker snr
Sutton		18	Thomas Clapham

Burials 1744/5

Fearby	Jan	16	Thomas Carter
Fearby		29	Jane wf Christopher Rudd
Swinton	Feb	6	William Whitelock snr
Healey		7	John Ascough
Masham		16	Margaret Rogerson, wid
Masham	Mar	2	Troth Harrison, wid
Masham		23	Alice d Thomas Theasby

Burials 1745

Healey	Mar	25	Mary wf Thomas Metcalf, blacksmith
Healey		26	Thomas Sayer
Masham	Apr	12	John Wardrop snr
Masham		26	David s Jane Broderick, wid
Masham	May	21	Elizabeth d John Atkinson
Low Roomer		22	William Harland
Masham	June	3	Frances d John Shepherd
Low Roomer	July	15	Ann wf Richard Batty
Lobley Hole	Aug	11	Phillis Glew
Lobley Hole		31	Ann wf John Walker
Ellingstring	Oct	27	James Milner from Baldersby late of Ellingstring
Masham		28	Dorothy d John Thompson, wright
Swinton	Nov	10	Thomasin Parker, wid
Ellingstring	Dec	4	Ann wf Richard Serjeant
Low Ellington		10	John Wilton
Masham		29	Francis Hardcastle

[p. 86]

Burials 1745/6

Masham	Jan	2	Elizabeth wf William Plews
Masham		10	Mary Gainforth

Swinton		13	Peter Hall, carpenter
High Ellington		14	Troth wf Christopher Cotes
Masham		15	Susanna Hodgson
Birks pa. East Witton		18	Jane wf Ralph Lampton
Masham		21	Mr Charles Hardcastle
Aldburgh	Feb	27	Joseph Wilson
Low Ellington	Mar	8	Margaret Williamson
High Ellington		13	Christopher s Christopher Jackson
Swinton		20	Robert Ryder, shoemaker

[p. 87]

Burials 1746

Ellingstring	Apr	11	Jane d John Ascough
Masham	May	17	Ann d John Shepherd
Ilton		18	Frances d William Blackburn
		20	A Boy of about 2 years old the son of a Dumb woman a stroler and a entire Stranger
Swinton	June	22	Elizabeth Imeson
Fearby		25	Isabel Margely
Masham	July	21	Mrs Mary Johnson, wid
Masham	Sept	8	Susanna d Richard Hanly
Masham		11	Eleanor Ryder, wid
Masham		29	John s Abraham Illingworth
Aldburgh	Oct	5	Thomas Wilson
Fearby		20	John Walker
Masham		22	John s Samuel Bowes
Masham		25	Ann wf John Plews
Swinton	Nov	4	John Bennet
Healey		24	Esther wf John Carter
Masham	Dec	19	Robert Stodder, mason
Masham		22	Thomas s Matthew Wardrop

Burials 1746/7

Fearby	Jan	1	Elizabeth d Robert Blackburn, wright
Low Ellington		1	George s George Williamson
Swinton	Feb	6	William King
Swinton		24	John Burnet
Masham	Mar	2	Thomas Kay
Healey		3	Elizabeth d Matthew Place

BURIALS

Burials 1747

Healey	Mar	28	Maudlin wf Matthew Place
Healey	May	24	Frances d George Metcalf
Gollinglith	June	4	John Walker
Ilton		17	Isabel wf Ralph Horseman
Millstone Bank House		30	Thomas Bellerby
Masham	July	7	George s John Gill
Masham		21	Christopher s John Gill
Ellingstring		26	Ann wf Edward Blackburn
Warthermarske	Sept	15	Ruth Kendrew, wid
Masham	Oct	7	Robert Boddy
Masham		26	Mary wf William Lupton
Kell Bank	Nov	9	Mary d Mary Walker, wid
Fearby		9	Edward s Marmaduke Wintersgill
Fearby		14	Christopher Dawson
Masham	Dec	9	Benjamin Elwood

Burials 1747/8

Healey Mill	Jan	9	Jane wf John Vitty
Masham		12	Mary Rodwell, wid
Masham		25	William s Susanna Gaines, wid
Masham		28	Margaret Boddy, wid
Sutton		31	Ursula wf Robert Dawson
Warren House	Feb	2	Matthew Parrot
Masham		21	Ann Pickersgill
Masham		23	William Hunter
Masham		26	Thomas Hagstone
Ilton	Mar	18	Richard Baine

Burials 1748

Swinton	Apr	2	Christopher Gregg, gent
Masham		9	Mary Smithies, wid
Stotfold	May	3	William Metcalf of Stotfold s George Metcalf late of Grimes Gill deceas'd
Masham		14	John Plumb, officer of excise
Ilton		14	William Moreland
Swinton	June	28	John s William Whitelock
Stotfold	July	13	Mathew Metcalf
Sutton		17	William s Christopher Whorleton

Swinton		22	Cicely Imeson, wid
Fearby	Aug	10	Hannah d John Ryder
Swinton		24	John Burnet
Ellingstring	Oct	14	Mary Jeff
North Stainley pa. Ripon		14	John Mankin
Ellingstring	Nov	20	Ann wf Robert Plews
Ilton		24	Richard s Hannah Baine, wid
Skelton Close	Dec	8	Martin Thwaites
Ilton		10	Francis Dodsworth

Burials 1748/9

Summerside	Jan	3	Humphrey King
Masham		20	Ann d William Terry
North Cote		25	Alice Metcalf, wid

[p. 90]

Sutton	Feb	7	Robert Dawson
High Roomer		21	Jane d John Houseman
Ripon	Mar	19	Anthony Beckwith, gent

Burials 1749

Masham	Mar	28	Dorothy wf Joseph Atkinson
Swinton	Apr	6	Marmaduke Smith, a Papist
North Cote	May	19	Eleanor wf Thomas Metcalf
Ilton	June	6	Ann d Jonathan Lobly
Ilton		20	Thomas Watson
Ilton		23	Ann d Ralph Horseman
Masham	July	6	Henry Hebden

[p. 91]

Stotfold	Sept	5	Mary d Robert Ruecroft
Masham	Oct	30	Simon s John Shepherd
Helm Ing pa. Watlass	Nov	3	Hannah d Thomas Ballan
	Dec	28	John Brown a Traveller
Ripon		30	Elizabeth wf William Spence

Burials 1749/50

Masham	Jan	27	Mrs Margaret Bateman, wid
Fearby	Feb	4	Robert Clayton
Ilton	Mar	19	John s Jonathan Lobly

Burials 1750

High Ellington	Apr	8	Robert s Christopher Jackson
Fearby		9	Margaret Blades, wid
High Roomer	May	17	Ann wf John Ouzeman
Masham	June	20	Laurence Pickersgill
Masham	July	15	Sarah Mitchel, wid
Warthermarske		18	William Metcalfe
Masham	Aug	9	Elizabeth wf James Metcalfe
Masham		12	Joseph s John Atkinson

[p. 92]

Fearby		22	Jane d John Wintersgill
Swinton	Sept	1	Hannah d Hugh Robinson
High Ellington		14	Thomas Thompson
Healey		25	Christopher s Robert Smorthwaite
Swinton		27	Esther wf William Whitelock
Masham	Oct	14	Thomas s Peter Robinson
Healey		16	Christopher Frier
Fearby	Nov	10	Robert Blackburn
Swinton		17	John Tunbull [sic]
Grewelthorpe		29	Elizabeth Burnet, wid
Stotfold	Dec	1	Richard Burrill

Burials 1750/1

Masham	Jan	10	Henry s Geffrey Clarkson
Masham		16	Barbara Banks, wid
Pickersgill		21	Martha d John Gill
Swinton		24	Mary wf George Imeson
High Ellington		30	Abigail Durham, wid
Masham	Feb	2	Margaret wf Robert Ripley

[p. 93]

Masham		4	William Lewis
High Ellington		5	Elizabeth Thompson, wid
High Ellington		6	Bridget wf Robert Smorthwaite
Masham		21	John Robinson
Swinton	Mar	14	The Hon. Abstrupus Danby Esq.

Burials 1751

Healey	Apr	19	John Ascough
Masham		28	Edward s Edward Croft
Masham	May	25	Margaret Thwaites

Sourmire		26	Jacob s John Barker
Aldburgh	June	11	Mary Wilson, wid
Ellingstring	Aug	12	Thomas s Peter Jackson
Masham		18	James s John Atkinson
Tanfield		23	Barbary d James Buck
Masham	Oct	11	Miss Anne Hildyard
Masham	Nov	7	Anne d Michael Beckwith jnr
Masham		16	Mary d John Thompson
Masham	Dec	25	Ann d Richard Hanley
Summerside		29	Richard s Richard King

Burials 1752

High Ellington	Jan	15	Isaac s Thomas Towler
Masham		20	John Burnit
Ilton		24	Jonathan s Jonathan Lobley
Swinton		27	Ralph Lambton
Sourmire		30	Ann wf Thomas Barker
Healey	Feb	7	Magdalen Smorthwaite
Masham		25	Joseph s Joseph Atkinson
Body Close	Mar	22	Dorothy wf Mark Plews
Stotfold	May	6	William s Thomas Ascough
Birks		7	Ellen Burnit, wid
Masham		12	Robert Wilson
Ellingstring		23	[*blank*] d Thomas Fawbert

[p. 94]

Masham		29	Thomas Winn
Masham	June	23	Jane d John Burn
Masham		30	Mary wf John Burn
Masham	July	7	Jane bastard d Sarah Body
Stone Fold		12	John s John Blackburn
Masham		12	Mary d Thomas Thwaites
Masham		13	Joseph s William Pickersgill
Sutton Penn		14	Thomas s Austin Hodgson
Masham		17	Peter s Thomas Theaseby
Bedale		19	William s John Plews
Masham	Aug	4	Elizabeth d Jeffrey Clarkson
Masham		12	Mary d William Robinson
Masham		13	Thomas s John Chapman
Low Ellington		19	Jane d William Ashton
Low Ellington		21	Ann d William Ashton
Masham		23	Elizabeth d Thomas Halfpenny
Masham		24	Mary d Thomas Banks
Masham		24	William s Thomas Rider

Masham	Sept	21	Catharine d Robert Jaques
Ilton	Oct	5	Joseph s Edward Blackburn
Fearby		6	William s George Jackson
Fairthorn		11	Hannah d Ellen Scaife
Ilton		14	Thomas Milner
Fairthorn		17	Jane d Ellen Scaife
Masham		20	Mary d Mary Ascough, wid
Pickersgill	Nov	19	Jane wf John Mallaby
Ellingstring		30	Martha d Ann Emmerson
Brigwith	Dec	17	Dorothy Brown

Burials 1753

Swinton	Jan	12	William Holliday
Healey		16	Anna d Robert Smorthwaite
North Cote		26	Jane wf Thomas Metcalfe
High Ellington	Feb	13	Ellen d Christopher Jackson
Grewelthorpe		15	Mary d Thomas Ascough
Healey	Mar	8	Dorothy d Christopher Wharlton
Gollinglith		13	Robert Walker

[p. 95]

Masham		25	Joseph s Michael Beckwith
Settle	Apr	8	Charles Ward
Low Ellington		15	Jane Horner
Body Close	May	15	John Walker
Ilton		24	James s George Prest
Warthermarske		25	Elizabeth wf William Oliver
Masham		27	Ann d Sicily [sic] Staveley
Ellingstring	June	17	Elizabeth wf John Jackson
Ellingstring	July	25	Richard Williamson
Masham	Aug	25	Judith d William Body
Healey	Sept	9	Elizabeth wf Thomas Plews
Swinton Mill	Oct	17	Jane d Robert Hodgson
Sourmire		23	John Barker
Leighton		27	Mary wf Robert Ruecroft
Masham		30	Elizabeth d Henry Thompson
Masham	Nov	29	Mary Ascough, wid
Burton Constablery		29	Joseph s Joseph Norridge
Masham	Dec	10	Ellen Sturdy, wid
Masham		10	Thomas Rider
Ilton		11	Frances d George Prest
Masham		24	Jane wf Thomas Clarkson
Masham		24	Elizabeth Hardcastle, wid
Healey		26	Christopher s Robert Smorthwaite

Burials 1754

Ilton	Jan	7	Ann Hauxwell
High Ellington		23	Jane d Christopher Jackson
Ilton		29	Rachel d Edward Blackburn
Fearby	Feb	12	William Blackburn
Stainley		17	Anne wf John Walton
Masham	Mar	12	Frederick s Thomas Theaseby
Ilton		16	Jane wf Matthew Taylor
Fearby		25	Edward Hawxwell
Fearby	Apr	3	Christopher Hodgson
Millstone Bank		5	William s John Bellerby
Stainley pa. Ripon		15	John Vitty
Masham	June	16	Thomas s Mr John Bolland
Masham	July	6	Lucy Gainforth
Ilton	Aug	16	Elizabeth wf John Atkinson
Swinton	Sept	10	Mary Reynard, wid
Pickersgill	Oct	1	Frances wf Thomas Gill
Healey		4	Robert Jackson
Ellington		10	Ellis Fennick
Sutton Penn		16	Ralph Eden
Ellingstring	Nov	12	John Hinley
Masham		12	Matthew s Jeffrey Clarkson

Burials 1755

Masham	Jan	4	William Oliver
Masham		8	John Plews
Swinton		13	Mary d Humphrey Wood
Masham		24	Thomas s Thomas James
Masham		25	Mary Smith, wid
Fearby	Mar	11	Jane Blackburn, wid
Masham		13	Thomas Banks, yeoman
Masham	Apr	29	John Wrather, grocer
Ellingstring	May	9	John Buckten
Masham		18	Elizabeth d George Pickersgill
Healey		21	Mary Wintersgill
Healey	June	3	Esther d Thomas Smorthwaite
Breary Banks		29	Elizabeth d Robert Ruecroft
Huc usque Examin. per E.P. C:			
Ellingstring	July	29	Susanna Hinley, wid
Masham	Aug	14	George Webster
Masham	Nov	17	Charles Hird
Fearby	Dec	24	Edward Williamson

Burials 1756

Masham	Jan	2	Christopher s Jeffrey Clarkson
Swinton		5	Marmaduke s Marmaduke Smith
Masham		5	Margaret bastard d Ann Body
Swinton Mill		26	Miriam d Robert Hodgson
Masham	Feb	9	Dorothy Hebden, wid
Fearby		13	Thomas Cundall
Fearby		22	Isabel d Samuel Smithson
Healey		25	Elizabeth Ascough
Masham		29	Ann wf Hugh Robinson
Ellingstring	Mar	28	Elizabeth Greathead, wid
Ilton	Apr	12	Rachel d Edward Blackburn
Masham		13	Ann wf Joseph Atkinson
Masham	May	7	Richard s William Hardcastle, gent
Masham		31	William s Peter Young
Ilton	June	3	Elizabeth d Peter Hutchinson
Fearby		3	Mary d Samuel Smithson
Ellingstring		4	Margaret wf Peter Jackson
Masham		6	Thomas Clarkson snr
Masham		15	Mary Body, wid
Ellingstring		15	Mary wf George Ascough snr
High Ellington		16	Thomas Jackson
Fearby		17	Jane wf Thomas Bowes
Masham		27	Margaret d John Harrison
Masham		28	Mary d George Medley
Low Ellington	July	6	Ursula wf Thomas Jackson

Huc usque Ex: per Ed. Place Com[missarium]

Grewelthorpe		22	John Auton
Millstone Bank	Aug	5	John s John Bellerby
Masham	Aug	8	Ann wf George Pickersgill
Fearby		11	Ann bastard d Susan Breary
Masham		18	Isaac s John Robinson
Body Close	Sept	3	Elizabeth d William Walker
Healey	Oct	11	Jane Ascough, wid
High Ellington		20	Thomas s Aaron Jackson
Masham		29	Elizabeth Banks, wid
Masham	Nov	3	Elizabeth wf Robert Plews
Fearby		8	George Jackson
Masham		8	William Plews

Healey		9	Catharine Ascough, wid
Healey		14	Dorothy wf Roland Hutchinson
Masham	Dec	11	Elizabeth d Joseph Atkinson
Aldburgh		20	Ellen wf Thomas Beecroft

Masham	29	William Robinson

Burials 1757

Masham	Jan	4	Mary Robinson, wid [of William *above*]
Ilton		21	Mary Keaton, wid
Fearby	Feb	1	Jane d Humphrey Blackburn
Ilton		5	William Johnson, tailor
Ilton		11	Elizabeth Braithwait, wid
Swinton		13	Mrs Margaret Gregg, wid
Gollinglith		22	Christopher Walker
Burton	Mar	8	Dorothy wf Joseph Norridge
Masham		10	Elizabeth Lambert, wid
Masham		23	Martha wf William Joy
Healey		25	Jane Metcalfe, spr
Ilton	Apr	8	Thomas Buckle, bach
Masham		27	Ann d William Joy
Ripon	May	14	Robert Wilson
Masham		18	John s Anthony Thwaites
Low Ellington		22	James s Henry Thompson

Huc usque Exam. per E.P. Com[missarium]

Low Ellington		29	Mary wf Henry Thompson
Ellingstring	June	27	George Ascough snr
Masham	July	13	Jane Ascough, wid
Warthermarske	Aug	8	Elizabeth wf Thomas Jackson
Fearby		16	Timothy s John Rider
High Mains		31	Jane wf Robert Rider
Low Ellington	Oct	15	Elizabeth Clapham
Lobley Hole	Nov	20	John Walker
Masham		28	Sarah Carter, wid
Masham	Dec	15	Mr Henry Procter
Ellingstring		20	Christopher King
Masham		27	Ann d Thomas Norridge

[p. 99]

Burials 1758

Breary Banks	Jan	8	Elizabeth d Thomas Wintersgill
Low Ellington	Feb	3	Matthew Hammond
Masham		22	Elizabeth d George Thirkill
Masham	Mar	7	Susanna Kimpton
Masham		19	Hannah d John Banks
Ilton	Apr	13	Mary Darby, wid
Masham		18	Thomas s John Jackson

Ellingstring		19	Mary Williamson, wid
Ripon		25	Mr Marmaduke Beckwith
Swinton	May	2	Sythe Burnet, wid
Masham		16	Isabel wf John Chapman
Middleham		25	John Metcalfe
Swinton	June	15	William s Christopher Pickersgill
Masham	July	7	Margaret Gill, wid
Masham		7	Jane d Revd Mr Robert Radclyffe
Masham		22	Elizabeth d William Frier
Ellingstring	Sept	8	Jane wf William Metcalfe
Masham		22	William Beckwith, an apprentice
Healey	Oct	8	Thomas Plews
Masham		23	William Fawcet
Breary Banks	Nov	1	Thomas Wintersgill
Masham		3	Mary & Barbary twin dd John Banks jnr
Swinton		4	Christopher Jackson
Sourmire		25	Esther Barker
Masham		26	John Grey
Stainley		26	John Walton
Fearby		30	Samuel Smithson
Pickersgill	Dec	23	Ann Watson
Masham		25	Isabel d John Banks
Ellingstring		29	Mary wf Thomas Jackson

Burials 1759

Pickersgill	Jan	9	William Watson
High Ellington		10	Ann Johnson

[p. 100]

Healey		28	Christopher Rudd
Warthermarske		30	Jane wf John Hanley
Healey	Feb	16	Jane wf Thomas Metcafe
Ilton		18	Elizabeth Bell, wid
Healey	Mar	17	Elizabeth Hodgson, wid
Masham		20	John s William Hardcastle, gent
Masham		27	Thomas Banks
Leighton		30	Robert Ruecroft
Pickersgill		31	Jane Wilson
High Burton	Apr	1	John Baines
Healey		4	Mary Metcalfe, wid
Swinton		21	Miss Ann Danby
Masham		23	Grace wf Robert Wardrop
Ellington		23	Elizabeth wf Thomas Plews

Marriage 1754 [continued]

May 13   George Pickersgill and Ann Pickersgill, btp, banns published Apr 28, May 5, 12 by Robert Radclyffe, Curate. He marks, she signs. W: Thomas Langdale, Abraham Illingworth

[End of Register]

[Parish Register PR/MAS. 1/5]

[p. i]   Masham Parish Register Book (being Vol. bought by Mr Bolland & Mr Johnson Churchwardens June 22d 1759)

Robt. Radclyffe
Curate

[p. 1]   **Baptisms 1759**

Healey	June	24	Judith d George Metcalfe
Healey		24	Catherine d Francis Glew
Stean Beck Down		25	John s John Holdsworth
Swinton		25	Jenny d Christopher Jackson dec^d
Masham	July	1	Mary d Michael Beckwith
Masham	Aug	13	Michael s Thomas Clarkson
Quarry House		25	Joseph s William Lightfoot
Masham	Sept	1	Nancy d Thomas Todd
Sourmire		27	Mary d Peter Jackson
Masham		29	Dorothy d Francis Thompson
Warren House	Oct	18	John s John Kendall
Masham	Nov	16	John s Mr John Baines
Towler Hill		22	John s Matthew Burton
Fearby	Dec	8	Matthew s John Cundall
Healey		8	Mark s Mark Towler jnr
Masham		10	Mary d Thomas Gill
Masham		14	John s John Banks jnr
Ellington		23	Thomas s Matthew Crags
Ilton		27	Mary d Robert Ruecroft
Breary Banks		29	Elizabeth d Robert Walker
Healey		29	Robert s Edward Thorpe
Masham		30	Anne d Henry Thompson

[p. 2]   **Baptisms 1760**

Ellington	Jan	1	Elizabeth d Thomas Beckwith

Ellingstring	Feb	23	Edith d William Tempest
Warthermarske		28	Esther d John Ward
Sutton Penn	Mar	7	Anthony s Anthony Ballan
Swinton		9	Thomas s Peter Trees
Swinton		19	George s Thomas Dawson
Masham		19	John s Thomas Theaseby
Masham		21	Margaret d William Smith
Aldburgh		21	William s Thomas Geldart
Masham	Apr	11	Jane d Thomas Beckwith
Masham		20	Joseph s Mr John Bolland
Roomer		27	Hannah d John Ouzman
Ellingstring	May	10	Robert s Thomas Plews
Ellington		14	James s Jacob Towler
Ellingstring		24	George s Thomas Lye
Masham	June	1	Elizabeth d John Clarkson
Sourmire		7	Leonard s Mark Barker
Healey		7	Esther d Edward Smorthet jnr
Warthermarske		8	Ann d Thomas Jackson
Masham		8	John s Henry Hodgson
Masham		11	William s John Warrener
Masham		12	John s Revd Robert Radclyffe
Swinton		16	Rosamond d David Ashtood [*entry repeated on p. 3 after Hodgson baptism June 29*]

[p. 3]

Round Hill		29	Peter s Thomas Atkinson
Healey		29	Elizabeth d William Hodgson
Swinton	July	13	Rosamond d David Ashtood [*a cross against the entry cf. June 16 above*]
Masham		31	Elizabeth d Jefferey Clarkson
High Ellington	Aug	3	Jane d Thomas King
Swinton		10	John s William Glew
High Ellington		23	Elizabeth d John Jackson
Masham	Sept	7	Ann d William Joy
Low Burton		14	Susannah d Richard Hanley
Masham		14	John s John Close
Howe		26	Beatrice d Daniel Ianson
High Ellington		27	George s John Beck
Masham		28	John s William Imeson
Ellingstring	Oct	7	Mary d John Ascough
Masham		12	William s William Terry
High Roomer		19	Ann d John Renard
Masham		20	Henry s Henry Storrey
High Ellington	Nov	2	Mary d William Brignel
Masham		23	Peter s Thomas Jackson
Healey		30	Mary d Jonathan Lobley

Masham	Dec	26	William s George Fletcher

Baptisms 1761

Masham	Jan	25	John s Francis Wardrop
Masham	Feb	27	Betty d Thomas Bradberry
High Ellington	Mar	1	John s John Wilkinson
Ilton		15	Henry and Thomas twin ss Henry Scaife
Body Close		21	James s William Walker
Healey Pasture		21	Mary d Christopher Walker
Ilton		28	Peter s George Barker
Masham	May	3	George s Ralph Alderson
Swinton		10	John s John Carter
Pickersgill		10	Peter s John Mallaby

[p. 4]

Masham		31	Nancy d George Medley
Masham	June	21	Thomas s Thomas Edmondson
Ilton		28	Christopher s Christopher Walker
Masham		28	William s John Baines
Swinton		29	William s William Stephenson
Ellingstring	July	12	Cornelius s Thomas Plews
Breary Banks		19	Hannah d Robert Walker
Masham		28	Jane d Matthew Gill
Masham	Aug	2	Catherine d Humphrey Wood
Masham	Sept	6	Thomas s Thomas Hartley
Swinton		6	Hannah d Thomas Dawson
Masham		11	Elizabeth d John Atkinson
Masham		12	Michael s Luke Spence
Fearby		12	Mary d John Rider
Masham		12	Mary d James Hamilton
Masham	Oct	1	Henrietta d Mr William Hardcastle
Ilton		11	George s James Nicholson
Aberford		17	John s John Hunsley
Masham		18	John s John Snell
Masham		25	Mary d Caleb Powel
Masham		25	Thomas s Anthony Sturdy
Masham		25	Matthew s Christopher Sanderson
Masham	Nov	2	Marmaduke s Joseph Millar
Sutton Penn		15	Anthony s Anthony Ballan
Swinton		15	Thomas s Peter Trees

[p. 5]

Swinton Mill		21	Isabella d Robert Hodgson
Fearby		29	William bastard s Sarah Theackstone
Ilton	Dec	4	Ann d Thomas Jackson

Masham		13	Thomas s Thomas Alman
Masham		20	John s George Ferby
Ellingstring		22	George s Robert Bellerby
Masham		23	Henry Potter s Thomas Croft
Masham		26	Michael s Robert Railey
Healey		27	[*blank*] s Mark Towler

Baptisms 1762

Masham	Jan	12	Thomas s Thomas Gill
Warthermarske		15	Ann d George Leadley
Masham		17	Hannah d John Kidd
Masham		17	James s John Porter
Ellingstring		29	John s John Lye
Masham	Feb	12	Ann d John Banks
Masham		14	William s Thomas Woburn
Masham		14	Francis and Esther twin s & d Francis Wardrup
Healey		16	Mary d John Suttle
Masham		19	Francis d Francis Thompson
Low Roomer		21	Peter s Robert Stoney
Masham		21	Dorothy d Matthew Hagstone
Masham		22	Jane d Laurence Carter
[p. 6]			
Towler Hill		22	Elizabeth d John Smith
Masham		23	Gabriel s Gabriel Kay
Masham	Mar	5	Robert s William Smith
Masham		16	Thomas s Mr John Baines
Masham		18	Isaac s Thomas Todd
Healey		20	Esther d George Metcalfe
Healey		28	Hannah d Edward Smorthwaite
Ilton		28	William s Thomas Casling
Healey	Apr	2	Hammond s Thomas Metcalfe
Fearby		3	Ellen d John Cundal
Howe		12	Mary d Daniel Ianson
Swinton		17	Hannah d Benjamin Akers
Fearby		24	Elizabeth d Thomas and Elizabeth Alexander
Ellingstring		25	Thomas s John and Dorothy Tempest
Masham		25	Barnabas s John and Margaret Bolland
Warthermarske	May	1	Ruth d John and Ruth Ward
Masham		5	Mary d Francis and Ellen Buckle
Masham		9	Esther d George and Elizabeth Duffield
Fearby		13	Mary d Robert and Mary Blackburn
Masham		13	Thomas s Jeffrey and Mary Clarkson
Ellingstring		19	Ellen d Thomas and Mary Lye, bapt privately

Fearby	June	12	William s John and Mary London
Masham		13	Elizabeth d Edward and Susanna Nicholson
Healey Pasture End		28	Mary d John and Mary Metcalfe
Ellington	July	18	Mary d Thomas and Mary Beckwith
Masham		25	Henry s Henry and Eleanor Storah
Fearby	Aug	10	George s Christopher and Jane Imeson
Healey		15	Elizabeth d Marmaduke and Elizabeth Hammond
Masham	Sept	30	Edward s Edward and Elizabeth Moises, b Aug 23
Ellington	Oct	9	Mary d John and Ann Jackson
Swinton		15	Susanna d David and Ann Ashton
Healey		15	John s John and Jane Carter
[p. 7]			
Masham		22	Mary d Joseph and Lucy Milner
Warthermarske	Nov	4	George s George and Jane Nicholson
Healey Mill		9	Bryan s John and Ann Vitty
Ellingstring		13	Arabella d Thomas and Mary Plews
Ellingstring		20	John s Robert and Ann Bellerby
Ilton	Dec	4	Elizabeth d John and Ann Taylor
Warthermarske		22	Ann d William and Ruth Metcalfe

Baptisms 1763

Swinton	Jan	13	William s George and Ann Morrell
Masham		15	Henry s Henry and Elizabeth Thompson
Masham	Feb	6	John s George and Frances Fletcher
Swinton	Mar	5	Thomas and Ann twin children Matthew and Christiana Imeson
Ellington		6	Thomas s John and Ann Durham
Masham		10	David s John and Mary Jackson
Masham		11	Mary d Thomas and Tabitha Edmondson
Low Roomer		16	Thomas s John and Hannah Houseman
Swinton		18	Mary d William and Rosamond Stevenson
Ellington		25	Thomas and Ann twin children William and Hannah Brignell
Fearby		26	James s Robert and Mary Blackburn
Ellington		27	Barbara d Thomas and Margaret King
Masham		27	Hannah d William and Hannah Imeson
Ilton	Apr	9	Prudence d John and Sarah Metcalfe
Healey		17	Ralph s Robert and Mary Walker
Healey		20	Thamar d Jonathan and Elizabeth Lobley
Masham		26	Thomas s Matthew and Ann Jeff
Ellington		30	Esther d Thomas and Esther Parker
Masham	May	2	Robert and Elizabeth twin children of Christopher and Mary Marshal

Masham		3	Lucinda d William and Elizabeth Wrather
Healey		4	Dorothy d Matthew and Elizabeth Burton
Healey		12	Elizabeth d John and Elizabeth Mallaby
Warthermarske		18	Thomas s Thomas and Mary Theakston
Ilton		19	John s Matthew and Margaret Hutchinson
Swinton		23	William s John and Frances Carter
Ilton		30	Jacob s Robert and Judith Ruecroft
Masham	June	5	Mary d Henry and Rebecca Hodgson
Ilton	July	3	Betty d Robert and Sarah Bell
Healey		11	Barnabas s Christopher and Mary Walker
Swinton		28	William s William and Eleanor Glew
[*no place*]	Aug	7	William s William and Deborah Pybus
Masham		28	Ann d Matthew and Ann Hagston
Masham		28	Jane d George and Elizabeth Firby

[p. 8]

Masham	Sept	4	Ruth d George and Margaret Medley
Masham		12	John s Caleb and Elizabeth Powell
Ellington	Oct	1	Izabel d Jacob and Frances Towler
Masham		9	Ann d Luke and Jane Spence
Ellington		14	Jane d John and Esther Beck
Moorhead		16	Ellen d Thomas and Thomasin Atkinson
Healey		16	Jonathan s William and Rebecca Hodgson
Warthermarske		18	Jane d George and Jane Nicholson
Healey		28	Esther d John and Jane Carter
[*no place*]	Nov	20	Joseph s Joseph and Margaret Bartle
Ellingstring		22	William s Thomas and Ellen Rider
Gollinglith Foot		27	Eden d John and Mary Metcalfe
Masham	Dec	6	Elizabeth d Ralph and Mary Alderson
Masham		7	Joseph s Joseph and Elizabeth Burrill
Masham		22	Thomas s Thomas and Ann Court
Fearby		26	Christiana d Thomas and Ann Spence
Ilton		31	Catharine d John and Mary Hutchinson

Baptisms 1764

Ellington	Jan	6	Nancy d John and Ann Wilkinson
Breary Banks		12	Mary d Robert and Sarah Theakston
Masham		14	Joseph s Richard and Mary Geldart
Masham		29	Mary d Thomas and Mary Hartley
Fairthorn	Feb	11	Thomas s Thomas and Amy Scaife
Masham		12	Eneas illeg s Margaret Clarkson
Masham		15	Peter and Jane children William [*altered from* Robert] Smith
[*no place*]		25	Mary d Edward and Ann Onion

Warthermarske		19	Thomas s John and Sarah Metcalfe
Warthermarske		19	Elizabeth d John and Elizabeth Mallaby
Masham		26	Sarah d Robert and Jane Smith
Masham		26	Ann d William and Hannah Robinson
Masham	Mar	5	Mary d James and Mary Towler
Masham		9	Jane d John and Ann Baynes
Low Ellington		11	Christopher s Matthew and Ann Craggs
Warthermarske		17	William s George and Catherine Leathley
Swinton Mill		18	Thomas s John and Mary Harland
Fearby		24	Elizabeth d Christopher and Mary Dawson
Healey		24	Elizabeth d Anthony and Mary Plews
Masham		25	Dorothy d John and Susanna Warrener
Healey		25	William s Mark and Theodosia Towler
Masham	Apr	8	Thomas s Moses and Mary Jackson
North Cote		8	Deborah d Robert and Alice Metcalfe
Masham		15	William s James and Hannah Hamilton
Fearby		21	John illeg s Mary Burnholme
[p. 9]			
Fearby		23	Mary d Christopher and Jane Imeson
Ellington		23	Jane illeg d Ann Jackson
Masham		24	Thomas s Thomas and Jane Gill
Masham		29	Barbara d John and Barbara Banks
High Roomer		29	Sarah d John and Margaret Reynard
Masham		29	Ursula d John and Catherine Nelson
Healey	May	4	Christopher s Edward and Jane Smorthwaite
Masham		31	Sally d Francis and Mary Wardrop
Masham	June	3	Jane d Richard and Ann Pearson
Ilton		5	Isabel d Ralph and Margaret Horsman
Masham		10	Thomas s John and Elizabeth Atkinson
Ellington		10	Robert s Robert and Jane Wintersgill
[no place]		11	Ann d William and Sarah Umpleby
Ellingstring		17	Richard s Thomas Robinson
Swinton	Aug	5	John s Matthew and Christiana Imeson
Masham		17	Jane d William and Elizabeth [Jane crossed out] Wrather
Masham		25	Abigail and Elizabeth twin dd William and Martha Harrison
Ellingstring	Sept	8	John s John and Elizabeth Pickersgill
Moorhead		9	Ann d Matthias and Ann Burrill
Healey		16	Thomas s John and Elizabeth Suttill
Masham		16	Dorothy d John and Mary Jackson
Moorhead		18	Esther d Mark and Margaret Barker
Masham		19	Jane d Francis and Deborah Thompson
Swinton		25	Mary d Anthony and Ann Hill
Masham	Oct	7	Elizabeth d Francis and Ellen Buckley
Swinton		14	Ann d Benjamin and Ann Akers

Masham		14	William s Joseph and Lucy Milner
Masham		23	William s George and Elizabeth Bowness
Ilton		28	Mary d Henry and Elizabeth Scafe
Fearby		28	Robert s Robert and Mary Blackbourn
Masham	Nov	25	William s John and Elizabeth Banks
Ilton		26	Mary d William and Mary Horseman
Masham	Dec	22	Hannah d Caleb and Jane Purchase
Masham		25	Henry s Henry and Rebecca Hodgson

Baptisms 1765

Fearby	Jan	1	James s John and Mary London
Warthermarske		2	Elizabeth d William and Ruth Metcalfe
Ellington		11	John s John and Ann Jackson
Masham		13	Sarah d Thomas and Hannah Wilson
Swinton Mill		20	Matthew s Thomas and Elizabeth Jackson
Ilton		26	Anthony s John and Ann Taylor
[p. 10]			
Ellington		31	Ann d Thomas and Mary Beckwith
Healey	Feb	2	Thomas s John and Jane Carter
Gollinglith Foot		4	Elizabeth d John and Mary Metcalfe
Ilton		11	Ann d Thomas and Alice Casling
Masham		19	Francis s Gabriel and Sarah Kay
Low Mains		22	Robert s Timothy and Esther Rider
Masham	Mar	4	John s John and Margaret Gill
Ellingstring		6	Ann d John and Ann Steel
Masham		10	Ursula d Henry and Mary Leeming
Warthermarske		15	Hannah d John and Ruth Ward
Ilton		16	Ann d Robert and Sarah Bell
Swinton	Apr	9	Thomas s William and Rosamond Stevenson
Masham		9	Jane d Caleb and Elizabeth Powel
Swinton		26	Alethea d David and Ann Ashton
Warthermarske	May	8	George s George and Jane Nicholson
Masham		20	John s George and Ann Atkinson [*entered at bottom of p. 10 with indication to this point*]
Moorhead		22	Mary d Thomas and Amy Scaife
Ilton		22	Thomas s Thomas and Ann Taylor
Gollinglith		30	Edward s Joseph and Mary Thorpe
Fearby	June	8	Mary d Christopher and Mary Dawson
Masham		12	Margaret d William and Margaret Smith
Masham		23	John s Leonard and Jane Mudd
Masham		23	Frances d William and Mary Beckwith
Masham		23	Mary d George and Elizabeth Firby
Fearby		30	Christopher s Christopher and Jane Imeson

Healey Constablery		30	John s John and Elizabeth Mallaby
Breary Banks		30	Esther d Robert and Mary Walker
Fearby	July	6	Elizabeth d Thomas and Esther Parker
Healey Mill		17	Thomas s John and Anne Vitty
Masham		20	Francis s George and Frances Fletcher
Masham		28	Nancy d John Kidd
Masham		28	Abraham s George and Elizabeth Duffield
Masham	Aug	8	Mary d William and Hannah Robinson
Masham		13	Dorothy d Thomas and Margaret Martindale
Fearby		13	Mary d John and Elizabeth Mallaby
Masham		16	James s John and Elizabeth Atkinson
Masham		24	Elizabeth d Joseph and Margaret Bartle
Masham		30	Thomas and Jane twin children Ralph and Mary Alderson
Masham	Sept	8	Hannah d Joseph and Dorothy Thorns
Swinton		9	Mary d John and Frances Carter
Ellington		27	Thomas s John and Esther Beck
Ilton	Oct	11	Elizabeth d Thomas and Ann Jackson
[p. 11]			
Howe		13	John s Daniel and Ellen Ianson
Fearby		19	John s Thomas and Ann Spence
Masham		20	Joseph s Thomas and Ann Court
Masham		20	Jane d Richard and Jane Pickersgill
Masham		29	George s John and Jane Snell
Ellingstring	Nov	14	John s Thomas and Mary Plews
Burton Constablery		17	John s Thomas and Tabitha Edmondson
Masham		19	John s George and Elizabeth Blades
Masham		30	Samuel s Robert and Katherine Towler
Masham	Dec	8	James s James and Esther Wilkinson
Healey		16	John s John and Dorothy Ascough

Baptisms 1766

Swinton	Jan	5	Ann d Peter and Elizabeth Trees
Masham		11	James s Robert and Margaret Atkinson
Fearby		11	John s John and Ann Hutchinson
Masham		12	James s Luke and Jane Spence
Masham		12	Sarah d John and Mary Jackson
Masham		12	Thomas s John and Ann Place
Masham		25	Joseph s John and Susanna Warrener
Stone Fold		25	Betty d Thomas and Sarah Jackson
Masham		25	William s Edward and Elizabeth Moises, b Jan 10, [dead *added in darker ink*]
Swinton	Feb	1	Christiana d Matthew and Christiana Imeson

Ilton		8	Mary d John and Sarah Metcalf
Fearby		8	Thomas illeg s Ellen Horseman
Masham		25	Joseph s William and Martha Harrison
Warthermarske		28	Betty d George and Catherine Leathley
Pott	Mar	1	George s George and Ann Barker
Masham		31	Ann d Thomas and Elizabeth Webster
Masham		31	Elizabeth d Mr William and Elizabeth Wrather
Masham	Apr	6	Thomas s Matthew and Ann Hagston
Masham		11	Caleb s Caleb and Elizabeth Powel
Masham		13	Mark s James and Mary Towler
Masham		13	Thomas s Francis and Mary Wardrop
Healey		20	Rose d Jonathan and Elizabeth Lobley
Masham		20	Henry s Francis and Jane Brotherton
Swinton	May	4	David s David and Ann Ashton
Masham		11	Thomas s John and Elizabeth Banks
Low Mains		25	Thomas s Timothy and Esther Rider
Warthermarske	June	1	Margaret d Thomas and Mary Theakston
Fearby		15	Francis s William and Ellen Glew
Ellington		15	Abigail d Matthew and Ann Craggs
[p.12]			
Healey		22	Elizabeth d Edward and Jane Smorthwaite
Ilton		22	Maria d James and Elizabeth Taylor
Ellingstring		27	Thomas s Thomas and Ellen Rider
Masham	July	6	Ann d James and Hannah Hamilton
Ilton		11	John s Robert and Sarah Bell
Ellington		11	William s Thomas and Ann Beckwith
Ellington		11	Joseph s Jacob and Frances Towler
Masham		19	Charlotte d Mr William Hardcastle and Mercy his wf
Masham	Aug	1	Robert s William and Hannah Imeson
Masham		24	Mary d William and Mary Beckwith
Healey		26	Thomas s Marmaduke and Elizabeth Hammond
Masham	Sept	7	Ann d John and Mary Carlile
Masham		19	Margaret d John and Margaret Gill
Warthermarske	Oct	20	William s George and Jane Nicholson [*deleted entry*]
Ellingstring		12	Thomas s William Nelson
Ellingstring		12	Arabella illeg d Elizabeth Emerson
Masham		22	Mary d Thomas and Margaret Martindale
Masham	Dec	26	Mary d Thomas and Mary Kay
Masham		27	John s John and Letitia Wintersgill

Baptisms 1767

Masham	Jan	25	Anthony s Thomas and Jane Gill
Fearby		31	Eleanor d Christopher and Mary Dawson

Warthermarske	Feb	5	Mary d William and Ruth Metcalf
Ilton		8	Mary d Peter and Mary Hammond
Masham		11	Ave d Robert and Jane Smith
Fearby		14	Jane d Christopher and Jane Imeson
Healey		14	Barbara d Edward and Ann Binks
High Ellington		15	Jane d Robert and Jane Wintersgill
Round Hill		16	Joseph s Thomas and Thomasin Atkinson
Healey		16	John s John and Elizabeth Suttill
Masham		17	Mary d Henry and Mary Leeming
Low Wood		19	William s Jeffrey and Eleanor Horsman
Roomer		21	Elizaabeth d John and Hannah Houseman
Fearby		21	Betty d Robert and Judith Ruecroft
Healey		22	Jacob s Mark and Theodosia Towler
Masham	Mar	2	Jane d Joseph and Margaret Bartle
Fearby		5	Catherine d Robert and Mary Blackbourn
Fearby		5	Thomas s Robert and Elizabeth Blackbourn
Fearby		5	Mary illeg d Dorothy Tunstal
Stonefold		28	Sarah d Thomas and Sarah Jackson
Masham		30	Ellen d John and Jane Skurrah
West Closes	Apr	4	Edward s Joseph and Elizabeth Kirkley
High Ellington		5	John s Leonard and Elizabeth Wilkinson
[p. 13]			
[*no place*]		14	William Heslop s Henry Webb, comedian, and Mary his wf
Moorhead		21	Esther d Thomas and Amy Scaife
High Ellington		24	Robert s John and Ann Jackson
Masham	May	31	Ann d John and Ann Bane
Masham		31	Moses s Moses and Mary Jackson
Gollinglith	June	4	Esther d John and Mary Metcalf
Healey Pasture End		4	Esther d Christopher and Mary Walker
Warthermarske		10	Sarah d John and Ruth Ward
Swinton		11	John s Anthony and Ann Hill
Masham		14	Betty d George and Elizabeth Firby
Warthermarske		26	Jane d Joseph and Mary Thorp
Masham		26	Grace d Francis and Mary Wardrop
Masham		28	John s Thomas [John *crossed out*] and Hannah Wilson
Swinton		28	George s Thomas and Izabel Dawson
Swinton	July	19	Elizabeth d Matthew and Christiana Imeson
Masham		20	Elizabeth d Francis and Margaret Thompson
Masham	Aug	30	Sarah and Ann twin dd John and Susanna Warrener
Masham	Sept	1	Anthony s William and Martha Harrison
Healey		13	John s Anthony and Mary Plews
Ellingstring		13	Eden d John and Esther Emerson
Masham		16	William s Edward and Elizabeth Moises, b Aug 23
Ellington		19	Hannah d William and Hannah Brignall

Masham		26	Ursula d Thomas and Mary Hartley
Healey Cote	Oct	5	Robert s Peter and Ann Jackson
Masham		11	George s George and Elizabeth Clark
Masham		11	John s Joseph and Dorothy Thorns
Masham		11	Leonard s Leonard and Jane Mudd
Grimes Gill		27	George s Thomas and Isabel Ascough
Swinton	Nov	3	Martha d William and Rosamond Stevenson
Breary Banks		8	Mary d Robert and Mary Walker
Masham		16	Jane d John and Barbara Wintersgill
Low Mains		21	Joseph s Timothy and Esther Rider
Masham		22	Elizabeth d Joseph and Lucy Milner
Fearby		29	John s John and Elizabeth Mallaby
Fearby		29	Hannah d Francis and Sarah Mallaby
Masham	Dec	4	William s Caleb and Elizabeth Powel
Masham		13	William s Henry and Ellen Storah
Masham		14	Phyllis d Thomas and Margaret Martindale
Masham		25	Elizabeth d Richard and Jane Pickersgill
Ilton		26	Christopher s John and Ann Taylor
Masham		29	David s John and Mary Jackson
Ilton		29	Ann d Ralph and Margaret Horsman

[p. 14]   **Baptisms 1768**

Masham	Jan	24	Henry s George and Frances Fletcher
Masham		24	Samuel s William and Mary Beckwith
Low Burton	Feb	14	George illeg s Ann Grindale
Roomer		20	William s John and Margaret Reynard
Pott		27	Elizabeth d George and Ann Barker
Masham	Mar	13	James s James and Hannah Hamilton
Healey		20	Hannah d Thomas and Isabel Towler
Masham		25	Elizabeth d George and Elizabeth Blades
Healey	Apr	2	Peter s John and Jane Carter
Masham		3	Elizabeth d Thomas and Mary Kay
Ellingstring		6	Robert s Thomas and Margaret King
Masham		10	John s Thomas and Ann Court
Masham		17	Frances d John and Frances Carter
Summerside		19	Mary d Matthew and Ann Burrill
Swinton Mill	May	1	Elizabeth d Thomas and Elizabeth Jackson
Masham		22	Mary d Joseph and Margaret Bartlett
Masham		22	Mary d John and Barbara Banks
Masham		22	Ann d Francis and John Brotherton
Masham		28	Jane illeg d Mary Greenhough
Masham	June	5	Elizabeth d Peter and Jane Robinson
Warthermarske		10	John s George and Catherine Leathley

Low Wood		24	Jeffrey s Jeffrey and Eleanor Horsman
Ilton		26	Amy d John and Sarah Metcalf
Warthermarske		28	Ruth d William and Ruth Metcalf
Swinton	July	3	Alethea d David and Ann Ashton
Masham		3	Jane d John and Jane Scurrah
Masham		10	Mary d George and Ann Atkinson
Ilton		16	George s George and Grace Blackburn
Masham		20	Thomas s Matthew and Mary Rider
Ash Head		23	Margaret d George and Ann Plews
Masham	Aug	28	Ellen d George and Jane Reynard
[*no place*]	Sept	5	Ann d Benjamin and Frances Grange [*entered at bottom of p. 14 with indication to this point*]
Fearby		8	Mary d Robert and Elizabeth Blackburn
Masham		20	Ann d Robert and Margaret Atkinson
Healey		25	George s John and Dorothy Ascough
Masham	Oct	14	Matthew s Matthew and Ann Hagstone
Aldburgh	Nov	27	William s Thomas and Tabitha Edmondson
Ellington	Dec	4	John s Francis and Mary Deacon
Ilton		10	Robert s Robert and Sarah Bell
Swinton		15	George s George and Catherine Imeson
Masham		29	Marmaduke s John and Letitia Wintersgill

[p. 15]

Baptisms 1769

Ilton	Jan	21	Thomas s Thomas and Alice Casling
Masham		21	Mary d John and Elizabeth Thwaites
Masham		22	George illeg s Catherine Watson
Ilton	Feb	8	James s James and Elizabeth Taylor
Fearby		10	Christopher s Christopher and Mary Dawson
Masham		12	John s John and Susanna Warrener
Masham		22	William s John and Mary Jackson
Masham		26	Robert illeg s Mary Humble
Masham	Mar	9	Elizabeth d Thomas and Margaret Martindale
Warthermarske		12	Joseph s Joseph and Mary Thorp
Masham		19	George s William and Hannah Robinson
Masham		23	George s Thomas and Isabel Robinson
Masham		26	John s John and Margaret Kidd
Fearby		26	Isabel d John and Isabel Burnet
Ellingstring		29	Charles s Thomas and Ellen Rider
Healey	Apr	2	Elizabeth d Mark and Theodosia Towlard
Warthermarske		2	Ann d Thomas and Mary Theakston
Swinton		6	Matthew s Matthew and Christiana Imeson
Masham		16	Thomas s Christopher and Mary Marshal
Agill		19	John s Leonard and Dorothy Sedgwick

Lamb Hill		22	Mary d John and Mary Hill
Fearby		23	William s Robert and Mary Blackburn
Fearby		28	Thomas illeg s Elizabeth Wood
Ellington	May	10	Sally d Jacob and Frances Towler
Masham		11	Susanna d Edward and Susanna Nicholson
Masham		21	Charlotte d Mr William Watson and Rebecca his wf
Ellingstring	June	18	Samuel s John and Ann Lye
Ellington		30	Anthony s John and Ann Jackson
Masham	July	1	Joseph s Joseph and Dorothy Thorns
Low Mains		7	Esther d Timothy and Esther Rider
Ellingstring		9	Ellen d William and Ellen Glew
Masham		9	George s George and Elizabeth Firby
Healey		23	John s Jonathan and Elizabeth Lobley
Masham		30	Mary d Moses and Mary Jackson
Masham	Aug	1	Ann d Thomas and Ann Metcalf
Masham		6	Thomas s Thomas and Ann Matthews
Masham		6	Ann d Thomas and Hannah Wilson
Masham		8	Matthew and Charles twin ss Matthew and Mary Gill
Masham		25	Francis s Anthony and Elizabeth Sturdy
Ilton	Sept	1	Peter s Peter and Mary Hammond
Ellingstring		2	Thomas s John and Esther Emerson
[p. 16]			
Masham		24	Jane d George and Jane Reynard
Masham	Oct	8	Thomas s Henry and Eleanor Storah
Swinton	Nov	5	Anthony s Anthony and Ann Hill
Masham		8	Watson s Edward and Elizabeth Moises, b Sept 12
High Ellington		9	Jane d Thomas and Dorothy King
Masham		25	Thomas s George and Elizabeth Clark
Masham		26	William s William and Martha Harrison
Ilton	Dec	3	Isabel d Ralph and Margaret Horseman
Moorhead		7	Amy d Thomas and Amy Scafe
Masham		15	Jenny d Matthew and Mary Rider

52 [*annual total*]

Baptisms 1770

Masham	Jan	19	Ann d Thomas and Margaret Bradbury
Masham		24	Caleb s Caleb and Elizabeth Powel
Masham		25	Thomas s George and Jane Nicholson
Masham	Feb	2	Thomas s Francis and Margaret Wardrop
Masham		18	John s George and Hannah Gowthwaite
Masham		19	John s John and Ann Bane
Fearby		25	Elizabeth d Robert and Elizabeth Blackburn
Masham		27	William s John and Elizabeth Roundill
Breary Banks	Mar	4	Margaret d Robert and Mary Walker

Masham		11	George s George and Elizabeth Wintersgill
Swinton		11	John s Thomas and Isabel Dawson
Masham		18	Ralph s Ralph and Mary Alderson
Masham	Apr	1	William s Richard and Jane Pickersgill
Warthermarske		13	Sarah d William and Ruth Metcalf
Masham		24	Elizabeth d Edward and Isabell Blackburn
Masham		29	John s John and Ann Place
Masham	May	7	John s Thomas and Jane Gill
Swinton		12	Mary d William and Elizabeth Floor
Masham		18	Margaret d Thomas and Margaret Martindale
Gollinglith Foot		24	John and Thomas twin ss John and Mary Metcalf
Masham	June	6	Margaret d John and Barbara Banks
Pott		9	Ephraim s George and Ann Barker
Healey		10	Jane d Anthony and Mary Plews
Burton Constablery		14	Ann d Samuel and Cicely Wilkinson
Masham		26	Jane d John and Letitia Wintersgill
Masham	July	1	Ann d Leonard and Jane Mudd
Swinton		8	Rosamond d William and Rosamond Stevenson
[p. 17]			
Ilton	Aug	5	William s Ralph and Elizabeth Prest
Masham		5	Joseph s Peter and Jane Robinson
Leighton		5	Thomas s Thomas and Elizabeth Jackson
Masham		12	Joseph s William and Mary Beckwith
[*no place*]		21	Margaret and Hannah twin dd Samuel and Ann Thompson, vagrants
Fearby	Sept	2	Margaret d Christopher and Mary Dawson
Ilton		15	Ann d John and Ann Taylor
Masham	Oct	7	George s George and Jane Reynard
Ilton		20	John s John and Sarah Metcalf
Ilton		21	William s Thomas and Ann Taylor
Warthermarske		21	Rachel d John and Ruth Ward
Masham		28	Henry s Robert and Margaret Atkinson
Masham	Nov	14	William s Thomas and Ann Matthews
Masham		15	John s John and Jane Scurrah
Masham	Dec	16	Peter s Thomas and Isabel Towler

44 [*annual total*]

Baptisms 1771

Nutwith Cote	Jan	1	Emanuel s William and Elizabeth Bond
Warthermarske		5	Catherine d George and Catherine Leathley
Low Mains		19	Mark s Timothy and Esther Rider
Fearby		29	John s Joseph and Isabel Burneston
Nutwith Cote		30	Isabinda illeg d Jane Emerson
Masham	Feb	3	Abigail d William and Martha Harrison

Masham		10	Joseph Fairburn s Christopher and Mary Brown
Ilton		12	Mary d George and Grace Blackburn
Masham		24	John s Matthew and Ann Hagstone
Masham	Mar	3	Thomas s John and Frances Carter
Warthermaske		17	Thomas s Joseph and Mary Thorpe
Swinton		24	Robert s Matthew and Christiana Imeson
Masham		30	George s Thomas and Mary Kay
Ash Head		28	Thomas s Thomas and Mary Carter
Ilton	Apr	20	William s Ralph and Margaret Horsman
Masham		21	Jane d James and Hannah Hamilton
Fearby		30	Esther d Robert and Mary Rider
Colsterdale		30	Edward s John and Mary Metcalf
Fairthorn	May	6	Jane d Thomas and Amy Scafe
Ellingstring		7	John s George and Mary Ascough
Masham		19	Christopher illeg s Dorothy Place
Fearby	June	6	Susanna d John and Isabel Burnet
Masham		9	Benjamin s Joseph and Dorothy Thorns
Masham		13	Thomas s John and Sarah Chapman
[p. 18]			
Healey		17	Dorothy d John and Dorothy Ascough
Ilton		30	Christopher s Thomas and Alice Casling
Masham	July	7	Ann d Thomas and Ann Court
Moorhead		14	Peter s Peter and Esther Carter
Moorhead		14	Robert s Robert and Elizabeth Imeson
Masham		14	Sarah d Richard and Isabel Thompson
Ilton		26	John s William and Edith Lightfoot
Masham		30	Mary d Henry and Eleanor Charnock
High Ellington	Aug	2	John s Thomas and Dorothy King
Masham		4	Barbara d Christopher and Elizabeth Whorlton
Masham		17	James s Elias and Susanna Metcalf
Masham		18	Rosamond d George and Ann Atkinson
Masham	Aug	25	Margaret d John and Margaret Kidd
Masham	Sept	29	Martha d George and Elizabeth Firby
Masham	Oct	8	William s Robert and Jane Smith
Ilton		27	Robert s James and Elizabeth Taylor
Fearby	Nov	3	Jane d Robert and Elizabeth Blackburn
Fearby		3	John s Luke and Jane Spence
Masham		3	Thomas s Caleb and Elizabeth Powel
Masham		11	Charles s Edward and Elizabeth Moises, b. Oct 13 [dead *added in darker ink*]
Ellingstring	Dec	8	Jane illeg d Mary Rudd
Swinton		15	John s Henry and Dorothy Raper

46 [*annual total*]

Baptisms 1772

Healey Cote	Jan	1	Ann d Thomas and Dorothy Smorthit
Ellington		5	John s Thomas and Mary Jackson
Ellingstring		29	Ann d Emanuel and Ann Lye
[no place]	Feb	14	Elizabeth d George and Elizabeth Clark
Healey		16	Thomas s David and Ann Walker
Agill		20	Margaret d John and Margaret Topham
Masham	Mar	1	Mary d Christopher and Jane Merryweather
Masham		20	Thomas s Jeffrey and Ann Clarkson
Masham		22	Henry s Moses and Mary Jackson
Healey		29	George s Jonathan and Elizabeth Lobley
Stonefold	Apr	3	Mary d Thomas and Sarah Jackson
Low Roomer		5	Joseph s William and Ellen Reynard
Masham		5	Elizabeth d John and Barbara Banks
Fearby		12	James s Thomas and Ellen Nelson
Warthermarske		19	Kester alias Christopher s Ralph and Esther Pattison
Masham		19	Mary d John and Elizabeth Roundhall
Masham	May	3	John s David and Elizabeth Walker

[p. 19]

Masham		17	William s William and Mary Beckwith
Burton Constablery		17	Elizabeth d Thomas and Tabitha Glover
Swinton		24	William s Anthony and Anne Hill
Healey	June	7	Thomas s Richard and Hannah Thompson
Masham		14	Mary d John and Ann Place
Ilton		21	Ann d Ralph and Elizabeth Prest
Masham		26	Thomas s Edward and Isabella Blackburn
Swinton		28	Martha d David and Ann Ashton
Masham	July	12	Mary d Thomas and Anne Dowson
Healey		19	Francis s Mark and Theodosia Towler
Masham	Aug	2	Elizabeth d George and Hannah Gouthwaite
Warthermarske		9	Mary d George and Catherine Leathley
Low Ellington		10	Robert s Robert and Mary Jeff
Masham		23	Mary d George and Elizabeth Wintersgill
Ellingstring		26	John s John and Esther Emerson
Cross Lanes	Sept	11	George s Robert and Mary Rider
Fairthorn		12	John s Thomas and Amy Scafe
Low Ellington		13	Nancy d Jacob and Frances Towler
Colsterdale		13	Anna d John and Mary Metcalf
Breary Banks		13	Robert s Robert and Mary Walker
Masham		19	Matthew s William and Ellen Glew
Masham		19	Mary d George and Elizabeth Wintersgill
Masham	Oct	2	John s Mr Thomas and Margaret Martindale
Swinton		4	Thomas s John and Rachel Hall
Fearby		18	Nancy d Christopher and Mary Dawson

North Cote		23	Isabella d Samuel and Cecily Wilkinson
Masham	Nov	7	Elizabeth d George and Jane Reynard
Burton Constablery		8	William illeg s Mary Geldart
Masham	Dec	6	Ann d Thomas and Ann Dawson
Ilton		13	Elizabeth d Thomas and Alice Casling
Masham		27	John s John and Sarah Chapman

48 [*annual total*]

Baptisms 1773

Low Ash Head	Jan	7	Thomas s Mark and Elizabeth Hutchinson
Bramley Grange		22	Matthew s Joseph and Ann Walker
Masham		30	Thomas s John and Jane Scurrah
Ilton	Feb	7	Prudence d John and Sarah Metcalf
Swinton		11	Henry s William and Rosamond Stevenson
[p. 20]			
Fearby		14	Dorothy d Robert and Elizabeth Blackburn
Masham		18	Thomas s Thomas and Mary Clark
Masham		19	Thomas s Edward and Susanna Nicholson
Agill	Mar	4	Thomas s John and Margaret Topham
Summerside		4	Esther d Peter and Esther Carter
West Wood		20	Eleanor d Jeffrey and Eleanor Horsman
Ellingstring		20	George s George and Mary Ascough
Ilton	Apr	19	William s William and Edith Lightfoot
Masham		20	Reuben s William and Jane Parker
Masham		20	Richard s William and Elizabeth Bond
Masham	May	7	Richard s Richard and Ellen Whitelock
Swinton		8	Jane d Matthew and Christiana Imeson
Masham		9	William s Thomas and Ann Court
Masham		16	Elizabeth d John and Elizabeth Roundall
[*no place*]		23	Ralph s Benjamin and Mary Siddall
Masham		30	Rosamond d Robert and Margaret Atkinson
Masham	June	13	Thomas s James and Hannah Hamilton
Masham	July	2	Hugh s Edward and Elizabeth Moises, b June 8
Masham		4	Edward s Leonard and Jane Mudd
Swinton		7	John illeg s Ann Ashton
Masham		18	Matthew s Joseph and Dorothy Thorns
Ellington		18	Elizabeth d William and Hannah Brignall
Masham		18	Thomas s Richard and Isabella Thompson
Ellingstring		30	Samuel s Samuel Smith
Masham	Aug	1	Sarah d Caleb and Elizabeth Powel
Fearby		1	Mary d Anthony and Mary Plews
Warthermarske		6	John s John and Mary Metcalf
Masham		18	John s Edward and Ann Wright
Healey Cote		21	Thomas s Thomas and Dorothy Smorthit

Masham		22	John s William and Martha Harrison
Healey	Sept	14	Jane d John and Dorothy Ascough
Healey		14	Mary d Thomas and Phoebe Jackson
Masham		19	Ann d Jeffrey and Ann Clarkson
Healey		23	Adam s Adam and Mary Barnes
Masham		28	Hannah d Robert and Jane Smith
Healey	Oct	5	Mary d Thomas and Mary Carter
Towler Hill		9	Isabel d Marmaduke and Elizabeth Hammond
Masham		17	Christopher s George and Elizabeth Clark [*altered from* Jeffrey and Anne Clarkson]
Masham		17	Jane illeg d Elizabeth Hunter
Fearby		17	John s Robert and Mary Blackburn
[p. 21]			
High Ellington		24	Thomas s Thomas and Dorothy King
Masham		24	George s George and Mary Fenwick
Ellingstring		31	William s Robert and Ann Lancaster
Healey	Nov	7	John s John and Hannah Barnes
Sourmire		7	Elizabeth d Robert and Elizabeth Imeson
Masham		11	Joseph illeg s Mary Banks
Masham		14	Matthew s Matthew and Frances Parke
Ilton		17	Esther d Thomas and Ann Jackson
Masham		18	Margaret d George and Elizabeth Firby
Warthermarske		21	Mary d Joseph and Mary Thorpe
[*no place*]		26	Isabella d John and Margaret Benzey, travellers
Masham	Dec	28	William s John and Margaret Kidd
Leighton		28	William s Thomas and Elizabeth Jackson

58 [*annual total*]

Baptisms 1774

Fearby	Jan	1	Ellen d Thomas and Ellen Nelson
Masham		2	Bateman s George and Ann Atkinson
Masham		2	William s John and Ann Plews
Swinton		10	Elizabeth d John and Rachel Hall
Masham		23	Mary d Peter and Jane Robinson
Masham		24	John s John and Margaret Morrell
Stotfold	Feb	3	Peter s Matthias and Ann Burrell
Masham		5	John s Anthony and Elizabeth Sturdy
Masham		6	Thomas s Thomas and Mary Kaye
Masham		13	Christopher s Richard and Sarah Smith
Low Mains		15	Jane d Timothy and Esther Rider
Warthermarske	Mar	27	Mary d William and Ellen Reynard
Masham		27	Elizabeth d John and Ann Place
Masham	Apr	3	Hannah d John and Ann Bane
Summerside		6	Robert s William and Isabella Topham

Masham		10	Isabel d John and Isabel Crossley
Healey		16	Esther d Richard and Hannah Thompson
Healey		17	John s Luke and Jane Spence
Masham		17	Mary d Samuel and Mary Wrather
Masham		21	Susanna d Elias and Susanna Metcalf
Ash Head		29	Ann d Mark and Elizabeth Hutchinson
Ilton		29	Walker s Daniel and Elizabeth Ingleby
[p. 22]			
Masham	May	22	George s George and Esther Wilson
Masham		22	Jane d Thomas and Frances Hutchinson
Low Ellington		26	John s Henry and Isabel Lupton
Masham	July	17	Mary d Henry and Eleanor Storey
Masham		23	Henry s Henry and Eleanor Charnock
High Ash Head		24	John s Matthew and Margaret Ascough
Ellingstring		29	Christopher s George and Mary Ascough
Cross Lanes	Sept	18	Hannah d Robert and Mary Rider
Ilton		18	Peggy d James and Elizabeth Taylor
Masham	Oct	9	Ellen d Moses and Mary Jackson
Masham		9	Benjamin s Benjamin and Mary Siddall
Burton Constablery		16	Solomon Fawnes s Thomas and Tabitha Edmondson
Warthermarske		19	Frances and Hannah twin dd George and Catherine Leathley
Healey		25	Samuel s George and Elizabeth Wintersgill
Masham		30	William s John and Sarah Chapman
Masham	Nov	13	Jane d Christopher and Jane Merriweather
Masham	Dec	7	Joseph s John and Jane Scurrah
Masham		20	Thomas s Christopher and Elizabeth Whorlton
Fearby		26	Polly d Christopher and Mary Dawson

42 [*annual total*]

Baptisms 1775

Swinton	Jan	15	Thomas s James and Jane Lancaster
Fearby		16	Robert s Robert and Elizabeth Blackburn
Aldburgh		19	Mary d Thomas and Ann Judson
Healey Pasture End		28	James s Christopher and Mary Walker
Masham	Feb	3	Ann d George and Jane Reynard
Ellingstring		11	Elizabeth d Manuel and Ann Lye
Ilton		12	George s Ralph and Elizabeth Prest
High Mains		16	Jane d Peter and Jane Ballan
Ellingstring		16	Mary d Jeremiah and Elizabeth Metcalf
Swinton		21	William s Matthew and Christiana Imeson
Swinton	Mar	12	Rachel d John and Rachel Hall
High Ellington		17	Leonard s Leonard and Elizabeth Wilkinson
Ilton		21	Elizabeth d William and Edith Lightfoot

Healey		26	Christopher s Jonathan and Elizabeth Lobley
Masham		31	Ann d George and Mary Fenwick
Sutton	Apr	9	Ann d Leonard and Elizabeth Hodgson
Healey		11	Thomas s Thomas and Catherine Barrows
[*no place*]		30	George s John and Esther Fryar, travellers
Masham	May	14	Mary d Matthew and Ann Hagston

[p. 23]

Masham		21	John s Samuel and Elizabeth Wrather
Ellingstring		25	Christopher Horsman illeg s Ann Plews
Low Mains		27	Thomas s Timothy and Esther Rider
Ellington		28	James s Jacob and Frances Towler
Fearby	June	4	Elizabeth d John and Ann Hutchinson
Masham		4	Jeffrey s Jeffrey and Ann Clarkson
Healey Cote		5	Esther d Thomas and Dorothy Smorthit
Healey		6	Thomas s Thomas and Ann Wrather
Masham		8	George s Sampson and Dorothy Horner
Masham		18	Christopher and George illeg ss Eleanor Robinson
Masham		25	Robert s Richard and Eleanor Whitelock
Nutwith Cote		25	Margaret d Edmund and Margaret Kaye
Fairthorn	July	2	Henry s Thomas and Amy Scafe
Masham		16	George s William and Jane Parker
Warthermarske		23	Ann d Mark and Elizabeth Barker
Swinton		23	Barnabas s Anthony and Ann Hill
Masham		30	George s William and Rosamond Stevenson
Arnagill		30	Amy d William and Amy Suttill
High Ellington	Aug	2	Thomas s George and Jane Jackson
Masham		19	Charles s Edward and Elizabeth Moises, b Aug 10 (dead)
Fearby		27	George s Thomas and Jane Ascough
High Ash Head		27	Ann d Matthew and Margaret Ascough
Healey	Sept	12	David and Edward twin ss David and Ann Walker
Masham		17	Elizabeth d William and Mary Beckwith
Sourmire		17	Thomas s Robert and Elizabeth Imeson
Masham		24	Matthew s James and Dorothy Towler
Warthermarske		30	Mary d John and Mary Metcalf
Swinton	Oct	3	Edward s Edward and Elizabeth Horsman
Ellingstring		8	John s John and Ann Thirlway
Moorhead		12	John s Peter and Mary Hutchinson
Summerside		12	Ann d Peter and Esther Carter
Masham		12	William s Thomas and Mary Clarke
High Ellington		15	John s John and Jane Barwick
Masham		29	Frances d Matthew and Frances Park
Pott	Nov	2	Edmond s George and Ann Barker
Masham		5	Ann d Caleb and Elizabeth Powel
Fearby		24	Thomas s Thomas and Ellen Nelson

Masham	Dec	9	Margaret d John and Jane Clarkson
Summerside		11	Margaret d George and Mary Graham
Ash Head		11	Isabella d Mark and Elizabeth Hutchinson
Masham		21	Christopher s Thomas and Ann Court
[p. 24]			
Masham		27	Thomas s Thomas and Margaret Martindale
Masham		30	Jeremiah s Robert and Jane Smith

64 [*annual total*]

Baptisms 1776

Masham	Jan	1	Thomas s John and Sarah Chapman
Warthermarske		10	Sarah d Thomas and Mary Theakston
Masham		14	John s William and Martha Harrison
Ellingstring		20	Matthew s John and Esther Emerson
Masham		21	Mary d Thomas [Edward *crossed out*] and Ann Dowson
Masham		21	Rachel d James and Hannah Hamilton
Masham		28	Thomas s Thomas and Elizabeth Banks
Masham		29	Hannah d George and Ellen Thackwray
Fearby	Feb	5	William s Anthony and Ann Ingleby
Masham		9	George s Thomas and Ann Geldart
Masham		11	Fanny d George and Esther Wilson
Ilton		18	John s John and Ann Tayler
Masham		25	Ann d George and Elizabeth Firby
Masham	Mar	6	Robert s Robert and Margaret Atkinson
Masham		9	Ann d Richard and Jane Pickersgill
Healey		17	Ann d Adam and Mary Barnes
High Ellington		21	Jane d Matthew and Mary Slee
Fearby	Apr	7	Nancy d Robert and Elizabeth Blackburn
High Burton Lane		14	William s Thomas and Dorothy Finley
Brock Ridding		14	John posthumous s John Pybus
Sourmire		28	Esther d Matthew and Esther Barker
Masham		28	George s Richard and Sarah Smith
Ilton		11	Margaret d Ralph and Margaret Horseman [*with note*: omitted before]
High Ellington	May	22	William s Thomas and Dorothy King
Masham		26	Ann d Thomas and Mary Banks
Masham		26	Jonathan s John and Elizabeth Roundall
Healey		26	Hannah d Richard and Hannah Thompson
Healey		28	Esther d John and Hannah Barnes
Masham	June	3	Thomas s Edward and Ann Croft
Fearby		2	Esther d Thomas and Mary Carter
Warthermarske		15	Sarah d George and Catharine Leathley
Sutton Penn		3	Dorothy d Leonard and Elizabeth Hodgson
Masham		23	Ann d John and Ann Place

Fearby		16	James s Thomas and Ann Taylor
Ilton	July	7	George s John and Sarah Metcalf
Masham		19	Dorothy d Joseph and Dorothy Thorns
Masham		23	Thomas illeg s Margaret Court
Masham		28	Esther d John and Isabel Crossley
Sourmire	Aug	1	Esther d Edmund and Esther Barker
[p. 25]			
Low Mains		1	Matthew s Timothy and Esther Rider
Healey		5	Ann d William and Mary Bollum
Ellingstring		15	George s George and Sarah Hinley
Gollinglith		18	George s Michael and Ann Freer
Swinton	Sept	1	John s John and Rachel Hall
Masham		15	Mary d George and Elizabeth Clark
Masham		19	Jane d Leonard and Jane Mudd
Masham		19	David s Benjamin and Mary Siddall
Masham		22	William s William and Elizabeth Joye
Masham	Oct	20	George s George and Ann Atkinson
Swinton		21	William s William and Elizabeth Morton
Brock Ridding	Nov	3	John s Joseph and Sarah Rodwell
Healey		10	George s Thomas and Catherine Barrows
Summerside	Dec	14	Peter s George and Mary Graham
High Ellington		15	William s William and Hannah Brignall
Aldburgh		20	Ann d Thomas and Ann Judson
Masham		31	Elizabeth d Mr Samuel and Elizabeth Wrather

56 [*annual total*]

Baptisms 1777

Healey	Jan	7	Anna d John and Dorothy Ascough
High Ellington		19	Stephen s Leonard and Elizabeth Wilkinson
Masham		26	William s John and Jane Scurrah
Masham		26	Mary d Christopher and Hannah Clarke
Ripon		26	William s Edward and Dinah Robinson
High Ash Head	Feb	6	William s Matthew and Margaret Ascough
Quarry House		15	Mary d Thomas and Mary Lightfoot
Swinton		16	Margaret d Matthew and Christiana Imeson
Masham	Mar	5	Mary d Matthew and Mary Gill
Masham		10	Thomas s Thomas and Ann Dawson
Ash Head		13	Mark s Mark and Elizabeth Hutchinson
North Cote		14	Samuel s John and Ann King
Masham		16	Henry s Thomas and Mary Kay
Masham		23	William s George and Elizabeth Firby
Masham		23	Thomas s Henry and Elizabeth Lupton
Masham		23	Mary d William and Jane Parker
Ilton	Apr	5	Joseph s William and Edith Lightfoot

Swinton		13	William s David and Elizabeth Thompson
Swinton		13	Ann d Anthony and Ann Hill
Ellingstring		26	Esther d Thomas and Jane Ascough
Masham	May	4	David s David and Elizabeth Walker
Warthermarske		6	John s Mark and Elizabeth Barker
Masham		17	James illeg s Martha Hutchinson
[p. 26]			
Summerside		18	Anna d Peter and Esther Carter
Healey Cote		19	John s Thomas and Dorothy Smorthwaite
Fearby		19	George s Thomas and Ellen Nelson
Fearby		25	William illeg s Deborah Wintersgill
Masham		25	Hannah d William and Hannah Robinson
Masham	June	1	Thomas s Thomas and Ann Dowson
Masham		1	John s Thomas and Frances Hutchinson
Masham		1	George s Jeffrey and Ann Clarkson
Masham		22	William s Christopher and Jane Merryweather
Fearby		22	Robert s Christopher and Mary Dawson
Healey	July	20	Matthew s Thomas and Ann Wrather
[no place]		27	Jane posthumous d Thomas Gill and Jane his wf
Ellingstring	Aug	19	Dorothy d Jeremiah and Elizabeth Metcalf
Warthermarske		24	George s John and Mary Thorp
Swinton		24	Elizabeth d Edward and Elizabeth Horsman
Warthermarske		24	Sarah d John and Mary Metcalf
Nutwith Cote		31	Mary illeg d Dinah Ripley
Masham	Sept	3	Ralph s Henry and Eleanor Charnock
Grewelthorpe		4	James s Michael and Mary Grainger
Masham		7	George s John and Sarah Chapman
Masham		8	Elizabeth d George and Margaret Fenwick
Swinton		14	Rachel d John and Rachel Hall
Masham		14	Dorothy d John and Jane Clarkson
Masham		17	Esther d Richard and Eleanor Whitelock
Masham		21	John s Charles and Elizabeth Atkinson
Healey		29	Hannah and Elizabeth twin dd George and Elizabeth Wintersgill
Masham	Oct	5	Mary d Joseph and Ann Jackson
High Ellington		10	Elizabeth d William and Elizabeth Jeff
Masham		24	Thomas s Robert and Mary Rider
Fearby	Nov	2	Christopher s Matthew and Hannah Craggs
Ellingstring	Oct	31	Thomas s Thomas and Mary Plews
Masham	Nov	9	William s William and Martha Harrison
Sourmire		14	George s Edmund and Esther Barker
Masham		20	Edward s Edward and Ann Croft
Warthermarske		23	Elizabeth d William and Ellen Reynard
High Ellington		27	Jane d George and Jane Jackson
Masham		28	Mary d Edward and Elizabeth Moises, b Oct 27

High Ellington	Dec	3	Esther illeg d Jane Jackson
Masham		12	Jane d Caleb and Elizabeth Powel
[p. 27]			
Gildermires		14	Edward s William and Elizabeth Joye

64 [*annual total*]

Baptisms 1778

Breary Banks	Jan	1	Thomas s Robert and Mary Walker
Healey		18	Ellen d Richard and Hannah Thompson
Healey		18	Mary d George and Judith Tanfield
Healey		18	Christopher s David and Ann Walker
Summerside		23	Matthew s Matthew and Ann Burrill
Masham		25	Elizabeth d Thomas and Elizabeth Banks
Masham	Feb	22	William s Thomas and Mary Banks
Summerside	Mar	12	Mary d George and Mary Graham
High Ash Head		28	Thomas s Matthew and Margaret Ascough
Ash Head		28	Peter s Mark and Elizabeth Hutchinson
Ellingstring	Apr	2	Ann d Leonard and Ann Wilkinson
Masham		3	Jane d Thomas and Ann Geldart
Masham		5	Christopher s George and Esther Wilson
Cart Ring		5	Nancy d Thomas and Ann Taylor
Masham		8	Mary d John and Elizabeth Reed
Healey		22	Jane d Jonathan and Elizabeth Lobley
Masham		22	Frances d James and Ann Abbot
Masham		26	Thomas illeg s Agnes Richmond
Masham		26	Ann d John and Elizabeth Jackson
Arnagill	May	8	James s William and Amy Suttill
Low Wood		16	Edward s Jeffrey and Eleanor Horsman
High Ellington		16	Simeon illeg s Ellen Collins
Healey	June	9	Mary d William and Mary Bollum
Ellingstring		10	Jane d Emanuel and Ann Lye
Warren House		14	Christopher s Charles and Mary Kendall
Masham	July	5	George s John and Margaret Morrell
Masham		15	Grace d Thomas and Margaret Martindale
Sourmire		19	Jane d Matthew and Esther Barker
Northallerton		19	Ann illeg d Ann Reynard
Masham	Aug	2	William s Christopher and Hannah Clarke
Ilton		2	William s John and Ann Taylor
Sutton		2	Benjamin s Robert and Mary Jeff
Masham		23	Edward s Robert and Margaret Atkinson
Swinton		24	George s William and Elizabeth Morton
Ellingstring	Sept	6	Joseph s Thomas and Ann Robinson
Fearby		17	Elizabeth d William and Mary Hardisty
Masham		17	Joseph s Benjamin and Mary Siddall

Healey		29	Mary d Anthony and Mary Urwin
Fairthorn	Oct	4	John s Thomas and Amy Scaife
Summerside		10	William s William and Isabella Topham
Masham		11	Jane d James and Frances Duffield
[p. 28]			
Masham		17	Mary d John and Sarah Chapman
Sutton		18	Augustine s Leonard and Elizabeth Hodgson
High Ellington		21	Betty d Thomas and Dorothy King
Masham		26	Samuel s Samuel and Elizabeth Wrather
Ilton	Nov	8	James s George and Jane Metcalfe
Masham		15	Barbara d William and Rosamond Stevenson
Masham		29	Edward s Jeffrey and Ann Clarkson
Healey	Dec	17	Francis s John and Hannah Barnes
Swinton		27	Elizabeth d Anthony and Ann Hill
Fearby		30	Esther d Anthony and Ann Ingleby

51 [*annual total*]

Baptisms 1779

Ellingstring	Jan	20	George s John and Esther Emerson
Fearby		22	John s Ralph and Mary Edon
Masham		24	Ann d Thomas and Ann Dowson
Masham	Feb	13	Hannah d Ralph and Mary Pybus
Fearby		14	Mary d Thomas and Ellen Nelson
Quarry House		19	Hannah d Thomas and Mary Lightfoot
Low Burton		21	Dorothy d Thomas and Dorothy Finley
Warthermarske		26	Mary d Mark and Elizabeth Barker
Healey		28	George s Thomas and Ann Wrather
Healey		28	Thomas s John and Dorothy Ascough
Ilton		28	Peter s Thomas and Alice Casling
Masham	Mar	13	Jane d John and Elizabeth Metcalf
Ellingstring		15	Mary d Thomas and Mary Plews
Ash Head		20	Matthew s Mark and Elizabeth Hutchinson
Masham		20	John s William and Mary Parker
Warthermarske	Apr	4	John s John and Mary Thorpe
Masham		4	Mary illeg d Isabel Hawkswell
Brock Ridding		7	Henry s Joseph and Sarah Rodwell
Moorhead		17	Peter s Peter and Mary Hutchinson
Summerside		17	Hannah d Peter and Esther Carter
Masham		24	Jane d Robert and Mary Rider
Masham		24	Elizabeth d Thomas and Jane Clarke
Warthermarske		25	Catharine d Joseph and Elizabeth Atkinson
Masham		27	Jane d John and Jane Clarkson
Masham	May	2	Hannah d Christopher and Jane Merryweather
Fearby		5	John s Thomas and Mary Carter

Healey		20	Elizabeth d Francis and Elizabeth Glew
Healey Cote		24	Elizabeth d Thomas and Dorothy Smorthwaite
Ilton		28	Thomas s William and Edith Lightfoot
[p. 29]			
Masham	June	3	Rosamond d John and Isabel Crosley
Masham		13	George s John and Jane Scurrah
Masham		20	Catharine d Edward and Ann Croft
Masham		27	Ann d George and Ann Atkinson
Ellington	July	25	George illeg s Elizabeth Ashton
High Ellington		8	Richard s Matthew and Mary Slye
Masham		11	Ann d William and Mary Beckwith
Healey		11	Robert s Adam and Mary Barnes
Fearby		27	Charles s Michael and Ann Fryar
Sourmire	Aug	9	John s Edmund and Esther Barker
Masham		10	John s George and Elizabeth Clarke
Pickersgill		14	Stephen s Thomas and Hannah Towler
Ilton		18	James s Ralph and Elizabeth Prest
Masham		22	Ellen d Richard and Eleanor Whitelock
Ellingstring	Sept	1	Jeremiah s Jeremiah and Elizabeth Metcalf
Sheffield		12	James s Thomas and Christiana Thompson
Swinton		12	Jane d Thomas and Mary Benson
Swinton		19	Dorothy d Matthew and Christiana Imeson
Masham		20	Nottingham s John and Jane Simpson
Masham	Oct	11	Edward s Francis and Ann Thompson
Masham		11	Matthew s Leonard and Jane Mudd
High Ash Head		29	Matthew s Matthew and Margaret Ascough
Masham		31	Frances d Thomas and Mary Kaye
Warthermarske	Nov	7	Jane d William and Ellen Reynard
Masham		7	Thomas s George and Mary Shaw
Ellingstring		23	Jenny d George and Sarah Hinley
Masham		27	Mary d Thomas Banks, saddler, and Mary his wf
Masham		28	William s Robert and Jane Smith
Fearby	Dec	12	Jane illeg d Ann Snell
Masham		27	Mary d Richard and Jane Cornforth

59 [*annual total*]

Baptisms 1780

Healey	Jan	16	Christopher s Richard and Hannah Thompson
Masham		23	Edward illeg s Elizabeth Banks
Fearby		23	John illeg s Isabella Burnet
Towler Hill		23	Mary d Joseph and Sarah Lancaster
Masham		30	Sarah d John and Catherine Dennison
Masham		31	Charles s Caleb and Elizabeth Powel
Swinton	Feb	11	Jane d Edward and Elizabeth Horseman

Ellingstring		17	Joseph illeg s Jane Walker
[p. 30]			
Ellingstring		21	Elizabeth d Thomas and Ann Robinson
Swinton		21	Elizabeth d William and Elizabeth Morton
Swinton		27	John s Ralph and Ann Caldbeck
Masham		27	Margaret d Thomas and Frances Hutchinson
Low Ellington	Mar	2	Henry s Wilks and Ann Metcalf
Masham		5	John s William and Mary Parker
Ellington		19	John s Arthur and Mary Ashe
Ilton		21	Anthony illeg s Elizabeth Prest
Masham		26	Elizabeth d James and Elizabeth Towler
Masham	Apr	3	John s John and Beatrice Plews
Masham		8	Ann d George and Ann Truthit
Masham		9	Thomas s William and Elizabeth Carter
Masham		18	Joseph s Joseph and Margaret Horner
Sutton	May	7	Thomas s Leonard and Elizabeth Hodgson
Healey		16	Robert s George and Elizabeth Wintersgill
Ilton		17	Mary d Thomas and Sarah Metcalfe
Masham		21	John s Benjamin and Mary Siddall
Swinton		26	John s David and Elizabeth Thompson
High Mains	June	17	Margaret d William and Mary Ballan
Fearby		18	Ralph s Ralph and Mary Edon
High Ellington	July	8	George s George and Jane Jackson
Masham		23	Barnabas s William and Jane Parker
Low Ellington	Aug	1	Christopher s Charles and Ann Rumfitt
Masham		14	John s James and Jane Metcalf
Masham		17	William s Samuel and Elizabeth Wrather
Masham		17	Margaret d John and Margaret Morrell
Masham		21	Thomas s Thomas and Ann Geldart
Swinton		27	Joseph s Joseph and Elizabeth Atkinson
Masham	Sept	2	William s William and Elizabeth Hartley
Ellingstring		3	James s William and Elizabeth Outhwaite
High Ellington		3	Ann d William and Elizabeth Jeff
Masham		13	John s Peter and Mary Haw
Masham		17	Elizabeth d John and Sarah Chapman
Ash Head		23	Rebecca d George and Mary Graham
Sourmire		23	Mark s Mark [*altered from* Matthew] and Esther Hutchinson
Masham	Oct	1	Mary d William and Martha Harrison
Masham		19	Martha d Matthew and Mary Gill
Masham		22	William s William and Mary Husband
[p. 31]			
Masham		22	William s John and Jane London
Masham		22	John illeg s Ann Pratt
Masham	Nov	9	Catherine d Thomas and Margaret Martindale

Masham		19	Daniel s Robert and Margaret Atkinson
Summerside	Dec	1	Christiana d Matthew and Ann Burrill
Masham		10	Margaret illeg d Jane Young
Fearby		21	Mary d Peter and Ann Jackson
Lamb Hill		24	George illeg s Jane Urwin

54 [*annual total*]

Baptisms 1781

Ellingstring	Jan	29	Mary d Joseph and Ann Reynard
Ellingstring		29	George s John and Elizabeth Berry
Fairthorn	Feb	3	David s Thomas and Amy Scafe
Warthermarske		18	Mark s Mark and Elizabeth Barker
Masham		16	Mary d Christopher and Agnes Pickersgill
Masham		22	Margaret d George and Margaret Fenwick
Hall Garth House		26	Thomas s John and Mary Jackson
Masham	Mar	4	Robert s John and Elizabeth Jackson
Ellingstring		23	Jonathan s Thomas and Mary Plews
Ilton		24	Christopher s William and Edith Lightfoot
Masham	Apr	22	Richard s Thomas and Ann Dowson
Sourmire		27	Ann d Edmund and Esther Barker
Masham		29	John s William and Mary Atkinson
Masham		29	Elizabeth d James and Frances Duffield
Masham	May	2	Jane d Thomas and Jane Clarke
Masham		6	Mary d John and Jane Scurrah
Healey		27	Catharine d Francis and Elizabeth Glew
Fearby		27	Mary d Charles and Mary Kendall
Masham	June	8	Mary d Francis and Ann Thompson
Masham		14	Thomas s John and Alice Craven
Nutwith Cote		24	Thomas s Thomas and Hannah Allanson
Masham	July	30	Edward s Thomas and Elizabeth Clarkson
Masham		29	Thomas s George and Esther Wilson
Masham	Aug	19	Anthony s George and Elizabeth Firby [*later pencil note*: died after 1873]
Masham		21	James illeg s Elizabeth Richardson
Warthermarske	Sept	2	William s John and Mary Thorpe
Masham		10	Matthew s Jeffrey and Ann Clarkson
Towler Hill		17	Matthew illeg s Elizabeth Burton
Nutwith Cote		30	Thomas s Thomas and Sarah Metcalf
Low Ellington	Oct	20	Matthew s Robert and Elizabeth Imeson
[*no place*]		28	John s Richard and Marianne Ward, strolling players
Masham	Nov	4	James illeg s Jane Croft
Masham		10	William s Robert and Mary Rider
High Ellington		11	Dorothy d Thomas and Dorothy King

[p. 32]

Gollinglith		24	Elizabeth d Joseph and Sarah Lancaster
Masham		24	Dorothy d Christopher and Jane Merryweather
Masham	Dec	2	Frances d John and Catharine Dennison
Quarry House		14	Elizabeth d Thomas and Mary Lightfoot
Healey		15	Charles s Edward and Judith Rudd
Ellingstring		26	Jane illeg d Jane Beckwith

40 [*annual total*]

Baptisms 1782

Ellingstring	Jan	1	John s Immanuel and Ann Lye
Ellingstring		1	Esther d John and Esther Emerson
Low Ellington	Feb	2	James Court illeg s Mary Craggs
Masham		3	Thomas s Henry and Elizabeth Lupton
Fearby		9	William s William and Mary Ballan
Fearby		9	John s Michael and Ann Fryer
Ellingstring		10	Thomas s Thomas and Ann Harrison
Swinton		12	Mary d William and Elizabeth Morton
Healey		16	Henry s Richard and Hannah Thompson
Fearby		16	William s Peter and Ann Jackson
Masham	Mar	3	Bella d Thomas and Mary Banks
Ilton		6	Thomas s Ralph and Elizabeth Prest
Masham		10	Esther d John and Beatrice Plews
Masham		17	Mary d William and Mary Ashton
Masham		24	John s Thomas and Elizabeth Banks
Masham		31	William s George and Elizabeth Clarke
Ilton	Apr	8	John s George and Jane Metcalf
Low Burton		7	Elizabeth d Thomas and Dorothy Finley
Ilton		8	Thomas s John and Mary Metcalf
Masham		21	Lister s Robert and Jane Smith
Masham		28	Thomas s John and Isabella Crossland
Ilton	May	5	George s Joseph and Mary Hanley
Ellingstring		8	William illeg s Margaret Burton
Masham	June	2	Ann d Joseph and Ellen Leeming
Masham		9	Ann d Richard and Eleanor Whitelock
Masham		15	Thomas s Samuel and Elizabeth Wrather
Summerside		16	Jane d Peter and Esther Carter
Arnagill		16	Jane d William and Mary Suttill
Swinton		27	William s Edward and Elizabeth Horsman
Masham	July	7	Hannah d Benjamin and Mary Siddall
[p. 33]			
Masham		10	William s John and Sarah Shaw
Masham		14	Agnes [*altered from* Mary] d Christopher and Agnes Pickersgill
Masham		14	Elizabeth d Robert and Mary Morton

Spout House		15	Ann d Peter and Esther Barker
Masham		27	Elizabeth d William and Elizabeth Gibson
Healey		28	David s Adam and Mary Barnes
Masham		28	Peter s Peter and Jane Robinson
Masham	Aug	4	Leonard s Leonard and Jane Mudd
Masham	Sept	7	Ann d Thomas and Alicea Tennant
Masham		15	James s James and Mary Henderson
Swinton		15	Ralph s Ralph and Ann Caldbeck
Masham		29	Thomas s William and Elizabeth Joye
Masham		29	Margaret illeg d Esther Duffield
Ash Head	Oct	5	George s George and Mary Graham
Nutwith Cote		8	John s Thomas and Sarah Metcalfe
Ilton		12	James s William and Edith Lightfoot
Masham		13	Henry s John and Sarah Chapman
Masham	Nov	9	Margaret d Thomas and Jane Geldart
Masham	Dec	1	Jane illeg d Dorothy Thompson
Masham		20	Maria d George Woodd esq., and Gertrude his wf
Ellingstring		27	Thomas Plews s Joseph and Ann Reynard

51 [*annual total*]

Baptisms 1783

Fearby	Jan	1	John s Charles and Mary Kendall
Low Ellington		5	Francis s Jacob and Frances Towler
Masham		5	Jane d William and Isabel Carter
Masham		12	Ellen d Thomas and Jane Clarke
Nutwith Cote		19	Dinah d Thomas and Hannah Allanson
Masham		26	Isaac s Isaac and Mary Towler
Healey	Feb	8	John s George and Judith Tanfield
Masham		19	Ann d George and Mary Pickersgill
Sourmire		22	Elizabeth d Edmund and Esther Barker
Swinton Green		23	Jane d Thomas and Ann Browne
Masham	Mar	9	James s James and Jane Metcalf
Low Ellington		9	Ann d Arthur and Mary Ashe
Masham		18	John s Peter and Mary Haw
Sutton Penn	Apr	6	George s Leonard and Elizabeth Hodgson
Healey		6	Francis s Francis and Elizabeth Glew
Swinton		19	Elizabeth d Joseph and Elizabeth Atkinson
Masham		19	Francis s Francis and Ann Thompson
Masham		27	George s James and Frances Duffield
Healey	May	4	Jane d Thomas and Ann Wrather
Healey		4	Ann d Richard and Hannah Thompson
Ellingstring		11	Ann d John and Elizabeth Berry
[p. 34]			
Warthermarske	Apr	21	Elizabeth d Mark and Elizabeth Barker [*marginal note:*

132

			misplaced, turn back]
Masham	May	25	James and Rachel twin children Thomas and Ann Dowson
Hall Garth House		25	John s John and Mary Jackson
Fearby	June	8	Esther d Thomas and Ellen Nelson
Masham		8	James s James and Elizabeth Towler
Masham		15	John s Richard and Elizabeth Topham
Fearby		20	Thomas s Ralph and Mary Edon
Masham	July	6	William s Francis and Elizabeth Terry
Masham		20	Henrietta d John and Henrietta Baines
Warthermarske		23	Elizabeth d George and Ann Truthit
Masham		25	George s Ralph and Mary Pybus
Masham	Aug	3	Ann d Christopher and Jane Merryweather
Masham		8	Alfred s William and Mary Parker
Ellingstring		16	Ann d Thomas and Mary Plews
Masham		20	Mary d William and Elizabeth Gibson
Masham		21	Hannah d William and Mary Husband
Ilton	Sept	22	William s Thomas and Ellen Scaife
Masham	Oct	26	Nancy d William and Dorothy Parkinson
Masham	Nov	2	George s George and Mary Shaw
Masham		21	William s Joseph and Ellen Leeming
Masham		21	William s George and Elizabeth Clark
Healey		26	Nancy d Anthony and Mary Urwin
Masham		30	James s Henry and Elizabeth Lupton
Swinton	Dec	5	Ann d William and Elizabeth Morton
Fearby		14	John s Michael and Ann Fryar
Masham		14	Hannah d Stephen and Mary Siddall
Masham		17	Edmund s Peter and Esther Barker
Masham		21	Jane d John and Elizabeth Imeson
High Ellington		30	Christopher s Robert and Mary Bellerby

51 [*annual total*]

Baptisms 1784

Warthermarske	Jan	11	Elizabeth d John and Mary Thorpe
Masham		20	Ann d Christopher and Agnes Pickersgill
Ellingstring		21	Alice illeg d Ann Lye
Fearby		31	Thomas s William and Mary Ballan
Masham	Feb	22	David s William and Mary Astwood
Masham		22	John s John and Ann Banks
High Ellington	Mar	4	Abraham s George and Jane Jackson
Ilton		7	Elizabeth d John and Esther Dummill
Masham		18	John s John and Jane London
Masham		26	Isabella d Thomas and Margaret Martindale
Masham		26	Margaret d Francis and Ann Thompson

[p. 35]

Masham		28	James s Isaac and Mary Towler
Masham		28	Rose illeg d Elizabeth Richardson
Masham		28	Mary d Thomas and Frances Hutchinson
Fearby		28	George illeg s Elizabeth Plews
Masham	Apr	4	James s John and Jane Scurrah
Masham		8	Thomas s Thomas and Alicia Tennant
Swinton		11	Jane d Joseph and Mary Hanley
Masham		11	William s Benjamin and Mary Siddall
Masham		21	Abigail d John and Jane Wood
Masham		25	Richard s George and Esther Wilson
Masham	May	2	Mary d William and Mary Clarkson
Gollinglith		3	Joseph Westmoreland s George and Sarah Lancaster
High Ash Head		8	Margaret d Matthew and Margaret Ascough
Leighton Park	June	2	Matthew s Matthew and Esther Barker
High Ash Head		3	George s Benjamin and Grace Allen
Quarry House		6	Thomas s Thomas and Mary Lightfoot
Ellingstring		6	Mary d William and Elizabeth Outhwaite
Ellingstring		6	Ann d Thomas and Ann Robinson
Masham		13	Elizabeth d Thomas and Mary Banks
Ilton		19	Mary illeg d Elizabeth Prest
Masham		24	Noah illeg s Ellen Croft, poor
Ellingstring		25	Ann d John and Esther Emerson
Swinton Green		27	Ann d Thomas and Ann Brown
Masham		27	John s George and Margaret Fenwick
Ash Head	July	17	Jonathan s George and Mary Graham
Masham	Aug	1	Margaret d Christopher and Sarah Wilson
Masham		8	Isabella d Robert and Jane Smith
Ilton	Sept	5	William s Henry and Mary Scaife
Masham		19	Mary d Jeffrey and Ann Clarkson
Masham	Oct	3	Ann d Thomas and Mary Croft
Ilton		3	George s George and Jane Metcalf
Healey		10	Mary d Francis and Betty Glew
Masham		11	Anna d John and Henrietta Baines
Ilton		22	Esther d John and Mary Metcalf
Ilton	Nov	7	John s Ralph and Elizabeth Prest
[*no place*]		14	Susanna illeg d Mary Butterfield
Masham		21	Mary d William and Mary Parker
Masham		23	Ann d Thomas and Mary Clarke
Healey		27	George s Edward and Judith Rudd

50 [*annual total*]

[p. 36]   **Baptisms 1785**

Masham	Jan	2	Barbara d William and Jane Parker

134

Masham		16	Jane d John and Beatrice Plews
Sourmire	Feb	5	Edmund s Edmund and Esther Barker
Masham		5	Ann d John and Ann Carter
Masham		6	George s John and Mary Jackson
Masham		6	Elizabeth d George and Mary Pickersgill
Masham	Mar	11	Jane d Christopher and Martha Peacock
Ellingstring		16	Emanuel s Emanuel and Ann Lye
Burton		22	Ellen d Thomas and Dorothy Finley
Healey	Apr	3	Thomas s Thomas and Hannah Steadman
Masham		3	George s James and Ann Towler
Masham		17	Ann illeg d Mary Dent, poor
Masham	May	1	Sarah d Francis and Elizabeth Terry
Healey		1	Elizabeth d Richard and Hannah Thomson
Low Ellington		4	Martha and William twin children Arthur and Ann Ashe
Ilton	June	4	William s Michael and Ann Walker
Ash Head		9	George s Matthew and Margaret Ascough
Summerside		9	Mary d Peter and Esther Carter
Summerside		9	Thomas illeg s Mary Nelson
Leighton		9	Mary d Peter and Elizabeth Hanley
Masham		12	Elizabeth d Joseph and Eleanor Leeming
Ellingstring		12	Elizabeth d Jeremiah and Elizabeth Metcalf
Masham		23	Robert s John and Isabel Crosley
Masham		26	Robert s Robert and Mary Rider
Masham		26	Thomas s Leonard and Jane Mudd
Swinton		26	Ann d Ralph and Ann Caldbeck
Fearby		26	Mary d Robert and Ann Plews
Ellington	July	3	Anthony s Anthony and Elizabeth Thwaites
Ellingstring		9	Joseph s Joseph and Ann Reynard
High Ellington		10	Christopher s Thomas and Mary Craggs
Masham		16	Richard s James and Jane Metcalf
Masham		17	Gabriel s Thomas and Mary Kaye
Masham		29	Benjamin s Robert and Margaret Atkinson
Masham	Aug	7	Isabella d John and Sarah Chapman
Masham		10	John s William and Mary Husband
Masham		11	Ann d Richard and Isabel Boynton
Masham		14	George s Thomas and Mary Dixon
[p. 37]			
Masham		19	William s Thomas and Margaret Martindale
Fearby		26	Margaret d Jacob and Margaret Ruecroft
Warthermarske	Sept	25	Sarah d Mark and Elizabeth Barker
Fearby		30	William s Ralph and Mary Edon
Fearby	Oct	14	John s William and Mary Ballan
[no place]		16	Ann d James and Christiana Walker, travellers
Masham		16	Mary illeg d Ann Morrell, poor
Roomer		28	Mary d Richard and Elizabeth Topham

Masham	Nov	1	Elizabeth d Christopher and Agnes Pickersgill
Masham		5	Christopher s Christopher and Jane Merriweather
Ilton		7	Elizabeth d Henry and Elizabeth Fryar
Ellingstring		17	Thomas s Thomas and Mary Plews
Masham	Dec	11	John s James and Frances Duffield, poor
Swinton		12	Lancelot-Harcourt s William and Elizabeth Morton
Ellington		18	John s John and Mary Howard
Healey		25	Hannah d Adam and Mary Barnes

54 [*annual total*]

Baptisms 1786

Swinton Mill	Jan	14	George s John and Hannah Wood [*altered from* Dawson]
Warthermarske	Feb	5	Edward s John and Mary Thorpe
Healey		6	Ann d George and Judith Tanfield
Masham		12	Mary d George and Mary Shaw
Masham		12	Mary d William and Dorothy Parkinson
Masham		19	Elizabeth d William and Mary Clarkson
Ellingstring		24	Thomas illeg s Margaret Plews
Masham		26	Thomas s Stephen and Mary Siddall
Masham		26	John s John and Elizabeth Imeson
Ilton	Mar	5	John s John and Esther Dumhill
Masham		12	John s William and Mary Astwood
Masham	Apr	16	Francis s Benjamin and Mary Siddall
Ilton		16	William s Joseph and Elizabeth Atkinson
Ellingstring		17	Mary d Thomas and Ann Robinson
Warthermarske		23	Margaret illeg d Mary Akers
Masham	May	28	Frances d Thomas and Mary Banks
Masham	June	9	Ann d William and Jane Parker
Ellingstring		18	William Thompson illeg s Ann Lye
Masham		25	William s John and Ann Banks
Healey		28	William s George and Elizabeth Wintersgill
Masham		30	Catharine d Thomas and Frances Hutchinson
[p. 38]			
Masham	July	8	William s Thomas and Ann Geldart
Masham		9	Mary d Thomas and Mary Croft
Masham		9	Michael s Isaac and Mary Towler
Gollinglith		13	William s Joseph and Sarah Lancaster
Swinton Green		16	Mary d Thomas and Ann Browne
Masham		23	Thomas s William and Sarah Pybus
Quarry House		30	Joseph s Thomas and Mary Lightfoot
Masham		30	Mary d Thomas and Alice Tennant
Swinton	Aug	6	Jane d Matthew and Sarah Sedgswick
Masham		9	Ann illeg d Ellen Croft, poor

Masham		13	John s Thomas and Dorothy Allanson
Masham		13	Elizabeth d Jeffrey and Ann Clarkson
Masham		13	Ann d Francis and Ann Thompson
Masham		13	Mary d John and Jane London
High Ash Head		17	Elizabeth d Benjamin and Grace Allen
Masham	Sept	1	William s John and Henrietta Baines
Fearby		7	Anthony s Anthony and Mary Urwin
Healey Pasture End		8	James s David and Elizabeth Walker
Arnagill	Oct	5	Francis s William and Mary Suttill
Ash Head		5	Esther d George and Mary Graham
Masham		8	Elizabeth d Benjamin and Elizabeth Akers
Fearby		14	Thomas s Michael and Mary Fryar
Fearby		15	Mary d Thomas and Hannah Steadman
Ilton		15	Henry s Henry and Mary Scafe
Masham		15	George s George and Isabella Robinson
Masham		29	Christopher s Ralph and Mary Pybus
Fearby		29	Anthony s Anthony and Eleanor Ballan
Masham	Nov	5	Thomas s Thomas and Jane Clarke
Masham		5	Isabella d George and Elizabeth Clarke, pauper
Healey Pasture End		6	John illeg s Elizabeth Metcalf
Masham		8	Mary d Christopher and Martha Peacock
Ellington		12	John illeg s Jane Wintersgill
Fearby		22	Joseph [*altered from* John] s Joseph and Mary Handley
Gollinglith	Dec	6	Peter s Peter and [*blank*] Mallaby

55 [*annual total*]

Baptisms 1787

Sourmire	Jan	22	Elizabeth d Mark and Esther Hutchinson
Hall Garth House	Feb	5	James s John and Mary Jackson
Masham		13	William s John and Jane Scurrah, pauper
Ellingstring		19	Luke illeg s Mary Jones
Masham		28	William s Thomas and Jane Parkinson

[p. 39]

Swinton	Mar	9	Thomas s Edward and Elizabeth Horsman
Leighton		9	Sarah d Peter and Elizabeth Hanley
Ellingstring		17	George s Cornelius and Ann Plews
Masham		27	Robert s William and Elizabeth Beckwith, pauper
Ilton	Apr	1	Prudence d Ralph and Elizabeth Prest
Masham		2	Robert s Thomas and Alice Raynwick
Masham		11	Elizabeth illeg d Mary Nottras, pauper
Healey		13	Francis s Francis and Elizabeth Glew
Swinton		15	Mary d John and Hannah Wood
Healey Mill		22	Henry s Henry and Jane Ripley
Warthermarske		29	Matthew s Mark and Elizabeth Barker

Sutton	May	6	John s Thomas and Elizabeth Stainthorp
Masham		11	John s John and Esther Richmond
Masham		13	Edward Nidd, an adult
Ellingstring		13	John s John and Dorothy Abbott
Roomer		22	Richard s Richard and Elizabeth Topham
Masham		27	Isaac Goodlad [*altered from* John Goodluck] s Henry and Ann Braithwaite
Sutton	June	4	Ann d William and Edith Lightfoot
Masham		28	Anise d Thomas and Ann Edmondson
Ellington	July	1	John s Thomas and Mary Craggs
Masham		2	Alice d Peter and Sarah Plews
Swinton		6	Mary d Thomas and Mary Imeson
Ilton		8	William Walker illeg s Catherine Hutchinson
Masham		8	William s William and Mary Parker
Ellingstring		15	Joseph s Joseph and Ann Reynard
Fearby	Aug	25	Anthony s William and Mary Ballan
Masham		26	Hannah d Thomas and Mary Dixon
Moorhead		29	Betty d John and Emmet Marsden
Masham	Sept	18	Joseph s Richard and Eleanor Whitelock
Masham		19	Francis s Francis and Elizabeth Terry
Masham		19	Christiana d William and Beatrice Hartley
Fearby	Oct	20	Thomas s Charles and Mary Kendall
Ellingstring	Nov	3	Henrietta illeg d Jane Ascough
Warthermarske		25	William s William and Ellen Reynard
Low Ash Head		29	Joseph s George and Mary Graham
Masham	Dec	27	Ann d Thomas and Mary Durham

41 [*annual total*]

[p. 40] **Baptisms 1788**

Masham	Jan	28	John s John and Mary Clarkson
Grimes Gill		30	George s Thomas and Mary Ascough [*altered from* Nelson]
Piper Hall	Feb	6	Ann d Thomas and Dorothy Finley
Ellingstring		17	Mary d John and Mary Howard
Masham		17	Ann d John and Beatrice Plews
Swinton		18	Martha d William and Elizabeth Morton
High Summerside		28	Catherine d Richard and Mary Hall
Sourmire		28	Joseph s Mark and Elizabeth Hutchinson
Masham		29	Agnes d Christopher and Agnes Pickersgill
Ellingstring	Mar	9	Dorothy d William and Elizabeth Outhwaite
Masham		23	Dorothy d Henry and Dorothy Croft
Masham		23	John and Robert twin ss John and Betty Ward, paupers
Masham		24	Catharine d Thomas and Mary Croft
Swinton		30	Ann d William and Mary Astwood

Masham	Apr	6	Stephen s Stephen and Mary Siddall
Ellingstring		10	Thomas s Emanuel and Ann Lye
Leighton		13	Thomas s Peter and Elizabeth Hanley
Ellington		27	John s Peter and Catharine Mallaby
Warthermarske	May	4	Joseph s John and Mary Thorpe
Ilton		4	Robert s John and Mary Metcalfe
Healey		4	Edward s Edward and Judith Rudd
Masham		11	James s Leonard and Jane Mudd
Masham		11	Ann d William and Mary Clarkson
Masham		17	Margaret d Christopher and Jane Merriweather, pauper
Low Ellington		18	Ann d John and Jane Barwick
Masham		19	John s John and Henrietta Baines
Masham		25	Mathew s Thomas and Dorothy Allanson
Fearby		25	Matthew s Thomas and Catharine Barrows
Masham	June	15	Anna d John and Elizabeth Imeson
Masham		22	George s Thomas and Mary Banks
Masham		22	William s William and Barbara Doxforth
Fearby		26	Mary d Ralph and Mary Edon
Summerside	July	12	Betty d Peter and Esther Carter
Quarry House		13	Robert s Thomas and Mary Lightfoot
Healey		20	Esther illeg d Mary Towler
Masham		20	Grace d George and Isabel Robinson
Masham		27	Elizabeth d George and Ann Imeson
Ilton		27	John illeg s Mary Metcalf
Healey	Aug	2	William s Richard and Hannah Thompson, pauper
Swinton		3	Christopher s Thomas and Ann Brown
Ellingstring		8	Jane d Joseph and Mary Maynard
[p. 41]			
Masham		10	John s George and Mary Shaw
Masham		10	Thomas s James and Jane Metcalf
Masham		17	William s John and Mary Jackson
Fearby		22	Ellen d Anthony and Ellen Ballan
Sourmire	[blank]		Thomas s Edmund Barker
Ilton	Sept	19	Susanna d John and Elizabeth Spence
Ilton		21	John s William and Esther Dumbhill
Masham		21	Mary d Benjamin and Mary Siddall
Masham		28	Frances d Matthew and Eleanor Elsworth
Ellingstring	Oct	5	Ann illeg d Ann Lye
Ellingstring	Sept	7	Mary d George and Dorothy Pybus, misplac'd
Gildermires	Oct	9	Arthur s Arthur and Ann Ashe
Masham		12	John and Sarah twin children Joseph and Ellen Leeming
High Ellington	Nov	2	David s Robert and Mary Jackson
Healey		2	Hannah d Thomas and Ann Wrather
Masham		9	William s William and Jane Walburn
Masham	Dec	7	Elizabeth d James and Anne Webster

Ilton		12	Maria d William and Eleanor Nelson
Warren House		16	Sarah d George and Esther Kendall
Masham		18	William s Christopher and Sarah Wilson
Ilton		21	Elizabeth d Henry and Mary Scaife
Masham		23	Francis s Francis and Anne Thompson
Masham		27	William s Thomas and Jane Clark

65 [*annual total*]

Baptisms 1789

Fearby	Jan	11	Mary d Thomas and Bridget Taylor
Fearby		11	Elizabeth d Thomas and Hannah Steadman
Ellingstring	Feb	12	John s John and Mary Urwin
Masham		15	Thomas s Thomas and Frances Hutchinson
Swinton	Mar	22	Ann d Benjamin and Elizabeth Akers
Healey		25	John s Francis and Elizabeth Glew
Fearby	Apr	5	Michael s Michael and Mary Fryar
Ellingstring		9	Mary d Robert and Mary Bellerby
North Cote		16	Richard s John and Ann King
Masham	May	1	Mary d Peter and Sarah Plews
Gollinglith		6	Sarah d Joseph and Sarah Lancaster
Ilton		21	Elizabeth d William and Sarah Baynes
Warthermarske		24	Sarah d Mark and Elizabeth Barker
Ilton		31	Esther d Ralph and Mary Prest
Masham		31	Richard s Richard and Sarah Morland
[p. 42]			
Low Roomer	June	7	Joseph s Richard and Elizabeth Topham
Summerside		28	George s George and Hannah Wilkinson
Masham	July	23	Ann d George and Margaret Fenwick
Masham	Aug	9	Elizabeth d Henry and Elizabeth Lupton
High Ellington	Sept	17	William s John and Mary Durham
Masham	Oct	18	Elizabeth d Henry and Ann Braithwaite
Summerside		29	Margaret d Richard and Mary Hall
Swinton		31	Thomas s Thomas and Mary Imeson
Masham	Nov	18	Martha d Christopher and Agnes Pickersgill
Arnagill		21	Hannah d William and Mary Suttle
Masham		22	John s Abraham and Mary Duffield
Ilton		29	Elizabeth d George and Susanna Nicholson
Swinton	Dec	5	Frances d Ralph and Ann Coldbeck
Ilton		13	Mary d Joseph and Elizabeth Atkinson
Masham		20	Ann d Thomas and Rachel Binks

30 [*annual total*]

Baptisms 1790

Masham	Jan	6	Thomas s Thomas and Dorothy Allanson
Masham		8	John s Thomas and Mary Durham
Warren House		24	Jane d George and Esther Kendall
Ilton		25	William s Thomas and Isabella Heslop
Warthermarske		31	Mary d George and Mary Dawson
Ellingstring	Feb	16	Margaret d Joseph and Ann Reynard
Masham		18	Henry s Christopher and Martha Peacock
Masham		28	Margaret d William and Elizabeth Archer
Masham	Mar	12	Thomas s Robert and Elizabeth Welford
South Leighton		13	Matthew s Peter and Elizabeth Hanley
Fearby		20	George s Anthony and Mary Urwin
Gollinglith		21	William and Joseph twin ss John and Alice Clarkson
Masham		31	Thomas s Thomas and Mary Croft
Grimes Gill	Apr	9	Matthew s Thomas and Mary Ascough
Broadmires		11	Thomas s Thomas and Ann Wintersgill
Masham		13	Thomas Young illeg s Mary Wilkie, poor
Masham		25	Thomas s Francis and Elizabeth Terry
Masham		25	James s William and Jane Walburn
Ellingstring		29	William s George and Dorothy Pybus
Fearby	May	16	Elizabeth d James and Mary Taylor
[p. 43]			
Quarry House		20	Martha d Thomas and Mary Lightfoot
Masham		23	Elizabeth d William and Elizabeth Beckwith, pauper
Masham		23	George s Thomas and Jane Clark
Fearby		30	Nancy d Matthew and Frances Kearton
Swinton Green		31	Edward s Thomas and Ann Brown
Masham		31	Margaret d William and Barbara Doxford
Masham	July	4	Matthew s Robert and Ann Wintersgill
North Cote		6	Matthew illeg s Margaret King
Low Mains		14	Esther d Thomas and Esther Carter [*altered from* Rider]
Masham		25	James s William and Mary Atkinson
Swinton		25	William s William and Mary Astwood
Masham	Aug	16	James s John and Jane London
Fearby		21	Abraham s Ralph and Mary Eden
Masham		22	William s Thomas and Elizabeth Banks, pauper
Summerside	Sept	5	Ralph s Ralph and Mary Walker
Masham		17	John and Thomas twin ss Thomas and Mary Banks
Swinton		19	Hannah d Benjamin and Elizabeth Akers
Masham		19	Jane d Stephen and Mary Siddall
Masham	Oct	1	Ann d James and Ann Webster
Masham Mill		3	Elizabeth d John and Mary Jackson
High Ellington		5	John s John and Mary Durham
Masham		6	Sarah Anelay d John and Elizabeth Powell

Masham		20	Francis s Thomas and Mary Sturdy
Masham		30	Mary d John and Mary Heslington
Fearby		31	Thomas s Thomas and Bridget Taylor
Masham	Nov	3	Nanny d Richard and Sarah Morland
Masham		10	Mary d William and Beatrice Hartley
Ilton		14	Mary d John and Esther Dummill
Masham		14	Mary d George and Ann Imeson
Masham		14	Ann d Benjamin and Mary Siddal
Masham		19	William s Thomas and Dorothy Leathley
Warthermarske		21	Mary d John and Mary Thorpe
Breary Banks		24	Robert illeg s Mary Walker
Masham	Dec	5	Nanny d John and Betty Ward, pauper
Piper Hall		5	Mary illeg d Mary Dent, pauper
Ellingstring		26	Esther d Robert and Ann Horner

58 [*annual total*]

[p. 44]   **Baptisms 1791**

Moorhead	Jan	20	John s John and Emmet Marsden
Fearby		23	Mary d William and Ellen Smith
Warthermarske		30	Jane d Edward and Elizabeth Thorpe
Healey	Feb	13	Judith d Edward and Judith Rudd
Masham		27	Thomas s Thomas and Ann Edmondson
Masham	Mar	2	Jane d William and Mary Clarkson
Masham		20	John s Christopher and Jane Merriweather, poor
Masham	Apr	3	Mary d John and Elizabeth Imeson
Masham		10	Thomas s Isaac and Mary Towler
Langthorne		19	Barnet illeg s Elizabeth Metcalfe, poor
Masham	May	15	Hannah d Jeffrey and Ann Clarkson
Gildermire House		15	Alethea d Arthur and Ann Ashe
Masham		16	Christopher and Robert twin ss Robert and Elizabeth Welford
Ilton		22	Isabella d Henry and Mary Scaife
Masham		29	George s George and Elizabeth Grundill
Masham	June	5	Ann d Henry and Dorothy Croft
High Ellington		13	Thomas illeg s Jane Wintersgill
Low Roomer		14	Robert s Richard and Elizabeth Topham
Masham		19	Charles s Christopher and Sarah Wilson
Swinton		21	Jane d Thomas and Mary Imeson
Ellingstring		26	Eleanor d William and Ann Thompson
Masham		26	Ann d George and Mary Shaw
Ilton	July	17	Hannah d Daniel and Elizabeth Ingelby
Masham		23	Joseph s John and Beatrice Plews
Masham		23	Joseph s Thomas and Dorothy Allanson
Fearby		27	John s Anthony and Mary Urwin

Fearby		27	Ann d Thomas and Ann Rider
Ellingstring	Aug	21	John s Robert and Mary Bellerby
Fearby		28	Mary and Jane twin dd William and Jane Casling
Summerside	Sept	8	Mary d Ralph and Mary Walker
Ellingstring		18	Elizabeth d Joseph and Elizabeth Herring
Ellingstring		18	Mary d Joseph and Mary Maynard
Fearby		30	William s Michael and Mary Fryear
Ellingstring	Oct	5	Margaret d Joseph and Ann Reynard
Masham		23	Jane d William and Ann Trees
Masham	Nov	6	Edith d Joseph and Isabella Towler
Masham		6	William s Matthew and Eleanor Elsworth
Masham		20	Henry s Henry and Elizabeth Loftus
Swinton		23	Ann d Robert and Anne Plews
Masham	Dec	5	John s John and Mary Wilkinson
Body Close		7	William s David and Elizabeth Walker, born as affirmed (by those who were present at the birth) in the Month of April 1789 and bapt, pauper
Masham		22	Sarah d Peter and Sarah Plews

44 [*annual total*]

[p. 45]   **Baptisms 1792**

Sykes House	Jan	1	Anne d George and Susanna Nicholson
Ilton		1	Peter s Ralph and Elizabeth Prest
Masham		8	Mary d Thomas and Mary Durham
Fairthorn		24	Amy illeg d Jane Scaife
Masham		28	John s Abraham and Mary Duffield
Masham	Feb	12	Jane d John and Mary Heslington
Ilton		26	John illeg s Ann Taylor
South Leighton	Mar	1	Peter s Peter and Elizabeth Hanley
Fearby		1	John s Joseph and Sarah Lancaster
Fearby		7	George s Thomas and Mary Jackson
Masham		11	William illeg s Sarah Towler, poor
Masham		12	Betty d Christopher and Martha Peacock
Masham		27	Mary d James and Ann Webster
Masham		28	Mary d Thomas and Rachael Binks, poor
Masham		29	Hannah d Thomas and Dorothy Leadley
Masham	Apr	8	Alice d Anthony and Dorothy Buckden
Masham		11	George s Robert and Ann Wintersgill
Ellingstring		11	John s Thomas and Ann Robinson
Ellingstring		16	Matthew s John and Mary Howard, poor
Masham		29	John s Anthony and Mary Shuffield
Masham	May	6	John s Thomas and Jane Clark
Warthermarske		20	John s George and Mary Dawson
Fearby		26	Ellen d William and Ellen Smith

Fearby		30	Sally d James and Mary Taylor
Swinton	June	2	Benjamin s Benjamin and Elizabeth Akers
Mile House		12	Thomas s Thomas and Esther Carter
Masham		24	Mary d Robert and Elizabeth Welford
Summerside		24	Sally d George and Hannah Wilkinson
Warren House		28	John s George and Esther Kendall
Masham		28	John s William and Beatrice Hartley
Masham		30	Moses s George and Mary Walker
Ellingstring	July	22	John s John and Ann Thompson
Masham		22	William s Robert and Esther Robinson
Fearby		29	Ann d Thomas and Bridget Taylor
Swinton	Aug	12	Margaret d William and Mary Astwood
Ellingstring		19	Thomas s George and Dorothy Pybus
Ellingstring		19	Elizabeth d William and Elizabeth Outhwaite
Healey		29	George s Francis and Elizabeth Glew
Healey		29	George s George and Elizabeth Wintersgill
Summerside		30	Thomas s Richard and Mary Hall
Body Close	Sept	9	Mary d David and Elizabeth Walker, pauper
Marfield House		16	James s James and Aletha Nicholson
[p. 46]			
Masham	Oct	7	Henry s Thomas and Mary Croft
Ilton		7	Stephen s William and Eleanor Nelson
Masham		21	Mary d Joseph and Eleanor Leeming, poor
Masham		28	Samuel s Isaac and Mary Towler
Swinton Green		28	Joseph s Thomas and Ann Brown
Masham		29	Elizabeth d Nicholas and Elizabeth Carter
Summerside	Nov	11	John s Peter and Esther Carter
Masham		14	William s William and Elizabeth Beckwith, poor
Warthermarske		18	Thomas s Mark and Elizabeth Barker
Masham		20	Edmund s William and Sarah Pybus
Masham		23	Ann d Gabriel and Elizabeth Kay
Masham		25	Thomas s Benjamin and Mary Siddal
Masham		30	Thomas s Thomas and Mary Sturdy
Masham	Dec	14	Susanna d Christopher and Jane Merriweather, poor
Masham		19	William s John and Margaret Charlton, poor
Healey		23	John s William and Ann Gill
Ilton		30	Joseph s John and Esther Dummil
Masham		27	William s Richard and Sarah Morland

60 [*annual total*]

Baptisms 1793

Masham	Jan	5	Mary d George and Isabella Clarkson
Masham		6	Jane d Matthew and Jane Jackson
Masham		9	Edmund s John and Mary Jackson

Ilton		10	James s James and Esther Metcalfe, poor
Masham		18	Mary d William and Mary Brewster
Ellingstring		22	Ann d James and Isabinda Stockdale
Masham		27	Mary illeg d Esther Barningham, poor
High Ellington		29	Ann d John and Mary Durham
Fearby	Feb	2	Ann d John and Ann Horner
Grimes Gill		9	Betty d Thomas and Mary Ascough
Masham		15	Sarah d Christopher and Agnes Pickersgill
Masham		17	William s William and Mary Atkinson
Masham	Mar	3	Ralph s Stephen and Mary Siddal
Sykes House		10	Mary d George and Susanna Nicholson
Masham		10	Ann d George and Elizabeth Grundill
Gollinglith		16	Hannah d Ralph and Mary Walker
Masham		17	Catharine d Henry and Dorothy Croft
Warthermarske		24	Mary d Edward and Elizabeth Thorpe
[p. 47]			
Masham		31	Margaret d John and Elizabeth Imeson
Masham		31	Margaret d Anthony and Ann Hill
Healey	Apr	4	Elizabeth and Hannah twin dd Edmond and Mary Jackson
Masham	May	7	Hammond Metcalfe s John and Mary Heslington
Healey		21	Mary d George and Elizabeth Roe
Masham	June	10	Joe s Thomas and Jane Clark
Masham		23	Elizabeth d William and Ann Nicholson
Masham		30	Margaret d William and Mary Clarkson
Nutwith Cote	July	1	William illeg s Sarah Reynard
Masham		2	John s John and Mary Trevor, pauper
Low Roomer		6	William s Richard and Elizabeth Topham
Masham		14	Francis s Ralph and Mary Pybus
Masham		21	John s John and Susanna Fletom
Healey		26	Alice d George and Mary Bateman
Ellingstring	Aug	12	Esther d Joseph and Mary Warrener
Low Roomer		12	Mary d John and Ann Jackson
Ilton		18	Alice d Donkin and Isabella Cameron
Fearby		18	Joseph s John and Mary Court
Masham		25	Mary d William and Agnes Crowder
Swinton		28	Matthew s Thomas and Mary Imeson
Healey	Sept	2	John s John and Hannah Ascough
Ellington		22	William illeg s Mary Staindrop
Low Ellington		22	George s John and Jane Barwick, poor
Ellingstring		29	William s Joseph and Mary Maynard, poor
Masham		29	Jane d William and Barbara Doxford
Fearby	Oct	4	James s William and Jane Weighill
Masham		6	Mark s James and Ann Towler
Masham		18	Mary d Robert and Ann Wintersgill

Masham		25	Elizabeth d Thomas and Denan Fletcher
Masham		27	Mary d George and Dorothy Pouter
Healey	Nov	7	Hannah d Edward and Judith Rudd
Healey Mill		11	Phillis d Edmund and Isabella Caygill
Masham		12	George s George and Esther Nelson
Fearby		18	Alice d William and Jane Casling
Masham		24	Elizabeth d Thomas and Dorothy Allanson
Masham		28	Richard s William and Alice Thwaites
North Cote	Dec	3	Sarah illeg d Anne King
Masham		12	Henry s John and Beatrice Plews
Masham		29	Robert s Thomas and Mary Durham
Masham		29	James s George and Mary Shaw

59 [*annual total*]

[p. 48] **Baptisms 1794**

Fearby	Jan	1	John s William and Mary Woodd
Arnagill		18	Elizabeth d William and Mary Suttle
Masham		19	Mercy d Joseph and Isabella Towler
Masham		19	Alice d Thomas and Dorothy Casling
Fearby	Feb	1	Ann d John and Ann Horner
Masham		3	Jane d Henry and Elizabeth Lofthouse
Masham		23	Ann d Christopher and Sarah Wilson, poor
Masham	Mar	7	Ann d James and Alethea Nicholson, poor
Ilton		9	James s James and Ann Jefferson
Ilton		9	William s John and Anne Davis
Ellingstring		16	Christiana d John and Edith Milner
Ellingstring		23	William s John and Mary Howard, poor
Ellingstring	Apr	13	Christopher s Joseph and Elizabeth Herring
Ellingstring		13	Robert s Robert and Mary Bellerby, poor
Ellingstring		13	Ann d Richard and Elizabeth Cunningham
Healey Mill		19	Margaret d Lawrence and Elizabeth Heap
Masham		20	Mary illeg d Elizabeth Leeming, poor
Summerside		27	Charlotte d George and Hannah Wilkinson
Masham	May	11	Mary d George and Mary Walker
Masham		13	Christopher s Christopher and Martha Peacock, poor
Masham	June	8	Elizabeth d Robert and Elizabeth Welford
Swinton		8	Ann d John and Jane Hill
Fearby		8	Thomas s Thomas and Ann Rider
Swinton		15	Thomas s Benjamin and Elizabeth Akers
Masham		15	Thomas s Matthew and Jane Jackson
Roomer		17	Thomas s Christopher and Hannah Hall
Masham		20	Mary d John and Mary Wilkinson
Ilton	July	6	Thomas s William and Eleanor Nelson
Masham		7	Mary d William and Ann Trees

146

Masham		18	Sarah d George and Ann Vicarman, poor
Healey		18	Jane d Robert and Jane Hudson
Ilton		20	Charles s Henry and Mary Scaife
Fearby		25	James s Michal [*sic*] and Ann Fryear
Warthermarske		27	Mary d John and Catharine Hodgson
Masham	Aug	6	William s William and Hannah Wood
Summerside		9	John s Richard and Mary Hall
Fearby		15	Mary d Thomas and Mary Jackson
Ilton		22	Mary d Ralph and Elizabeth Prest
Masham		31	James s Thomas and Mary Croft, pauper
Ellingstring	Sept	7	Elizabeth d George and Dorothy Pybus [*later note*: died July 3 '95]
High Ellington		19	Dorothy d John and Jane Walker
Masham		23	George s George and Isabella Clarkson

[p. 49]

North Cote	Oct	9	Mary d John and Margaret Boston
Masham		19	Michael s William and Elizabeth Beckwith
Ellingstring		23	William s William and Ann Thompson
Fearby		26	Solomon Fawnes s Thomas and Ann Edmondson
Swinton	Nov	9	Anna d John and Sarah Shields
Healey		16	Mary d Barnard and Ann Bulcock
Gildermires		24	William s Anthony and Anne Hill
Broadmires		29	George s Thomas and Ann Wintersgill
Masham	Dec	3	William s Anthony and Mary Shuffield
Fearby		7	Elizabeth d Thomas and Bridget Taylor
Healey		16	Ann d Francis and Elizabeth Glew
Gollinglith		18	Thomas s John and Elizabeth Wintersgill
Warthermarske		18	Mary d Robert and Mary Walker
Masham		25	Mary d Robert and Esther Robinson

56 [*annual total*]

Baptisms 1795

Warthermarske	Jan	4	Mary d George and Mary Dawson
Mile House		6	John s Thomas and Esther Carter
Masham		11	Sarah d Thomas and Mary Sturdy
Fearby		16	Christopher s Ralph and Mary Eden
Warthermarske		22	Catharine d Edward and Elizabeth Thorpe
Burton Cons[tablery]		27	John Mac'Fereson illeg s Elizabeth Edmondson
Healey Mill	Feb	15	John s John and Mary Greenwood
Masham	Mar	4	Jane d William and Agnes Crowder
Masham		22	Robert s Gabriel and Elizabeth Kay
Masham		22	Edward illeg s Ann Mudd
Masham		22	Jane d Benjamin and Mary Siddal
Fearby		29	Mary d Robert and Jane Russel

Foxholme House	Apr	7	Robert s Matthew and Elizabeth Imeson
High Ellington		9	Christopher s John and Mary Durham
[*no place*]		14	Joseph s Revd Joseph Burrill and Lucinda his wf who was the eldest daughter of the late Mr William Wrather of Masham b and bapt
Masham		15	Matthew s John and Susanna Fleetom
Masham		26	James illeg s Sarah Towler
Masham	May	3	George s John and Mary Beckwith
Ilton		3	Joshua s Joseph and Elizabeth Rider
Healey Mill		10	Ann d Lawrence and Elizabeth Heap
Fearby		31	William s Thomas and Esther Whitaker
Masham		31	Charles s George and Elizabeth Grundill
Healey Mill		31	Esther d Charles and Elizabeth Dovner
Masham	June	14	Thomas s John and Mary Heslington
Masham		28	William s Thomas and Elizabeth Drummer
[p. 50]			
Ellingstring	July	9	Thomas s Henry and Jane Ascough
Masham		12	Ann d William and Mary Brewster
Fearby		19	William s William and Mary Wood
Fearby		19	Mary d Edmond and Mary Jackson
Summerside		25	Matthew s Robert and Mary Walker
Burton Constablery	Aug	9	Dorothy d John and Dorothy Rogers
Healey Mill		9	Mary d John and Emmet Marsden
Warthermarske		16	William s John and Catharine Hodgson
Warren House	Sept	6	Thomas s George and Esther Kendall
Fearby		6	Thomas s Joseph and Ann Reynard
Masham		20	Thomas s Thomas and Hannah Clarkson
Swinton		21	Jane d John and Jane Hill
Masham		27	Ann d Henry and Dorothy Croft
Masham		27	James s James and Ann Webster
Masham		29	Matthew s Matthew and Hannah Imeson
Fearby	Oct	4	Ann d William and Jane Casling
Roomer		4	Margaret d Christopher and Hannah Hall
Masham		4	Thomas s John [*altered from* Thomas] and Elizabeth Imeson
Masham		6	George s Jane Merriweather
Masham	Nov	22	John s Thomas and Dorothy Leadley
Ellingstring		22	Elizabeth d William and Ann Gill
Healey		22	John s Robert and Jane Hudson
Fearby		22	Elizabeth d Matthew and Jane Terry
Fearby		22	Jane d Thomas and Ann Rider
North Leighton		26	Elizabeth d John [*altered from* Thomas] and Elizabeth Dallow
Healey		26	Mary d John and Hannah Ascough
Foxholme		29	William s William and Rebeccah Hill

Swinton	Dec	4	James s John and Sarah Shields
Masham		20	Isabella d Thomas and Jane Blackburn
Masham		21	Joseph s William and Hannah Mudd
Masham		26	William s John and Mary Trevor
Masham		26	William s William and Jane Ward
Ilton		27	Daniel s Donkin and Isabella Cameron

58 [*annual total*]

[p. 51]   **Baptisms 1796**

Masham	Jan	3	Mary d Thomas and Denas Fletcher
Masham		3	Margaret d William and Ann Nicholson
Masham		22	Peter s Peter and Sarah Plews
Low Roomer		24	George s John and Ann Jackson
Healey Mill		24	Ann d John and Mary Dindsdale
Ellingstring		30	Jane d John and Ann Thompson
Healey Mill		31	Matthew s Joseph and Sarah Lancaster
Masham	Feb	28	Thomas s Thomas and Martha Myers
Masham	Mar	6	Thomas s James and Elizabeth Stot
Burton Constablery		8	Elizabeth d Thomas and Ann Brown
South Leighton		12	Simon s Peter and Elizabeth Hanley
Spout House		12	Esther d John and Ann Wilson jnr
Healey		12	Mary d George and Elizabeth Wintersgill jnr
Healey		12	Samuel s Edward and Mary Taylor
Masham		12	Robert s Robert and Elizabeth Welford
Masham		13	Elizabeth d Matthew and Jane Jackson
Aldburgh		24	James [Henry D'Arcy *interlined*] s James Hutton and Mary his wf b and bapt [baptised James & christened James Henry D'Arcy Mar 23 1797]
Masham		27	Jane d Christopher and Sarah Wilson
Masham		27	Nanny d George and Abigail Hartley
Masham		27	John s Joseph and Isabella Towler
Low Roomer		27	Hannah d James and Mary Edrington
Swinton		28	Mary d William and Anna Jackson
Masham		31	Martha d Christopher and Martha Peacock
Masham		31	Ann d John and Mary Wilkinson
Foxholme House	Apr	2	William s Miles and Mary Lowley
Masham		7	Alethea d James and Alethea Nicholson
Fearby		17	Thomas illeg s Mary Clarke
Masham		27	Peter s Peter and Frances Smith
Masham		30	William s George and Isabella Clarkson
Masham	May	1	Ann d Thomas and Dorothy Allanson
Masham		1	Christopher s Thomas and Dorothy Casling
Masham		15	Frances d William and Mary Clarkson
Ellingstring		29	John s John and Edith Milner

149

Masham	June	1	Elizabeth d Henry and Elizabeth Lofthouse
High Ellington		2	Mary d John and Mary Durham
Masham		3	John s George and Ann Windrass
Healey Mill		5	George s Edmund and Isabella Caygill
Grimes Gill		11	Margaret d Jno. and Elizabeth Ascough
Ilton		12	Joseph s John and Esther Dummill
Masham		12	William s George and Mary Shaw
Healey Mill	July	10	Ann d William and Elizabeth Outhwaite
Masham		10	Ann d James and Ann Towler
Healey		15	Catharine d Edward and Ann Spence
Ellingstring		15	George s George and Dorothy Pybus
[p. 52]			
Swinton		20	Thomas s William and Ann Glew
Swinton		24	Joseph s Benjamin and Elizabeth Akers
Leighton Park		25	Esther d George and Esther Clarke
Burton Constablery	Aug	14	Christopher s Christopher and Jane Hansom
Ellingstring		21	Ralph s William and Ann Thompson
Masham		28	Mary d John and Mary Ellis
Masham		28	George s George and Mary Walker
Masham		31	William 2nd s Revd Joseph Burrill and Lucinda his wf (who was the eldest daughter of the late Mr William Wrather), b Aug 22
Swinton	Sept	4	George s William and Mary Astwood
Masham		14	James s Ralph and Ann Cummings
Masham		25	James s William and Mary Brewster
Burton Constablery	Oct	23	William s Thomas and Mary Fawcet
Masham		23	Mary d Anthony and Mary Shuffield
Warthermarske	Nov	6	Henry s Christopher and Mary Beckwith
Masham		13	Deborah d Thomas and Mary Banks
Masham		27	John s George and Esther Nelson
Ellingstring		27	Thomas s Thomas and Mary Craggs
Fearby		27	Mary d John and Ann Horner
Ilton	Dec	4	Matthew s Matthew and Esther Imeson
Masham		4	Elizabeth d William and Agnes Crowder
Masham		11	Catharine d Thomas and Mary Durham
Warthermarske		17	Joseph s Mark and Elizabeth Barker
Masham		26	Sarah d Christopher and Esther Clark

67 [*annual total*]

Baptisms 1797

Masham	Jan	1	John s Thomas and Mary Croft
Swinton		7	Ann d William and Mary Dinsdale
Gebdykes		15	Esther d Robert and Esther Robinson
Ilton		22	Mark s Daniel and Elizabeth Ingelby

BAPTISMS

Ellingstring		22	John s John and Dorothy Metcalfe
Burton Constablery		24	Richard s Matthew and Mary Wilson
Healey Mill		24	Margaret d Barnabas and Ann Bulcock
Ellingstring		24	Richard s John and Mary Howard
Warthermarske		29	Robert s Robert and Mary Walker
Gildermires	Feb	12	Anthony s Anthony and Ann Hill
Healey		12	Thomas s Edward and Judith Rudd
Burton Constablery		17	William s Hugh and Margaret Pattison
Masham		17	Elizabeth d John and Mary Dowson
Fearby		26	Martha d Thomas and Bridget Taylor
High Ellington	Mar	1	Christopher s Christopher and Mary Lambert
Masham		5	John s George and Margaret Kitchen
Warthermarske		5	Hannah d John and Catharine Hodgson
[p. 53]			
Masham		10	Matthew s Matthew and Hannah Carter
Masham		15	William s John and Beatrice Plews
Masham		15	Thomas s John and Dorothy Vitty
Fearby		19	John s Matthew and Jane Terry
Swinton	Apr	2	John s John and Jane Hill
Masham		9	Nanny d George and Dorothy Pouter
Healey Mill		9	Thomas s Charles and Elizabeth Dovner
Ellingstring		20	Ann d Robert and Mary Bellerby
Swinton		23	Sarah d George and Esther Imeson
Fearby		23	Robert s Michael and Mary Fryear
Fearby		30	Dorothy d Thomas and Ann Rider
Masham	May	12	John s Thomas and Mary Sturdy
Burton Constablery		13	Mary d Allanson and Mary Longstaff
Masham		14	Sarah d John and Mary Beckwith
Swinton Green		14	Esther d Thomas and Ann Brown
Fearby		21	William s John and Mary Court
Swinton	June	1	Charles s John and Sarah Shields
Healey		6	Elizabeth d George and Elizabeth Raw
Healey		6	Matthew s Peter and Christiana Pratt
Masham		11	Mary d George and Mary Hodgson
Ellingstring		27	David s John and Jane Walker
Ilton	July	9	Elizabeth d Thomas and Margaret Metcalfe
Masham		9	Elizabeth d George and Elizabeth Grundill
Gollinglith		23	Hannah d John and Elizabeth Wintersgill
Masham		30	Ann d Henry and Elizabeth Hodgson
Masham	Aug	6	Ann d John and Susanna Fleetom
Masham		10	Elizabeth d John and Hannah Hird
Grimes Gill		12	Matthew s John and Elizabeth Ascough
Masham		20	Matthew s Thomas and Elizabeth Hagstone
Nutwith Cote	Sept	3	Ann d John and Sarah Smith
Healey		7	Henry s Richard and Mary Hall

Healey Mill		10	Elizabeth d Lawrence and Elizabeth Heap
Healey		10	George s Joseph and Mary Maynard
Burton Constablery		10	Nancy d Francis and Elizabeth Metcalfe
Masham		24	Hannah d Thomas and Hannah Clarkson
Masham	Oct	1	Mary d Thomas and Ann Renwick
Masham		8	Gabriel s Gabriel and Elizabeth Kaye
Masham		15	George s Thomas and Martha Myers
Gildermires	Nov	6	Mary d William and Elizabeth Hill
Burton Constablery		6	John s Ralph and Ann Cummings
Healey		13	Thomas s Francis and Elizabeth Glew
Masham		13	Frances d Thomas and Denas Fletcher
Masham		26	John 3rd s Revd Joseph Burrill and Lucinda his wf, b Nov 16
Masham		30	Mary d William and Elizabeth Ward
Fearby	Dec	3	William s William and Jane Casling
[p. 54]			
Foxholme		10	Mary d Edward and Hannah Metcalfe
Masham		11	Mary d William and Elizabeth Wood
Burton Constablery		24	Ellis s John and Elizabeth Ponder
Low Ellington		30	Elizabeth d Robert and Esther Imeson
Ilton		31	Esther d John and Esther Dummil

67 [*annual total*]

Baptisms 1798

Masham	Jan	14	Mary illeg d Sarah Towler
Fearby	Feb	4	Sarah d Edmund and Mary Jackson
Masham		11	John s Thomas and Jane Clark
Summerside	Mar	3	Elizabeth d William and Mary Procter
Healey		3	Abigail d Robert and Jane Hudson
Fearby		3	Esther d Thomas and Esther Witaker
Masham		9	Thomas s Thomas and Jane Blackburn
Masham		14	Thomas s Matthew and Ann Imeson
Ilton		23	Willy s William and Hannah Mudd
Masham	Apr	1	George illeg s Jane Gill
Masham		8	Mary d William and Ann Nicholson
Masham		10	Thomas s Peter and Frances Smith
Masham		20	John s Anthony and Mary Urwin
Ilton		22	George s George and Susanna Nicholson
Healey Mill		28	Bellah d John and Emmet Marsden
Masham	May	3	John s John and Margaret Boston
Fearby		6	Jane d Thomas and Mary Jackson
Broadmires		13	John s Thomas and Ann Wintersgill
Ilton		17	Sarah illeg d Ann Taylor
Fearby		20	Hannah d William and Mary Wood

152

Burton		27	Catharine d John and Catharine Rooking
Masham		28	Mary d James and Elizabeth Stott
South Leighton	June	16	Betty d Peter and Elizabeth Hanley
Masham		19	Ann d John and Mary Trevor
Warthermarske	July	1	Ann d Charles and Mary Beckwith
Masham		8	Betty d Simon and Ann Pickersgill
Masham		22	Isabella d Joseph and Isabella Towler
Healey		27	George s Edward and Ann Spence
Fearby		27	Hannah d Thomas and Elizabeth Smorthit
Masham		29	Nanny illeg d Mary Thornberry
Warthermarske	Aug	12	Edward s Edward and Elizabeth Thorpe
Ellington		18	Ann d Marmaduke and Jane Hauxwell
Ellingstring		18	Eleanor d John and Ann Thompson
Masham		19	Rebecca d Henry and Jane Atkinson
Masham		26	Christopher s Christopher and Martha Peacock
[p. 55]			
Low Roomer		26	Ann d John and Ann Jackson
Masham		28	Ann d Bateman and Mary Atkinson
Masham	Sept	4	Christopher s Robert and Elizabeth Welford
Swinton		9	Isabel d William and Mary Astwood
Masham		16	John s Thomas and Dorothy Casling
Masham		19	Hannah d Robert and Ann Wintersgill
Masham		19	Martha d Matthew and Jane Jackson
Ellingstring	Oct	1	Elizabeth d John and Elizabeth Emerson
Ellingstring		1	Margaret d John and Dorothy Pybus
Masham		7	Susanna d Joseph and Mary Warrener
Ilton Knowle		12	Peter s George and Isabella Wintersgill
Ellingstring		14	Mary d William and Ann Thompson
Ellingstring		14	William s Thomas and Mary Craggs
Ilton		17	John s Joseph and Elizabeth Rodwell
Foxholme		25	Hannah d Miles and Mary Lowley
Ilton		28	Mary d Henry and Mary Scaife
Healey Mill	Nov	4	Alice d William and Elizabeth Outhwaite
Howe		8	Elizabeth d William and Esther Lightfoot
Warthermarske		10	Hannah d Robert and Mary Walker
Fearby		13	Charles s George and Elizabeth Nelson
Fearby		22	William illeg s Susanna Burnit
Masham		25	Ann d John and Mary Hargrave
Fearby	Dec	1	Dorothy d Matthew and Jane Terry
Fearby		1	George s George and Elizabeth Ascough
Masham		1	Rebeckah d George and Mary Hodgson
Low Ellington		2	John s John and Jane Ramsay
Swinton Mill		2	Elizabeth d George and Mary Dawson
Healey Mill		2	Katy d John and Mary Dindsdale
Masham		9	James s Thomas and Ann Renwick

Masham		14	Elizabeth d George and Dorothy Pouter
Fearby		16	Betty d Donkin and Isabella Cameron
Masham		24	William s William and Mary Brewster
Masham		27	William s Joseph and Eleanor Leeming
Masham		29	John s James and Rosamond Carver

69 [*annual total*]

[p. 56]   **Baptisms 1799**

Spout House	Jan	6	Peter s John and Ann Wilson
Masham		8	Sarah d Thomas and Dorothy Allanson
Masham		11	Sarah d James and Elizabeth Webster
Grimes Gill		14	Nanny d John and Elizabeth Ascough
Masham		19	Elizabeth d William and Elizabeth Ward
Masham		27	Ann illeg d Dorothy Buckden
Healey	Feb	13	Elizabeth d Edward and Mary Taylor
Fearby		24	Jane d William and Ann Stirk
Masham	Mar	3	Elizabeth d Christopher and Sarah Wilson
Swinton		10	Elizabeth d John and Jane Hill
Swinton		10	William s Benjamin and Elizabeth Akers
Ellingstring		17	Reuben s William and Mary Stanley
Masham		17	Roger s Roger and Hannah Kirkbride
Healey		24	James s Peter and Christiana Pratt
Masham		25	Ann d George and Margaret Kitchen
Masham		30	Ann d Anthony and Mary Shuffield
Low Mains		31	Esther d Mark and Sarah Rider
Masham	Apr	7	Ann d William and Agnes Crowder
Masham		7	Mary d George and Elizabeth Grundal
Ilton		17	William s Christopher and Sarah Taylor
Crab House		21	Robert s William and Mary Rider
Masham		27	Jane d George and Mary Walker
Gebdykes		28	Mary d Robert and Esther Robinson
Masham	May	12	Elizabeth d Thomas and Mary Croft
Fearby		19	Ann d Thomas and Bridget Taylor
Pickersgill	June	2	Matthew illeg s Mary Walker
Fearby		9	Jane d John and Nancy Horner
Masham		11	Mary d William and Dorothy Court
High Ellington		11	Thomas s John and Jane Jackson
Masham		17	Mary d John and Henrietta Baines
Ellingstring		23	George s Thomas and Ann Robinson
North Cote		26	Elizabeth d Christopher and Mary Procter
Masham	July	8	John s John and Sarah Shields
Healey Mill		8	John s Christopher and Jane Smith
Healey Mill		8	Matthew s John and Mary Howard
Masham		14	Elizabeth d Thomas and Mary Sturdy

Masham		14	Thomas s George and Esther Nelson
Ellingstring		17	William s William and Ann Gill
Fearby		21	William s Matthew and Mary Spence
Masham		21	Anthony s Thomas and Martha Myers
Masham	Aug	18	Thomas s Thomas and Dorothy Leathley
[p. 57]			
Burton		25	Elizabeth d William and Mary Bowran
Burton		25	Neddy s John and Mary Urwin
Swinton	Sept	1	John s William and Mary Dinsdale
Healey Mill		1	Ann d Lawrence and Elizabeth Heap
Healey		15	George s William and Ann Bearley
Ilton		22	Ann d Thomas and Margaret Metcalfe
Masham		26	Elizabeth d William and Elizabeth Wood
Gildermires		29	Elizabeth d William and Elizabeth Hill
Masham	Oct	1	John s John and Hannah Hird
Fearby		13	Elizabeth d William and Jane Casling
Masham		26	Margaret d Thomas and Margaret Bretwell
Roomer		27	Hannah d Christopher and Hannah Hall
Masham		27	Jane d John and Mary Heslington
Masham	Nov	7	Jane illeg d Mary Kaye
Masham		7	William s Matthew and Ann Glew
Masham		10	James 4th s Revd Joseph Burrill and Lucinda his wf, b Oct 29
Masham		17	William s John and Mary Wilkinson
Masham		23	Ann d Peter and Sarah Plews
Ilton		24	Jane d George and Susanna Nicholson
Healey		24	Ann d George and Elizabeth Raw
Masham		24	Sarah illeg d Mary Urwin
Masham		28	Jonathan s Thomas and Mary Bray
High Ellington		28	Thomas s John and Mary Durham
Gollinglith	Dec	22	Mary d John and Elizabeth Wintersgill
Fearby		22	Thomas s Thomas and Elizabeth Smorthit
High Mains		23	Ann d Robert and Elizabeth Jeff

66 [*annual total*]

Baptisms 1800

Healey Mill	Jan	12	John s Barnabas and Ann Bulcock
Fearby		26	Elizabeth d Michael and Ann Bell
Masham		26	William s John and Mary Hutchinson
Masham	Feb	2	Betty d Joseph and Betty Beckwith
Masham		5	Samuel s Francis and Jane Walker
Masham		5	Thomas s Thomas and Mary Durham
Warthermarske		7	Thomas s Thomas and Mary Theakston
Fearby		8	John s James and Rachel Dixon

Masham		9	Eleanor d Anthony and Frances Gill
Burton		23	Ann d Ralph and Ann Cummins
Howe		25	Joseph s William and Esther Lightfoot
Masham	Mar	13	John s Robert and Elizabeth Atkinson
Masham	Apr	5	Christiana d Christopher and Jane Wilson
[p. 58]			
Ellingstring		13	Jeremiah Metcalfe s Henry and Mary Hall
Burton		13	Susanna d James and Mary Buckle
Masham		13	Thomas s John and Mary Beckwith
Masham		17	Betty d Thomas and Dorothy Casling
Ellingstring		28	John s Henry and Jane Hammond
Ellingstring		28	Simon s Thomas and Ann Robinson
Ilton Knowle	May	4	Mary d George and Isabella Wintersgill
Masham		19	Esther d George and Elizabeth Wilson
Masham	June	1	Richard s Thomas and Hannah Clarkson
Broadmires		1	Hannah d Thomas and Ann Wintersgill
Healey		3	Robert s Robert and Jane Hudson
Healey		3	Catharine d John and Catharine Carter
Fearby		15	Thomas s George and Elizabeth Ascough
Masham		23	Edward s Thomas and Jane Blackburn
Ilton		29	Ann illeg d Ann Kettlewell
Masham	July	20	Mary illeg d Hannah Siddal
Healey		27	Elizabeth illeg d Hannah Wintersgill

[Visitation held at Masham July 30 Revd W. Lawson Commissary]

Quarry House	Aug	3	John s John and Hannah Smorthit
High Ellington		9	Maria d Thomas and Ann Morrell
Healey		10	Hannah d Charles and Elizabeth Dovenor
Fearby		10	William s George and Elizabeth Nelson
Masham		16	Ann d Henry and Elizabeth Lofthouse
Ellingstring		17	Esther d Robert and Mary Bellerby
Masham		26	Ann d Henry and Sarah Pulleyn
Masham	Sept	7	James s James and Elizabeth Stott
Masham		13	Margaret d John and Mary Trevor
Fearby		14	Thomas s William and Mary Wood
Masham		20	Sarah d William and Elizabeth Ward
Warthermarske		21	[blank] d Charles and Mary Beckwith
Healey		28	Jane d Edward and Judith Rudd
Foxholme		28	Thomas s Edward and Hannah Metcalfe
Healey	Oct	6	Matthew s Matthew and Elizabeth Wintersgill
Fearby		6	Matthew s Matthew and Jane Terry
Leighton		11	John s Matthew and Hannah Carter
Swinton Green	Nov	9	William s Thomas and Ann Brown
Warthermarske		16	Elizabeth d Robert and Mary Walker
[p. 59]			
Swinton		30	Martha d William and Mary Astwood

Masham		30	Ann d Matthew and Ann Imeson
Masham	Dec	3	David s James and Alethea Nicholson
Masham		15	Elizabeth d Robert and Ann Wintersgill
Masham		25	Anna illeg d Jane Pybus

54 [*annual total*]

Baptisms 1801

Masham	Jan	2	Jane d Anthony and Mary Shuffield
Masham		20	Eleanor d George and Dorothy Pouter
Summerside		31	Hannah d George and Jane Metcalfe

[p. 60]   **An account of the Publications of Banns**

[*entries 1779-1788 are signed by Edward Moises, Vicar; from 1789 onwards by J. Burrill, Curate*]

1779

John Leeming of Sessay and Mary Lye otp published 14, 21, 28 July
Thomas Clarke of East Witton and Rosamond Ashton otp published 4, 11, 18 Aug
Thomas Robinson and Sarah Kendrew btp published 5, 12, 19 Sept
William Lupton and Margaret Windall btp published 19, 26 Sept, 3 Oct
William Hartley and Elizabeth Kaye btp published 26 Sept, 3, 10 Oct
Richard Bowes and Mary Johnson btp published 10, 17, 24 Oct
Peter Lofthouse of Kirkby Malzeard and Ann Gill otp published 17, 24, 31 Oct
Charles Rumfitt and Ann Jackson btp published 7, 14, 21 Nov
John Kaye of Fewston and Isabella Ascough otp published 28 Nov, 5, 12 Dec
John London and Jane Pickard btp published 5, 12, 19 Dec
Matthew Thompson of Bedale and Sarah Sturdy otp published 5, 12, 19 Dec

1780

Thomas Metcalf and Sarah Neesham btp published 9, 16, 23 Jan
Peter Jackson and Ann Vitty btp published 9, 16, 23 Jan
[p. 61]   Joseph Rayner of East Witton and Ann Plews otp published 26 Mar, 2, 9 Apr
Charles Reynard of East Witton and Martha Hutchinson otp published 30 Apr, 7, 14 May
Thomas Clarkson otp and Elizabeth Huntington of Easby published 25 June, 2, 9 July
John Berry of East Witton and Elizabeth Bellerby otp published 8, 15, 22 Oct
Thomas Medcalf and Sarah Ward btp published 5, 12, 19 Nov
Isaac Towler and Mary Carmichael btp published 10, 17, 24 Dec

Simon Thompson of West Tanfield and Isabel Henderson otp published 10, 17, 24 Dec

1781

John Knubley otp and Jane Appleby of Kirkby Malzeard published 4, 11, 18 Feb
Joseph Hanley and Mary Rider btp published 11, 18, 25 Feb
Matthew Jackson and Mary Harland btp published 18, 25 Mar, 1 Apr
Edward Rudd and Judith Metcalf btp published 1, 8, 15 Apr
Joseph Maynard and Mary Prest btp published 1, 8, 15 May
Richard Boynton of Well and Isabel Richmond otp published 29 May, 5, 12 June

[p. 62]　William Astwood and Mary Gill btp published three several Sundays
William Bradberry and Isabella Ramsey btp published three several Sundays
William Archer and Elizabeth Nicholson btp published three several Sundays

1782

Thomas Brown and Ann Geldart btp published 10, 17, 24 Mar
Peter Barker and Esther Wilson btp published three several Sundays
George Wilkinson and Hannah Mallaby btp published three several Sundays
John Banks and Ann Hardy btp published three several Sundays
Charles Bainbridge of Middleham and Ann Jackson otp published three several Sundays
Thomas Scafe and Eleanor Howred btp published three several Sundays
Robert Raley and Sarah Horsman btp published three several Sundays
Christopher Wilson and Sarah Reynard btp published three several Sundays

1783

John Wood of Kirkby and Jane Sedgwick otp published three several Sundays
Henry Scafe and Ann Pybus btp published three several Sundays
[p. 63]　Stephen Siddall and Mary Gill btp published three several Sundays
William Pybus and Sarah Hebden btp published three several Sundays
Henry Scafe and Mary Pickersgill btp published three several Sundays
George Lye of East Witton and Prudence Lye otp published three several Sundays

1784

John Abbot of East Witton and Dorothy Fawbert otp published three several Sundays

158

BAPTISMS

Francis Whorlton and Catharine Robinson btp published three several Sundays
Michael Walker and Ann Snell btp published three several Sundays
Arthur Ashe and Ann Astwood btp published three several Sundays
Michael Hammond of East Witton and Mary Metcalf otp published three several Sundays
Thomas Johnson Hopper and Hannah Slee btp published three several Sundays
Christopher Walker and Dorothy Smith btp published three several Sundays
Cornelius Plews and Ann Brockhill btp published three several Sundays
Thomas Craggs and Mary Cook btp published three several Sundays

[p. 64]   [1785]

Henry Fryar and Elizabeth Davy btp published three several Sundays
Benjamin Akers and Elizabeth Beckwith btp published three several Sundays
Joseph Herring and Elizabeth Tempest btp published three several Sundays
Samuel Hauxwell of Burneston and Hannah Kidd otp published three several Sundays
John Wood and Hannah Dawson btp published 9, 16, 23 Oct
Thomas Allison and Dorothy Warrener btp published 30 Oct, 6, 13 Nov
John Vitty and Dorothy Longstaff btp published 13, 20, 27 Nov
William Robinson of Ripon and Mary Firby otp published 4, 11, 18 Dec

1789

William Gilling of Northallerton and Isabel Burnet otp published 6, 13, 20 Dec
George Grundill and Elizabeth Coldbeck btp published 13, 20, 27 Dec

1790

Ralph Walker and Mary Burrel btp published 27 Dec 1789, 3, 10 Jan
Thomas Carter and Esther Rider btp published 31 Jan, 7, 14 Feb
John Glew otp and Ann Ferguson of Burneston published 31 Jan, 7, 14 Feb
[p. 65] Thomas Leathley and Dorothy Leeming btp published 14, 21, 28 Feb
Jeremiah Metcalfe and Elizabeth Slie btp published 23, 30 May, 6 June
Samuel Sidgwick of Patrick Brompton and Mary Scaife otp published 19, 26 Sept, 3 Oct
Henry Loftus and Elizabeth Pickersgill btp published 26 Sept, 3, 10 Oct
William Thwaites of Kirkby Malzeard and Alice Brown otp published 24, 31 Oct, 7 Nov
James Beck of Kirkby Malzeard and Prudence Reynard otp published 7, 14, 21 Nov
John Thompson and Alice Slater btp published 7, 14, 21 Nov

William Casling and Jane Oselton btp published 7, 14, 21 Nov

1791

John Lye otp and Ann Heslington of Leek published 10, 17, 24 Apr
John Barnes otp and Ruth Dorner of the chapelry of Middlesmoor published 13, 20, 27 May

1794

Jonathan Autherson otp and Hannah Millner of Wensley published 2, 9, 16 March
Joseph Thorpe and Mary Alexander btp published 23, 30 Mar, 6 Apr
Thomas Whitaker and Esther Baines btp published 6, 13, 20 Apr

[p. 66]

1795

John Skurrah otp and Ann Beckwith of Ripon published 25 Jan, 1, 8 Feb
John Ramshaw and Jane Mallaby btp published 25 Jan, 1, 8 Feb
Christopher Lambert otp and Mary Winn of Thornton Steward published 9, 16, 23 Aug

1796

William Dinsdale of Darton and Mary Jackson otp published 24, 31 July, 7 Aug
Henry Atkinson otp and Jane Prest of Osmotherley published 21, 28 Aug, 4 Sept
Thomas Renwick otp and Ann Snowden of Otley published [ ] Oct, 6, 13 Nov

1798

Joseph Smith otp and Sarah Bellwood of Wath published 4, 11, 18 Mar
Leonard Barker and Elizabeth Jackson btp published 15, 22 Apr [sic]
Bateman Atkinson and Mary Storrah btp published 15, 22 Apr [sic]
[William inserted in pencil] Court and Dorothy Clarkson btp published 15, 22 Apr [sic] [pencil annotation: married May 1]
William Hanley of East Witton and Mary Parker otp published 22, 29 Apr, 6 May
Joseph Clarkson and Mary Winn btp published 22, 29 Apr, 6 May
James Clark and Isabella Bage btp published 6, 13, 20 May

1799

Samuel Harte otp and Mary Barritt of Calvary published 3, 10, 17 Mar
Patterick Milburn otp and Margaret Potts of Scruton published 27 Oct, 3, 10 Nov
Christopher Thompson and Jane Myers btp published 3, 10, 17 Nov
Marmaduke Croft and Jane Pickersgill otp published 3, 10, 17 Nov
George Parker and Elizabeth Grime of Witton published 10, 17, 24 Nov
Simon Thwaites and Elizabeth Robinson btp published 10, 17, 24 Nov
William Topham of Kirkby Malzeard and Amy Suttill otp published 24 Nov, 1, 8 Dec

1800

Joseph Ponder and Ann Jackson btp published 2, 9, 16 Feb
Richard Thompson otp and Sarah Stroddard of Ripon published [ ] Mar, 6, 13 Apr
Peter Graham and Sarah Procter btp published 30 Nov, 7, 14 Dec

Burials 1759

Masham	May	10	Rebecka wf Matthew Place
Swinton		10	Ann Hall
Masham		17	Hannah d William Imeson
Masham		18	Dorothy Thornberry, wid
Masham		18	Isabel wf Francis Horner
Masham	June	3	Elizabeth wf Gabriel Kay
Masham		5	Hannah wf Mr William Horner
Ilton		9	James Teasdale
Ellingstring		13	John Williamson
Ellington		13	Jillian d Aaron Jackson
Fearby		20	Isabel Carter
Ellington		29	Elizabeth Pickersgill, spr
Swinton Green	July	5	Mary wf Christopher Hanley
Masham		6	Sarah wf Adam Barns
Sourmire	Sept	4	Frances Barker, wid
Masham		6	Thomas Norridge, comber
Ellingstring		14	Mary d William Metcalfe
Masham		25	Margaret wf Richard Smith
Swinton	Oct	8	Thomas Smith of the Lodge
Ilton		25	Thomas s Thomas Caseling
Leighton	Nov	22	Edmond s Matthew Jackson
Ellington		27	Abigail d John Durham
Masham		28	Eleanor wf Edward Nicholson

Burials 1760

Masham	Jan	17	Margaret Bearper
Ilton		18	William Blackburn
Ellington		31	Thomas s John Beck
Masham	Feb	20	John Banks
Masham		23	Elizabeth wf Marmaduke Smorthet
[p. 69]			
Masham	Mar	20	William Watson
Ilton		23	Ann Prest
Masham	Apr	1	Mathew s William Robinson
Ilton		3	Elizabeth wf Christopher Pickard
Masham		13	William Horner
Masham		15	Ursula d Thomas Croft
Masham	May	2	Marmaduke Smorthet
Masham		3	Dorothy d Christopher Sturdy
Fearby		5	Ann wf John Blackburn
Masham		16	Dorothy d George Thornberry
Ellington		17	James s Jacob Towler
Masham		25	Thomas s Adam Barns
Masham	June	13	John s Revd Rob[er]t Radclyffe
Ellington		17	Anthony Jackson
Masham	July	13	George Wilson
Masham	Aug	1	Ann d Edward Durham
Masham		1	Elizabeth d Jeffrey Clarkson
Swinton		2	Hannah wf Benjamin Akers
Fearby		3	Mary wf John Wintersgill
Masham		7	Ann d Ralph Alderson
Sutton		30	Anthony s Anthony Ballan
Masham	Sept	1	John s Thomas Rogerson
Masham		2	Thomas s Thomas Rogerson
Swinton		7	Hannah d Benjamin Akers
Helming		13	Mary d Thomas Balland
[p. 70]			
Ilton		23	Margaret wf William Broadley
Swinton		23	George s Thomas Dawson
Masham	Oct	8	Robert s Henry Thompson
Swinton		14	Thomas s Peter Trees
Masham		14	Ann d William Joy
Masham		18	Mary Strother
Masham		26	John Rogerson
Low Ellington		27	Henry Thompson
Masham		29	Henry s Henry Storrey
Fearby	Nov	4	Thomasin d Grace Carter
Lobley Hole		13	Ann Burril

Ellington	Dec	2	Jane Jackson
Ellingstring		4	George s George Ascough
Quarry House		8	Joseph s William Lightfoot
Masham		13	Ann Rayley

Burials 45

Burials 1761

Masham	Jan	2	Jane Hammond
Masham		12	Ann Ward
Ilton		22	Edward Blackburn
Body Close		25	Sarah Walker
Fearby	Feb	2	Thomas Bowes
Masham		25	Mary Hebdin
Stotfold	Mar	2	Ann wf Thomas Ascough
Helming		7	Prudence d Thomas Balland
Masham		15	William s William Terry
[p. 71]			
Masham		26	George s Ralph Alderson
Masham	Apr	1	Mary wf Mr George Nares
Masham		24	John s Francis Wardrop
Healey	May	2	George Metcalfe
Healey	July	7	Ann wf William Hudson
Ilton		12	John s William Broadley
Masham	Aug	16	Thomas Wilson
Masham	Sept	11	William s Thomas Clapham
Masham		26	Joseph Calvert
Fearby	Oct	4	Elizabeth Hauxwell
Kirkby Malzeard		11	Frances Wrather, wid
Colsterdale		14	Margaret Walker
Masham		19	Elizabeth d John Atkinson
Healey		26	Mary Bennet
Masham	Nov	6	Thomas Clapham
Masham		6	Marmaduke s Joseph Millar
Fearby		23	Mercy wf John Burnet
Low Burton		23	Ann d Richard Hanley
Masham	Dec	1	John Clarkson
Masham		17	Mr John Beckwith
Masham		22	Thomas Metcalfe
Masham		24	Isabel wf John Gill

31 Burials in the year 1761

[p. 72]		**Burials 1762**	
Masham	Jan	2	Jane Wardrup, wid

163

Masham	Feb	11	Esther d Francis Wardrup
Aiscough		25	Ann Haw, wid
Ellingstring	Mar	3	Robert Plews
Ilton		28	John Place
Ellingstring		30	Thomas Jackson
[no place]	Apr	5	Francis s Francis Wardrup
Fearby	May	17	Elizabeth d Thomas and Elizabeth Alexander
Fearby		27	Elizabeth Dawson
Lamb Hill	June	5	Mr William Beckwith
Swinton		20	William Robinson
Ellingstring	July	11	Ann wf Robert Norwich
Fearby		13	Ann d John and Mary London
Ilton		15	John Atkinson
Masham		21	Robert Ripley
Swinton		29	Elizabeth wf William Imeson
Healey	Aug	27	Mary wf Mark Towler
Masham		28	Jane wf Christopher Saunderson
Masham		31	Elizabeth wf William Fryar
Masham	Sept	3	Jane d Thomas and Mary Rider
Ellingstring		12	Christopher s Thomas and Sarah Fawbert
Masham		20	Matthew Place
Masham	Oct	19	Ellen Horner
Fearby		25	Mary Towler
Warthermarske	Nov	17	George s George and Jane Nicholson
Ellington		19	Edward Place

26 Burials

Burials 1763

Body Close	Jan	6	Elizabeth wf William Walker
Ellingstring		13	Arabella d Thomas and Mary Plews
Masham		28	Nancy d George and Margaret Medley
Masham	Feb	1	Ann d Thomas and Margaret Bradbury
Masham		3	Jane wf Robert Smith
Fearby		13	Ann d Thomas and Elizabeth Alexander
[p. 73]			
Masham	Mar	12	George s George and Ann Bowness
Healey		16	Mary wf Christopher Mallaby
Masham		17	Robert and Margaret children William and Margaret Smith
Healey		18	Esther d George and Jane Metcalfe
Moorhead		22	Peter Burrell
Masham		24	David s John and Mary Jackson
Ellington	Apr	8	Robert Clapham
Ellingstring		9	Mary wf Moses Jackson

164

Masham		10	John Jaques
Ellington	May	14	Elizabeth wf John Beck
Ilton		15	Prudence d John and Sarah Metcalfe
Ellington		22	Thomas Plews
Masham	June	3	Mary d James Hamilton
Masham		12	Ann wf George Bowness
Masham	July	14	Dorothy d John and Frances Croft
Ellington		18	Elizabeth King
Masham	Aug	5	Elizabeth Beckwith
Masham		18	Michael Beckwith
Masham	Sept	7	Thomas Watson
Masham		15	Mary d Henry and Rebecca Hodgson
Masham	Oct	4	John Thompson
Masham	Dec	9	Catharine Johnson
Moorhead		11	Richard Handley
Masham		22	Elizabeth d Ralph and Mary Alderson
Masham		30	Thomas Croft

32 B[urials]

Burials 1764

Masham	Feb	17	Jane d William and Margaret Smith
Masham		18	Peter s William and Margaret Smith
[*no place*]		23	Miss Jane Danby
Low Ellington	Mar	3	Elizabeth wf Thomas Thwaites
Masham		3	Mary wf George Blades
Masham		9	Ann Plumb
North Cote		15	Dorothy Robinson
Fearby	Apr	5	Esther Jackson
Masham		8	Jane wf Mr Simon Wrather
Ilton		11	Mary Temple
Ellingstring		20	Ann Watson
Ellington	May	8	Thomas Towler
Masham	June	11	Ann d Thomas and Mary Court
Well		11	Francis Horner
Masham		21	Robert Jaques
Masham	July	7	Sally d Francis and Mary Wardrop
Ellingstring	Aug	14	John Ascough
Swinton		17	William Burneston
Masham		18	George Kay
[p. 74]			
High Burton		28	James Pickersgill
Leighton		28	Mary wf Matthew Jackson
Ilton	Sept	4	Nancy d John and Ann Taylor
Ellington		11	Elizabeth Pickersgill

Fearby	Oct	11	Christopher s John and Elizabeth Cundall
Fearby	Nov	1	Elizabeth Teasdale
Masham		16	Jane Plews
Low Ellington		21	Alice Thompson
Swinton		27	Lucy Smith
Ellington	Dec	9	Alice Robinson
Moorhead		15	Marmaduke Metcalfe
Swinton		29	Isabel Walker

31 Burials in 1764

Burials 1765

Ilton	Jan	4	Mary d William and Mary Horseman
Healey		15	John Carter
Swinton		24	Edmund Atkinson
Ellingstring	Feb	8	Ellen wf George Ascough
Ellington		11	Ann d Thomas and Mary Beckwith
Masham		24	Mary wf John Wrather
Masham	Mar	3	Frances Jaques
Ellingstring		4	Ann Steel
Low Ellington		27	Christopher s Matthew and Ann Craggs
Moorhead	Apr	18	Hannah Wintersgill
Fearby		25	John Ianson
Masham		30	George Bowness
Masham	May	1	Jane d Caleb and Eliz[abeth] Powel
Swinton		4	Alethea d David and Ann Ashton
Ellingstring		22	Elizabeth Fawbert
Tanfield		28	Dorothy d Robert and Alice Metcalfe
Masham	June	5	Mary d Joseph and Lucy Milner
Masham		12	Margaret wf William Smith
Masham		15	Mary d John and Thomasin [Isabel *crossed out*] Robinson
Ilton	Aug	11	Ann d Robert and Sarah Bell
Masham		22	Elizabeth wf Thomas Woburn
Masham		26	Elizabeth d Joseph and Margaret Bartle
Masham	Sept	5	Jane d Ralph and Mary Alderson
Swinton		24	Thomasin wf Peter Hammond
Ilton	Nov	3	Mary wf Edward Blackbourn
Crab House		7	Mary Theakston
Fearby		21	John Breary
Masham	Dec	9	Samuel Beckwith
[p. 75]			
Ilton		23	Mary Wintersgill

29 Burials in 1765

166

Burials 1766

Brigwith, pa. East Witton	Jan	1	Thomas Plews
Ellingstring		16	Esther Walker
Masham	Feb	18	Robert Norwich
Ash Head		19	Francis Plews
Masham	Mar	12	William s Edward and Elizabeth Moises [*note about misplaced entries below*]
Masham		21	Hannah Banks
Healey		27	Elizabeth Metcalf
Masham	Apr	15	Christopher Hanley
Masham		20	George Hagston
Warthermarske	May	27	George s George and Jane Nicholson
Fearby	Feb	28	Ellen Hodgson
Healey		28	Matthew Wynne
Healey	June	24	Jane wf Edward Smorthwaite
Warthermarske	July	11	Margaret wf Anthony Barker
Masham		18	Frances wf John Croft
Masham		20	Catharine d Humphrey and Catherine Wood
Ellington	Aug	8	Gillian wf Aaron Jackson
Healey		15	Elizabeth d Edward and Jane Smorthwaite
Healey		28	Elizabeth wf Marmaduke Hammond
Healey		31	Thomas s Marmaduke Hammond
Masham	Sept	11	Francis s Gabriel and Sarah Kay
Healey		14	Edward Smorthwaite
Warren House	Oct	18	Sarah wf John Kendal
Masham		20	John Blades
Fearby		24	Mary d Christopher Imeson
Masham	Nov	1	Thomas s Jeffrey and Mary Clarkson
Masham		7	William s George and Elizabeth Bowness
Masham		9	George Pickersgill
Masham		29	Elizabeth wf Mr William Wrather
Masham	Dec	2	Ann d John and Barbara Banks
Masham		17	Caleb s Caleb and Elizabeth Powel
Breary Banks		18	Thomas Lye
Round Hill		23	Thomasin Burrill, wid

33 Burials in 1766

Burials 1767

Masham	Jan	9	Thomas s John and Margaret Clarkson
Fearby		17	Thomas Breary
Masham		22	Susannah wf William Thomas
Healey		23	Christopher Whorlton

Masham		23	Sarah d John and Mary Jackson
[p. 76]			
Fearby	Feb	1	Mary d Christopher and Mary Dawson
Low Mains		1	Thomas s Timothy and Esther Rider
Healey		9	Barbara d Christopher Whorlton
Fearby		16	Mary d John and Elizabeth Mallaby
Pickersgill		19	John Gill
Richmond		22	William s Thomas and Ann Beckwith
Masham	Mar	3	Jane d Joseph and Margaret Bartle
Masham		18	Ann d James and Hannah Hamilton
Masham		28	Abigail d William and Martha Harrison
High Ellington	Apr	12	Thomas s John and Esther Beck
Masham		12	Robert s William and Hannah Imeson
Masham		13	Ursula d Henry and Mary Leeming
Healey	May	1	Christopher s Thomas and Ann Craggs
Ilton	June	11	Mary wf William Horseman
Low Ellington	July	1	Sarah d Smithson and Margaret Wynne. Vide below [*reference to June 16 entry*]
Masham		6	Mary wf Francis Wardrop
Ilton	June	16	William Taylor
Warthermarske	July	28	Anthony Barker
Moorhead	Aug	1	Mark Barker
Masham		21	Margaret wf Francis Thompson
Masham	Sept	13	William Thirkill
Ilton		30	John Sly
Moorhead		30	Mary Burrill, wid
Masham	Oct	4	Grace d Francis Wardrop
Warthermarske		18	Ann wf Richard Cass
Fearby	Nov	2	Hannah wf Robert Blackburn
Low Ellington		12	Joseph s Thomas Thwaites
Masham		26	Eleanor d John and Jane Scurrah
Masham		28	Mary d William and Elizabeth Pickersgill
Low Ellington	Dec	4	Thomas Thwaites
Masham		10	Robert Wardrop
Masham		14	Anthony s Thomas and Mary Ballan
Masham		14	William s Henry and Ellen Storah
Masham		24	Mary Scurrah

39 Burials in 1767

Burials 1768

Ilton	Jan	2	Jane Leatham
Masham		7	Thomas s John and Margaret Bolland
Masham		17	Jane d John and Margaret Bolland
Masham		26	Margaret wf Mr John Bolland

Fearby	Feb	3	Mary Dawson, wid
Low Mains		9	Joseph s Timothy and Esther Rider
Masham		12	Jonas Metcalf
Ellingstring		18	Ellen d Thomas and Alice Moor
Masham		26	Francis Sturdy
Masham	Mar	8	David s John and Mary Jackson
[p. 77]			
Masham		10	Thomas s James and Hannah Hamilton
Masham		16	John s Ralph and Mary Alderson
Masham		25	Francis Thompson
Masham		26	Thomas s Francis Wardrop
[*no place*]	Apr	6	Ann Beckwith, wid
Ellingstring		20	James s Thomas and Alice Moor
Masham	May	11	Richard s Thomas and Mary Rogerson
Masham		11	George Fletcher
Burneston		17	Thomas s Thomas and Esther Parker
Masham		17	George s Ralph and Mary Alderson
Masham		21	Thomas s Ralph and Mary Alderson
Swinton	June	25	David s David and Ann Ashton
Masham		30	Jane wf Francis Brotherton
Swinton	July	4	William Glew
Masham		23	Ellen Calvert, wid
Fearby		27	William Marshal
Fearby		29	Margaret wf Henry Rushton
Hunton	Sept	3	Mary wf William Dennison
Masham		8	Margaret wf John Gill
Masham		26	Hannah Brignall
Masham	Oct	20	Ann wf Edward Raper
Masham		22	Judith Baxter, servant
Healey		25	Ann wf Mark Plews
Masham	Nov	23	John s Joseph and Dorothy Thorns
Masham	Dec	4	Thomas Oliver
Masham		4	Mr Richard West
Masham		5	John Wintersgill
Masham		5	Elizabeth d Peter and Jane Robinson
Swinton		16	George s George and Catherine Imeson
Ellington		22	Mary wf John Thackeray
Ellington		26	Esther wf John Beck

41 Burials in 1768

[p. 78]

Burials 1769

Leighton	Jan	6	Matthew Jackson
Masham		16	Elizabeth Thompson
Masham		23	Thomas s Thomas and Mary Ballan

Hunton	Feb	4	Anna wf [*blank*] Heslop
Masham		5	George s William and Hannah [Ann *crossed out*] Robinson
Masham		5	William s John and Margaret Bolland
Ellington		16	Judith wf Henry Lupton
Ellington	Mar	1	Ann Mennel
Breary Banks		21	Mary wf Stephen Smith
Gebdykes		26	Mary d Henry and Mary Leeming
Ellington	Apr	6	John Beck snr
Masham		22	George s William and Hannah Robinson
Millstone Bank		26	Margery Bellerby, wid
Masham		27	Ann d John and Susannah Warrener
Ilton	May	3	Isabel d Ralph and Margaret Horsman
Masham		25	Jane wf John Cooper
Healey	June	4	Mark Plewis
Masham		7	Ann wf William Wade
Masham		28	Thomas Machel
Ellington	July	3	Anthony s John and Ann Jackson
Masham	Aug	13	Jane wf Peter Robinson
Masham		21	Isabel Hagston, wid
Masham	Oct	5	Matthew s Matthew and Mary Gill
Ellington	Nov	4	Elizabeth wf James Metcalf
Masham		22	William Wade
Masham	Dec	1	William s William and Martha Harrison
Ellingstring		5	George Kendrey jnr
Swinton		7	George Imeson
Ellington		9	Ursula Watson
Nutwith Cote		18	John Bartlett, gent
Masham		27	Elizabeth Spence

31 Burials in 1769

Burials 1770

Masham	Feb	20	Charles s Matthew and Mary Gill
Ellingstring		23	Elizabeth Chambers
Fearby	Mar	5	Ellen wf Joseph Atkinson
Ellington		17	William Ashton
Masham		20	Ralph s Ralph and Mary Alderson
Fearby		25	Thomas illeg s Elizabeth Wood
High Ellington	Apr	14	Aaron Jackson
Masham		17	Thomas Webster
Ilton	Apr	17	George Prest
Masham		26	Robert Plews
Ellingstring		27	Mary Grayson

[p. 79]

170

BURIALS

Ilton	May	13	Ralph Chambers
Masham	June	30	Henry s Frances Fletcher, wid
Fairthorn	July	5	Amy d Thomas and Amy Scafe
Masham		12	Frances Hagston, wid
Masham		31	Edward Raper
Ellingstring	Aug	19	Margaret wf Thomas King
Warthermarske	Sept	8	John Ward
Masham		27	Mr Thomas Wrather
Masham	Oct	11	Mary wf John Jackson
Masham	Nov	8	Peter Robinson snr
Masham		21	Ann wf William Robinson
Ellingstring	Dec	2	Dorothy wf Henry Procter
Healey		13	Mary Rudd
Ellingstring		12	Margaret wf George Kendrew
Leyburn		15	Laurence Pickersgill
Sourmire		18	George Barker
Ilton		25	Anthony Watson

28 Burials in 1770

Burials 1771

Healey	Jan	5	Elizabeth Wilson
Breary Banks		19	Stephen Smith
Birks		25	Mary d Thomas and Mary Wintersgill
Masham		28	Jane Clapham, wid
Masham	Feb	2	William s Thomas and Ann Matthews
Healey	Mar	13	Catharine wf Joseph Windrass
Gebdykes		22	Rebecca d Henry and Mary Leeming
Towler Hill		27	Matthew Burton
Masham	Apr	6	Thomas Hutchinson
Sykes in Middlesmoor chapelty		25	John Walker
Ilton		29	Ralph Horsman
Sykes in Middlesmoor chapelry		30	William Walker
Swinton	May	15	Thomas s John and Rachel Hall
Masham	June	30	John Haste
Bedale	July	13	Simon Wrather
Masham	Aug	3	Mary Robinson
Breary Banks		6	George s George and Dorothy Smith
Ilton	Oct	13	Christopher s Thomas and Alice Casling
Masham		13	William s Robert and Jane Smith

19 Burials in 1771

Burials 1772

Healey	Jan	15	William Suttill
Healey		26	Ann Ascough, wid
[p. 80]			
Ellington		31	John Thackeray
Fearby	Feb	21	Mary wf Thomas Atkinson
Lamb Hill		21	Mary wf John Hill
High Ellington		28	Moses Jackson
High Sutton	Mar	18	William Duffield
Healey		22	Thomas s David and Ann Walker
Fearby		23	Jane d Robert and Elizabeth Blackburn
Masham		30	Elizabeth d George and Elizabeth Clark
Masham	Apr	11	Charles s Edward and Elizabeth Moises
Masham		25	Ralph s Peter and Jane Robinson
Masham	May	1	Ann Norris
Nutwith Cote		7	Jane Harland, wid
Grewelthorpe, pa. Kirkby Malzeard		23	Richard Batty
[*no place*]	Sept	20	James Legard, vagrant
Low Mains		20	Robert Rider
Masham		21	Jane d William and Jane Parker
Fearby	Oct	15	Matthew Hutchinson
Masham		18	Elizabeth wf George Wintersgill
Ellingstring		23	Dorothy wf John Tempest
Masham	Dec	19	Ann Procter, wid

22 Burials in 1772

Burials 1773

Masham	Jan	5	Rosamond d George and Ann Atkinson
Masham		8	Isabella d Thomas and Grace Thwaites
Ilton		11	Ann Blades
Masham		21	Mary d John and Ann Place
Healey		24	Mary d George Wintersgill
Healey	Feb	23	Francis s Mark and Theodosia Towler
Masham	Mar	4	John Nicholson
Masham		27	Mary Banks, wid
Norton Conyers		28	James s John Maud
Ellington	Apr	3	Edward Plews
Grewelthorpe, pa. Kirkby Mazeard		22	Anne Winn
Masham		25	Richard s William and Elizabeth Bond
Ellingstring		29	Richard Sergeant
Ellingstring	May	3	Jane wf Robert Tempest

Ellingstring		11	Mary wf Jeremiah Metcalf
Masham		28	Ann d John and Rosamond Atkinson
Swinton	June	15	Mary wf William Danby esq.
Fearby		18	Hannah d Francis and Sarah Mallaby
[p. 81]			
Masham	July	5	Mr Johnson
Masham		21	Ann d Thomas and Hannah Wilson
High Mains	Aug	1	Jane Ballan, wid
Masham		26	Leonard s Leonard and Jane Mudd
Fearby		29	Sarah wf William Longstaff
Healey	Sept	5	Ann Richardson
Ilton		22	Catharine wf William Atkinson
Ilton		27	Elizabeth Chambers, wid, aged 100
Healey Cote	Oct	1	Ellen Scowthroup
Masham		19	Thomas Scowthroup
Masham	Nov	2	Hannah d Ralph and Bridget Siddall
Sourmire		12	Elizabeth d Robert and Elizabeth Imeson
Healey		18	Agnes d William and Margaret Hodgson
Masham		20	Ann d Robert and Margaret Atkinson
Masham		24	William s John and Elizabeth Roundell
Nutwith Cote	Dec	1	Thomas s Thomas and Rose Coates
Fearby		5	Ellen d Luke and Jane Spence
Ellingstring		11	Elizabeth Lye, wid
Masham		16	Elizabeth d John and Barbara Banks
Fearby		30	Robert Blackburn

38 Burials in 1773

Burials 1774

Masham	Jan	10	Ann wf John Plews jnr
Round Hill	Feb	5	Thomas Atkinson
Nutwith Cote		6	John Ascough
Ellington	Mar	17	Thomas s John and Ann Jackson
Ellingstring		19	Sarah d Thomas and Sarah Fawbert
Ilton		24	Mary Imeson, wid
Low Burton		25	Joan wf John Middleton
Roomer		29	Ann wf Thomas Trees
Masham	Apr	8	Thomas s John and Sarah Chapman
Swinton		14	Matthew Imeson
Ellington		16	Elizabeth d Christopher and Jane Jackson
Grewelthorpe		17	Thomas s Francis and Jane Metcalf
Healey	June	2	Thomas s George and Jane Metcalf
Masham		3	Ann d Thomas and Ann Court
Masham	Aug	11	Thomas Lupton
Warthermarske		13	Elizabeth Ward, wid

Masham		27	Mr John Wrather, aged 88
Fearby		29	Mary Breary, wid, aged 86
[p. 82]			
Warthermarske	Oct	20	Frances d George and Catherine Leathley
High Ellington		23	Christopher Coates
Ellington	Nov	5	John Tunstal
Warthermarske		8	Hannah d George and Catherine Leathley
Spelderbanks		10	Dorothy Wintersgill
Fearby		24	John Burnet
Healey	Dec	9	Ralph Walker
Pickersgill		28	Isabel wf John Smith

26 Burials in 1774

Burials 1775

Ellington	Jan	6	Robert Smorthwaite, aged 87
Masham		6	William s John and Sarah Chapman
Masham		21	Dorothy d William and Dorothy Terry
Masham		29	Thomas Theasby
Roomer	Feb	16	John Kipling
Fearby	Mar	17	Dorothy d Robert and Elizabeth Blackburn
Masham		29	George Morrell
Swinton	Apr	6	Rachel d John and Rachel Hall
Healey		13	Thomas s Thomas and Catherine Barrows
Ilton		20	Ann Simpson, wid
Fearby		24	Robert s Robert and Elizabeth Blackburn
Masham	May	16	Mary Roe, wid
Ellingstring	June	12	Christopher Horseman Plews
Masham		16	Jane d William and Martha Harrison
Ellingstring		18	Richard s Thomas Robinson
Masham	July	17	Elizabeth d Laurence and Elizabeth Carter
Breary Banks	Aug	5	Hannah d Robert and Mary Walker
Masham		23	Charles s Edward and Elizabeth Moises
[no place]	Sept	3	Thomas Lockhart esq.[1]
Masham		15	Ann d George and Mary Fenwick
Ellingstring		21	Robert Fawbert
Masham		22	Thomas s Christopher and Mary Jackson
Warthermarske		25	John Ward
Healey		26	Edward s David and Ann Walker
Brock Ridding		27	John Pybus
Masham	Nov	26	Ellen d Moses and Mary Jackson

---

[1] pencil note : 'Aged 36 as observed on his lead coffin, by me this June 30, 1879 [The marble monument says annos *prope triginta* natus]   G.M. Gorham'

Healey		29	David s David and Ann Walker
Fairthorn	Dec	6	John s Thomas and Emmy Scaife
Masham		6	Thomas Hartley
Masham		23	Hannah Hammond, wid, aged 96

30 Burials in 1775

[p. 83]   **Burials 1776**

Masham	Jan	11	Grace Thwaites
Masham		16	Hannah d Robert and Hannah Beech
Fearby		16	Ellen d Thomas and Ellen Nelson
Masham		16	Mary Shepherd, wid, aged 82
Ilton		18	Ann Blades, wid, aged 86
[*no place*]		25	Mrs Catherine Lister
Ellingstring	Feb	3	Mary wf Thomas Plews
Masham		6	Dorothy Lupton
Masham		22	Marmaduke s William and Dorothy Terry
Masham		22	Mary wf Thomas Walker
Masham	Mar	1	Matthew Wardrop
Masham		9	Hannah Plumb
Healey Cote		14	Thomas Plews
Masham		15	Mr John Bolland
Masham		31	Frances d George and Frances Thornberry
Masham	Apr	4	Martha wf William Towler
Fearby		11	William Langstaff, aged 89
Masham		14	Ellen Hamilton, wid
Ilton		28	Christiana d Thomas and Ann Spence
High Ellington		28	Elizabeth d William and Hannah Brignell
Masham		28	Ann d George and Elizabeth Firby
High Ellington	May	1	William King
Ilton		6	Ellen wf Marmaduke Smith, aged 83
Ellingstring		10	Reuben s John and Anne Lye
Masham		18	Mary wf George Fenwick
Masham		21	James Calvert
Masham		29	James Hamilton
Healey	July	11	Francis Glew
Masham		19	Dorothy wf Joseph Thorns
Middleham		23	Alice wf Thomas Thompson
Low Mains	Aug	1	Esther wf Timothy Rider
Swinton		24	Peter Trees
Masham	Sept	4	Ralph Alderson
Masham		5	Michael Windall
Masham		17	John Place
Masham	Oct	22	Elizabeth Johnson, wid
Healey Cote	Nov	1	Robert Barker

Ellingstring		7	Ann Sergeant
Masham		17	Mary Ripley
Masham		21	Edward Stephenson, aged 84
Masham		27	Margaret Henderson
[p. 84]			
Healey Cote	Dec	14	Isabel Barker, wid
Healey		21	Ellen Pickersgill, aged 95
Low Bishopside pa. Ripon		22	Christopher Dawson

44 B[urials] in 1776

Burials 1777

Ellington	Jan	9	David Ashton
Masham		12	Mary wf James Hird
Masham		19	Mary d John and Hannah Richmond
Grewelthorpe		20	Jane wf Francis Metcalf
Masham		26	Mary Thirkill, wid, aged 82
Ellingstring		28	James Bartlett
Fearby	Feb	11	Dorothy wf Austin Hodgson
Warthermarske		13	Sarah d George and Catherine Leathley
Healey	Mar	3	William Hudson, aged 80
Masham		10	Thomas Gill
Masham	Apr	17	Dorothy d Matthew and Ann Hagston
Masham		26	Thomas Burneston
Warthermarske		26	Michael Hammond
Masham	May	6	Margaret Geldart, aged 92
High Ellington	June	8	William s Thomas and Dorothy King
Masham	July	9	Abraham Ellingworth, sexton, aged 79
Ilton		20	Elizabeth Norris, wid, aged 91
Ilton	Aug	6	Mary wf Samuel Sly, aged 88
Ilton		6	Elizabeth wf James Taylor
Fearby		12	Ann Breary, wid, aged 105
Ellingstring		18	John Walker
Healey		29	Michael s Luke and Jane Spence
Masham	Sept	5	Ralph s Henry and Eleanor Charnock
Millstone Bank		24	Mary wf John Bellerby
Ilton	Oct	6	Peter Scaife
Masham	Nov	29	George s John and Sarah Chapman
Ilton	Dec	7	Samuel Sly

27 Burials in 1777

Burials 1778

Masham	Feb	26	Thomasin wf John Robinson

Burton Constablery	Mar	2	Annis Fawnes
Ilton		10	John Stot
Masham		13	Mary d Caleb and Elizabeth Powel
Aldburgh		26	Ann wf Thomas Judson
Swinton	Apr	5	Elizabeth Trees, wid
Masham		19	Edward s Edward and Ann Croft
Low Burton		29	George s Thomas and Dorothy Finley
High Burton	May	30	Robert Kellet
[p. 85]			
Warthermarske	June	5	Elizabeth Hammond, wid
Masham		9	Ann wf Samuel Bowes
Gollinglith Foot		20	John s John and Mary Metcalf
Masham		21	James Towler
Masham	July	16	Ann wf John Weighill, aged 89
Masham		17	Jane d Caleb and Elizabeth Powel
Masham		26	Jane Hird, wid
Fearby	Aug	6	Humphrey Blackburn
Healey		17	Mary Wynne, wid, aged 82
Swinton		25	Ann d Ralph and Ann Caldbeck
Healey		26	Mary d William and Mary Bollum
Masham	Sept	6	Elizabeth Wardrop, wid
Fearby		21	Christopher Dawson
Summerside	Oct	4	Hannah d Peter and Esther Carter
Masham		5	Thomas s Henry and Elizabeth Lupton
Masham		12	Ann wf William Terry, carpenter
Masham		23	David Bell, aged 81
Masham		30	Elizabeth Towler, wid, aged 94
Ellingstring	Nov	4	George Ascough, aged 80
Masham		19	Hannah wf William Lightfoot

29 Burials in 1778

Burials 1779

Healey	Jan	14	Jonathan Lobley
Fearby	Feb	6	Mary Horsman, wid
Masham		9	Ann d Thomas and Grace Thwaites
Ellingstring		16	John s Christopher and Ann Hinley
Gebdykes	Mar	1	John Weighill, aged 91
Masham		8	Robert Crow
Moorhead		15	Thomas Ascough
Masham		25	John s William and Mary Parker
Masham		26	Dorothy d John and Mary Jackson
Masham		29	Robert Smith, aged 85
Fearby	Apr	3	Elizabeth d William and Sarah Longstaff
Swinton		20	Mary Clarke

Masham		21	William Beckwith
Masham		25	Thomas s Thomas and Ann Dawson
Masham		30	William Leeming, aged 93
Masham	May	4	Jane d John and Jane Clarkson
Masham		12	Jane wf John Clarkson
Swinton		14	Francis Coates
Warthermarske		30	Catharine Thorpe
[p. 86]			
Ilton	June	3	Mary Stott, wid
Spelderbanks		7	Jane d Marmaduke and Jane Wintersgill
Ellingstring		10	Ann Emerson
Summerside	July	1	Matthew s Matthew and Ann Burrill
Masham		1	Elizabeth Kaye, wid
Masham		5	Ann Slye, wid
Low Ellington	Aug	8	Smithson Wynne
Masham		18	Edward s Edward Blackburn
High Ellington		22	William Brignall
Swinton	Nov	14	John Harland
Masham	Dec	3	Thomas Thwaites jnr
Masham		10	Elizabeth wf Christopher Whorlton
Bramley		16	Thomas Lupton
Ellingstring		24	Leonard s John and Ann Lye
Healey		24	Barbara Whorlton

34 Burials in 1779

Burials 1780

Masham	Jan	6	Ann Johnson
Masham		29	Ann Place, wid
Fearby	Feb	13	Christopher Ripley
Swinton		21	Mary Smith, aged 95
Galphay		27	Alice wf Robert Metcalf
Masham	Mar	18	Thomas Thwaites
Middleham		26	Richard s Thomas Thompson
Masham	Apr	13	Ann d John and Ann Place
Masham		24	Ann d George and Ann Atkinson
Healey	May	10	John s William and Margaret Hodgson
Ellington		10	George illeg s Elizabeth Ashton
Masham		31	John Warener
Sutton	July	6	Margaret d Anthony and Frances Ballan
Swinton	June	14	Jane Iminson, wid
Masham		18	John s John and Mary Atkinson
Masham	July	8	Edward Croft
Masham		31	Mary wf Revd Robert Radclyffe
Masham	Aug	6	Widow Morrell

BURIALS

Ilton		10	Thomas s Henry and Hannah Fryar
Masham		17	Margaret wf John Morrell
Masham	Sept	18	John s Peter and Mary Haw
Masham		27	Mr William Wrather
Low Ash Head		30	Rebecca d George and Mary Graham
Healey	Oct	15	Edward Metcalf
Masham		29	Thomas Rogerson
Moorhead	Nov	10	John Topham, aged 84
Masham		12	Margaret Beckwith, wid, aged 85
[p. 87]			
Masham		19	William s John and Ann Plews
Ellingstring	Dec	4	Joseph Steel, aged 86
Ellingstring		8	Mary Exelby, aged 85
Fearby		14	Isabel Hodgson, aged 87
Masham		22	Jane Ripley
Fearby		26	Ellen d Christopher and Mary Dawson

33 Burials in 1780

Burials 1781

Fearby	Jan	14	Mary Dawson
Fearby	Feb	27	John Cundall
Masham	Mar	18	Mrs Dorothy Wrather, wid, aged 87
Swinton	Apr	22	William Danby esq.
Masham		24	Rebecca Leeming, wid
Masham	May	8	Dorothy wf John Wardrop
Fearby	June	18	Jane wf Luke Spence
Fearby		27	Mary wf Thomas Carter
Ellingstring		29	Ann Buckton
Healey Cote	July	21	Thomas Smorthwaite
Masham		31	Edward s Thomas and Elizabeth Clarkson
Masham	Aug	11	Thomas Hudson
Fearby	Sept	2	Isabella Gill, wid
Fearby		28	John s Thomas and Mary Carter
Masham	Oct	3	Elizabeth Webster, wid
Fearby		4	Robert Jackson
Masham		4	Mary Bell, wid
Masham	Nov	8	Margaret wf Thomas Burnett
Healey	Dec	16	Charles s Edward and Judith Rudd

19 Burials in 1781

Burials 1782

Ilton	Jan	6	Samuel Stables
Masham		8	Catharine d Edward and Ann Croft

Masham		13	Elizabeth Clarkson
Masham		18	James illeg s Jane Croft
Ilton		21	Marmaduke Smith
Grewelthorpe		28	Mary wf John Court
Fearby		28	Christopher s Christopher and Mary Dawson
Masham	Feb	11	Benjamin Sivers
Swinton Green		12	Mary Coates
Healey		18	Henry s Richard and Hannah Thompson
Masham	Mar	8	Christopher Sturdy, aged 90
Masham		23	James Hird, aged 82
Fearby		28	Ann wf Robert Blackburn, aged 88
[p. 88]			
Masham		31	William Hardcastle, gent.
Masham	Apr	5	Thomas Sedgwick
Masham		23	Ann wf Joseph Raley
Fearby		23	Thomas Cundall
Sheffield		28	Christiana wf Thomas Thompson
Ilton	May	24	Isabel wf Peter Hutchinson
Masham		29	Lister s Robert and Jane Smith
Ellingstring	June	3	Christopher Hinley
Warren House		9	John s John Kendall
Fearby		26	John s Michael and Ann Fryar
Masham	July	5	George s Robert and Mary Rider
Masham		14	Elizabeth wf Henry Scafe
Masham		15	Peter Jackson, aged 90
Masham		17	Thomas s Henry and Elizabeth Lupton
High Ellington		18	Christopher Jackson, aged 84
Masham		21	Dorothy d Richard and Elizabeth Brown
Masham	Aug	2	William s George and Elizabeth Clarke
Masham		3	Edward Croft
Ellingstring		3	Thomas s Thomas and Mary Plews
Masham		5	Ann d Henry and Mary Leeming
Masham		10	James illeg s Elizabeth Richardson
Masham		10	Dorothy d Christopher and Jane Merryweather
Masham		12	Ursula d Henry and Mary Leeming
Swinton		17	Mary illeg d Mary Glew
Masham		23	William s William and Sarah Shaw
Leighton	Sept	9	Mary Metcalfe, wid, aged 85
Fearby		9	Elizabeth Taylor, wid, aged 87
Masham		14	Margaret Bell
Masham		18	Joseph Thorne
Masham		19	James s James and Esther Wilkinson
Masham		29	Margaret d George and Margaret Fenwick
Masham	Oct	14	Barnabas Metcalf
Masham	Nov	16	Catharine Mailman

Low Ellington		19	Jane Coldbeck
Masham		20	William s William and Mary [Jane *crossed out*] Parker
High Ellington		30	Dorothy d Thomas and Dorothy King
Masham	Dec	11	Jane illeg d Dorothy Thompson
Masham		14	William Beckwith snr
Fearby		24	Peter Jackson
Fearby		26	Margaret Hodgson, aged 95
Masham		28	Francis Thompson

54 Burials in 1782

[p. 89]

Burials 1783

Sourmire	Jan	5	Ann d Edmond and Esther Barker
Fearby		18	Isabel wf Joseph Burneston
Masham		23	Samuel Bowes
Masham	Feb	21	Mary wf James Henderson
Sourmire		21	George s Edmond and Esther Barker
Masham		27	Catharine Theasby
Masham	Mar	4	Elizabeth wf Thomas Clarkson jnr
Masham		21	Mary wf Peter Haw
Healey Pasture End		31	Robert s Christopher and Mary Walker
Masham		31	Agnes d Christopher and Agnes Pickersgill
Masham	Apr	7	William Robinson
Masham		18	Mary wf Thomas Court
Masham		21	Francis s Francis and Ann Thompson
Masham		23	James Henderson
Pottgate, pa. Ripon	May	14	Francis Metcalfe
Healey		25	Francis s Francis and Elizabeth Glew
Summerside		30	Sarah wf Richard Hall
Brompton	June	1	Sarah wf Thomas Robinson
Masham		25	Dorothy wf Thomas Hagston, aged 89
Masham	July	4	Ann wf Thomas Dowson
Lamb Hill		7	Mary Heslington, wid, aged 89
Warthermarske		31	Catharine wf George Leathley
Masham	Aug	5	John Plews snr
Masham		27	Mary Alderson, wid
Masham	Sept	3	William Whitelock
Masham		10	Mary Ascough
Masham	Oct	2	Margaret d William and Margaret Smith
Ilton		7	Hannah wf Henry Fryar
Ilton		7	Hannah d Henry Fryar
Roomer		21	Robert Stoney
Fearby		26	Nancy d Christopher and Mary Dawson
Masham	Nov	9	Barnabas Bolland

Low Ellington		13	Mary wf Arthur Ashe
Masham		26	William s Joseph and Ellen Leeming
Masham		30	Hannah d William and Mary Husband
High Ellington	Dec	3	John Plews
Masham		26	Alfred [Edward *crossed out*] s William and Mary [Peter and Esther *crossed out*] Parker
High Ellington		30	John Durham

38 Burials in 1783

[p. 90]   **Burials 1784**

Masham	Jan	21	Mary wf Moses Jackson
Healey		24	Mary d John and Dorothy Ascough
Masham		25	Catharine Croft, wid, aged 81, pauper
High Ellington	Feb	8	Ann d John and Ann Jackson
Masham		24	Sarah d Caleb and Elizabeth Powell
Colsterdale		21	Samuel Ascough
Masham	Mar	31	Isabella d Thomas and Margaret Martindale
Fearby	Apr	22	Margaret d Christopher and Mary Dawson
Low Ellington		24	Mary Thompson
Masham	May	1	Mr John Lonsdale, aged 82
Ellingstring		2	Thomas Fawbert, aged 81, pauper
Masham		7	Elizabeth wf Thomas Jackson
Masham		16	Daniel s Robert and Margaret Atkinson
Fearby		18	Mary d Thomas and Mary Carter
Masham	June	9	Thomas Clarkson
Masham		16	Agnes d John and Hannah Richmond
Ellingstring		24	Thomas Plews snr
Masham	July	25	Mary Carter, pauper
Masham		28	Thomas Beecroft
Masham		28	Barnabas s William and Jane Parker
Healey	Aug	10	Sarah wf Mark Towler snr, pauper
Masham		16	Frances Hagston, wid
Warren House		20	Mary wf George Kendall
Masham	Oct	17	Richard Geldart, aged 83, poor
Masham	Nov	2	Robert Rider
Gollinglith		3	[*blank*] wf John Mallaby snr
Ilton		3	Mary illeg d Elizabeth Prest
Ilton		17	Esther d John and Mary Metcalf
Swinton	Dec	18	Benjamin Akers
Low Ellington		25	Ann Ashton

30 Burials in 1784

BURIALS

Burials 1785

Masham	Jan	3	Mary Braithwaite
High Ellington		31	Elizabeth Thwaites, aged 84
Masham	Feb	5	John Metcalfe
Masham		7	Ann wf John Carter
Masham		15	The Reverend Robert Radcliffe, clerk
Masham		27	Thomas Metcalfe, aged 92, poor
Ellingstring	Apr	3	Thomas Ascough
Masham		5	William s John and Jane Scurrah
Low Ellington	May	28	Thomas Jackson late of Low Ellington, aged 85
[p. 91]			
Healey	June	7	Hannah wf John Barnes
Masham		15	Luke Hutchinson
Masham		19	Hannah wf Thomas Allanson
Summerside		21	Matthew Burrill
High Ash Head	July	5	George s Matthew and Margaret Ascough
Low Ellington		5	Elizabeth wf Anthony Thwaites
Masham		8	Ann d Thomas and Mary Croft
Masham		19	Sarah wf Richard Smith, poor
Masham		20	Noah illeg s Ellen Croft, poor
Masham	Aug	6	Hannah d Benjamin and Elizabeth Akers
Nidd		10	John Wells
Masham		14	James illeg s Eleanor Colling, poor
Masham		17	Charles Allicock
Masham		26	William s Thomas and Margaret Martindale
High Mains		31	John Ballan
Swinton	Sept	1	Ellen wf Henry Smith, aged 88, poor
Masham	Oct	8	Robert s Robert and Mary Jackson
Masham		18	Elizabeth Oram alias Urwin
Masham		29	John s Peter and Mary Hawe
Binsoe	Nov	25	Ann wf George Marsh
Pateley Bridge	Dec	6	Dorothy Metcalf, wid, aged 92

30 B[urials]

Burials 1786

Masham	Jan	5	William Pickersgill, pauper, aged 80
Masham		11	Thomas Hutchinson snr, poor
Masham		11	Isabella Robinson, poor
Fearby	Feb	5	Christopher Mallaby
Masham		15	Thomas s Thomas and Hannah Allanson, poor
[no place]		15	Susanna illeg d Mary Butterfield, poor
Sutton Penn	Mar	1	Leonard Hodgson
Swinton		15	Christopher Pickersgill

183

Place	Month	Day	Name
Ilton		15	Mark Hutchinson, aged 81
Swinton		18	David Astwood
Healey		21	Mary Walker, wid, poor
Masham		22	Ann d John and Ann Carter
Cathorpe	Apr	1	Hannah wf Samuel Hawkswell
Cathorpe		12	Hannah d Samuel Hauxwell
Ellingstring		12	George Kendrew
Warthermarske		20	Elizabeth d John and Mary Thorpe
Healey Pasture End		21	Christopher Walker
[p. 92]			
Masham	May	10	William s John and Margaret Kidd
Masham		17	Elizabeth Wrather, wid
[no place]		28	Martha d Arthur and Ann Ashe
Masham	June	15	Jane d Robert and Mary Rider
Healey		28	Frances Watson, wid, aged 91
Fearby	July	6	Jane Hutchinson, wid, aged 88
Warthermarske		9	Sarah d Mark and Elizabeth Barker
Masham		16	Thomas Geldart
Masham		17	Thomas Langdale, pauper
Bedale		27	Rachel wf Henry Rodwell
Fearby	Aug	2	Esther wf James Robinson, aged 90, pauper
Bramley Grange		16	John Bell, aged 81, pauper
Ilton	Sept	3	Sarah Kirton, aged 98, pauper
Masham		8	Thomas s William and Sarah Pybus
Ellington		8	Elizabeth Astwood
Sutton Penn		26	Anthony Ballan
Masham	Oct	8	Hugh Robinson, pauper
Fearby		25	James Robinson, aged 88, pauper
Colsterdale	Nov	30	Isabella Ascough, wid, aged 88
Swinton	Dec	28	Henry Smith, aged 90, pauper

37 Burials in '86

Burials 1787

Place	Month	Day	Name
Masham	Jan	2	George s George and Isabella Robinson
Low Mains		2	Robert s Timothy Rider
Ilton		19	Ann Greathead, pauper
Warthermarske		23	Thomas Gill
Masham	Feb	7	Ann Blackburn, wid
Ilton		7	Sarah wf John Metcalf
Ellingstring		10	Elizabeth wf Jeremiah Metcalf
Masham		11	Marmaduke Lupton
Swinton		22	Ann Harland, wid, aged 82, pauper
Ellingstring	Mar	3	William Thompson illeg s Ann Lye
Masham		4	Thomas Ripley, pauper

Masham		21	Mary Rogerson, wid
Masham		30	Isabel Lupton, wid
Masham		31	Ann illeg d Ellen Croft, pauper
Fearby	Apr	1	Ann d Robert and Ann Plews
Masham		2	William Hamilton, pauper
[*no place*]	Mar	25	Isabella d Thomas and Alice Leadham, a poor traveller
Ellington	Apr	6	Ann illeg d Mary Craggs
Masham		7	John s Thomas and Dorothy Allanson
Fearby		8	Matthew s John Cundall
[p. 93]			
Masham		11	Ann d Christopher and Jane Merriweather, pauper
Ilton		11	Ann wf Thomas Jackson
Masham		12	Catherine Becroft, wid
Masham	[*no date*]		William Boddy, aged 85, pauper
Leighton		16	Sarah d Peter and Elizabeth Hanley
Masham		17	Robert s Thomas and Alice Raynwick
Warthermarske		23	Ann Gill, wid, aged 98, pauper
Ellingstring		24	John Walker
Masham		24	John Atkinson
Masham		24	William s William and Martha Harrison
Masham		28	Alice wf Thomas Rainwick
Masham	May	13	Margaret Calvert
Breary Banks		24	Mary d George and Dorothy Smith
Masham	June	4	Catharine d Thomas and Frances Hutchinson
Masham		8	Ann d Thomas and Ann Dawson
Ellingstring		19	Robert Bellerby
Masham		19	Thomasin Jackson, wid
Masham		20	Jeffrey Clarkson
Masham	July	24	Elizabeth Clarkson
Masham		29	Hannah wf John Richmond
Masham	Aug	16	Jane d William and Dorothy Woodall
West Summerside		19	Richard King, aged 84
Masham	Sept	12	John Anderson
Ellington	Nov	17	Daniel illeg s Ellen Thompson
Fearby		22	Ann d Robert and Ann Smorthit, pauper
Masham	Dec	9	Elizabeth wf William Joye
Azerley		22	Robert Metcalf

47 Burials

Burials 1788

Masham	Jan	5	John Holmes
Masham		9	Elizabeth Bearpark, wid, pauper

Burrill		20	Robert Blackburn, aged 89
Fearby	Feb	4	William Atkinson
Masham		17	Christiana d William and Beatrice Hartley
Masham	Mar	4	Mary wf Henry Kendrew, aged 81
Masham		6	John Thompson
Masham		14	Mary wf Thomas Clarkson
Healey		18	Magdalen Barker, aged 81, pauper
Masham	May	6	Isabella Crowe
Masham	June	3	Thomas Court
[p. 94]			
Fearby		9	Thomas Nelson
Masham		10	Elizabeth d John and Elizabeth Roundhill
Masham		24	Elizabeth wf Laurence Carter
[*no place*]		27	John s John and Ellen Varley, travelling tinker
Masham	Aug	7	Ellen Peel, wid, aged 80
Masham		22	Mary d John and Margaret Kidd
Ellingstring		26	Jane Prest, wid
Masham		27	Jane d John and Ann Baine
Masham		28	Henry s Henry and Elizabeth Thompson
Fearby	Sept	12	William Balland
Healey		23	William s Richard and Hannah Thompson, pauper
Masham	Oct	3	Ann d John and Margaret Kidd
Ellington	[*no date*]		Ann Barker, wid, aged 82
Masham		15	Ann d Thomas and Mary Pickering, pauper
Masham		20	Mary Clarkson, wid
Masham		23	Margaret wf William Lupton
Fearby	Dec	5	Elizabeth Williamson, aged 83, pauper
Healey		23	Elizabeth wf William Simpson, aged 84, pauper
Masham		24	Mary wf Thomas Pickering, pauper

30 Burials

Burials 1789

Healey	Feb	17	Hannah wf Richard Thompson, pauper
Healey		20	Edward s Edward and Judith Rudd
High Ellington		27	Jane wf Christopher Jackson
Masham	Mar	6	Robert s William and Elizabeth Beckwith, pauper
Masham		8	Elizabeth illeg d Sarah Towler, pauper
Masham		10	Catharine d Thomas and Mary Croft
Masham		11	Thomas s George and Elizabeth Clark
Masham		19	George Truthit, pauper
High Ash Head		20	William Ascough
Masham		21	James s Leonard and Jane Mudd, pauper
Masham		26	Frances Delicate, wid

186

Ellingstring		27	Elizabeth Bartlet, wid
Masham	Apr	10	Mary d William and Mary Sherwood, pauper
Masham		10	Esther wf Peter Barker
Warthermarske	May	7	Mary d George Leathley
Masham		17	Mr Thomas Martindale
Ellington		28	Ann Wintersgill, wid, aged 88
Masham	June	9	Thomas s James and Jane Metcalf
[p. 95]			
Leeming		19	William s William and Barbara Doxford
Masham		30	Ellen Beckwith, pauper
Healey	July	2	Ann wf Thomas Craggs, aged 86
Masham	Aug	14	Peter s Peter and Mary Hammond
Healey Mill		23	Ann wf John Vitty
Healey		26	Frances Whorlton, pauper
Swinton	Sept	19	Deborah Glew, wid, pauper, aged 95
Masham	Oct	2	Hannah d Stephen and Mary Siddall
Masham		6	Benjamin s Robert and Margaret Atkinson
Masham		12	Thomas Walker
Masham		13	John s John and Margaret Kidd
Masham		14	Elizabeth wf Samuel Wrather
Masham		21	Elizabeth d Henry and Ann Braithwaite
Bramley, pa. Kirkby Malzeard		23	Sarah Bell, wid, pauper, aged 92
Masham		24	John s William and Mary Atkinson
Ellingstring		26	Thomas King, pauper
Ilton		28	Mary d Christopher and Elizabeth Lightfoot, pauper
High Ellington	Dec	3	Thomas s William and Ann Brignall
Masham		23	William s George and Elizabeth Clark, pauper
Ellingstring		31	Emanuel Lye

38 Burials in 1789

Burials 1790

Healey	Jan	12	Esther d Richard and Hannah Thompson, pauper, aged 12
Masham		13	Thomas s Thomas and Dorothy Allanson, infant
	Feb	11	The Revd Edward Moises, Vicar of Masham cum Kirkby Malzeard, died at York Feb 6 and bur. at Masham, aged 73
Brigwith, pa. East Witton		12	Mary Plews, aged 73
High Ellington		13	William s John and Mary Durham, infant
Ellingstring		15	Ann Hinley, wid, pauper, aged 73
Ilton		20	Eleanor wf William Atkinson, aged 56

Masham	Mar	2	Martha wf Anthony Thwaites, pauper, aged 89
Gollinglith		23	Joseph s John and Alice Clarkson, infant
Gollinglith		24	William s John and Alice Clarkson, infant
Masham	Apr	15	Elizabeth Pickersgill, wid, pauper, aged 81
Carlton in Coverdale		27	Augustin Hodgson, aged 91
Masham	May	1	Rosamond wf John Atkinson, pauper, aged 78
Sourmire		5	Peter Hutchinson, aged 98
Ellingstring		12	Margaret d Jos. and Ann Reynard, infant
[p. 97]			
Masham	June	18	Ann d John and Beatrice Plews, aged 3
North Cote	July	10	Matthew illeg s Margaret King, infant
Body Close		22	William Walker, aged 75
Low Ellington		30	Jane Ashton, wid, aged 86
Masham	Aug	10	Hannah d John and Mary Wilson, infant
Healey Pasture End		30	Ann Teasdale, aged 38
High Ellington	Sept	20	John Bellerby, aged 70, pauper
Fearby		28	Sarah Ripley, wid, aged 82
Fearby		29	Grace wf William Brentley, aged 62, pauper
Masham	Nov	2	Joseph Raley, aged 86, pauper

25 Burials in 1790

Burials 1791

Healey	Jan	28	Hannah Summers, wid, pauper, aged 78
	Feb	9	The Revd Richard Kirshaw B.D., Vicar of Masham cum Kirkby Malzeard, died at London Jan 27 & bur. at Masham, aged 47
Masham		15	Elizabeth wf Francis Terry, aged 41
Masham		20	Hannah wf William Rodwell, pauper, aged 82
Masham		25	John s Abraham and Mary Duffield, aged 1
Masham		27	Francis Wardrop, aged 72
Masham		28	Mary Spence, wid, pauper, aged 84
Masham	Mar	8	John Hill, aged 58
Masham		15	Thomas s George and Jane Nicholson, aged 21
Masham		16	Mary d William and Beatrice Hartley, infant
Masham		23	Jane wf Peter Jackson, aged 27
Masham	Apr	6	George s Richard and Sarah Smith, aged 15
Masham		9	Esther Robinson, wid, pauper, aged 80
Swinton		10	Mary d Edward and Elizabeth Horsman, aged 6
Masham		11	Thomas Trees, aged 78
Masham		15	Susanna Warrener, wid, pauper, aged 51
Masham		18	John Richmond, aged 32
Fearby		22	Esther d Thomas and Mary Carter, aged 15

BURIALS

Masham	May	29	Thomas Banks, pauper, aged 51
Masham	June	3	Thomas s John and Elizabeth Atkinson, aged 26
Masham		6	Christopher and Robert twin ss Robert and Elizabeth Welford, infants
Ilton		16	Elizabeth Prest, wid, pauper, aged 80
High Ellington		25	Samuel Beckwith, aged 82
Masham	July	27	John Ferguson, aged 34
Fearby		27	Robert Smorthwaite, pauper, aged 77
Healey		27	Rosamond Lobley, pauper, aged 25
Ilton		28	William Horsman, aged 76
Masham		31	William Rodwell, pauper, aged 85
Masham	Aug	7	William Lightfoot, aged 79
Masham		22	Francis s Francis and Anne Thompson, aged 2
[p. 97] Warthermarske		24	John Thorpe, aged 38
Pickersgill		29	John s Thomas and Hannah Towler, aged 4
Summerside	Sept	13	Mary d Ralph and Mary Walker, infant
Masham		15	John s Christopher and Jane Merriweather, pauper, infant
Masham	Oct	20	George Clark, pauper, aged 55
Fearby	Dec	21	John s Anthony and Mary Urwin, infant
Gollinglith		26	Thomas s John and Mary Metcalfe, aged 21
Healey		30	Mark Towler, pauper, aged 85

39 Burials in 1791

Burials 1792

Masham	Jan	3	Michael s William and Elizabeth Beckwith, pauper, aged 15
Low Ellington	Feb	3	John Mallaby, pauper, aged 88
Masham		26	Elizabeth Beckwith, aged 63
Masham	Mar	2	John Wardrop, aged 78
Masham		30	Thomas s Agnes Richmond, pauper, aged 14
Masham	Apr	2	Thomas Jackson, miller, aged 72
Ellingstring		9	Mary d Joseph and Mary Maynard, pauper, infant
Ilton		17	Christopher s Ralph and Elizabeth Prest, aged 14
Masham	May	12	John s Thomas and Jane Clark, infant
Swinton		20	William Iveson (killed from a tree), aged 20
Ellingstring	June	19	Jane Faubert, wid, pauper, aged 85
Masham	July	10	Margaret Vayro, aged 20
Masham	Aug	3	Jane d John and Mary Heslington, infant
Ellingstring		7	Sarah wf George Hinley, pauper [*no age given*]
Masham	Oct	31	Jane d William and Ann Trees, aged 1
Gollinglith	Dec	3	Anna d John and Mary Metcalfe, aged 20

Masham		14	John s William and Beatrice Hartley, infant
Ilton		17	Elizabeth Horsman, spr, aged 69
Ilton		22	James Metcalfe, aged 40
Masham		22	Margaret Buntin, wid, aged 78
Ellingstring		27	Joseph Procter, aged 74

21 Burials in 1792

[p. 98]   **Burials 1793**

Masham	Jan	12	Jane Clarkson, spr, pauper, aged 70
Masham		16	Thomas s Christopher and Mary Marshall, pauper, aged 23
Masham		19	Deborah wf Edward Blackburn, aged 58
Fearby		27	Elizabeth Burnit, wid, pauper, aged 52
Fearby		29	Solomon Fawns, bach, aged 70
Gildermire House		30	Alethea d Arthur and Ann Ashe, poor, aged 2
Warthermarske	Feb	4	Mary d George and Mary Dawson, aged 3
Warthermarske		6	John s George and Mary Dawson, aged 1
Masham		11	Gabriel Kay, pauper, aged 87
High Ellington		24	Mary d John and Ann Jackson, aged 30
Fearby	Mar	2	Ann d John and Ann Horner, infant
Masham		10	Mary Rider, wid, pauper, aged 80
Masham		17	William s William and Jane Walburn, poor, aged 4
Fearby	Apr	3	Mary Burnistone, wid, pauper, aged 89
Healey	May	3	Elizabeth d Edmund and Mary Jackson, infant
Fearby		7	Jane Ianson, spr, aged 73
Ash Head		18	Mary wf George Graham, aged 47
Bedale		22	William Bell, aged 37
Swinton		30	John Duffield, aged 36
Warren House	June	5	John Kendall, aged 84
Masham		17	William Walburn, pauper, aged 31
Masham	July	17	William s Thomas and Ann Geldart, aged 7
Masham	Aug	2	Joseph s William and Elizabeth Beckwith, poor, aged 14
Ellingstring		7	Sarah wf John Nelson, aged 48
Leeds		7	Mary wf Francis Sturdy, aged 40
Masham		12	William Gee, pauper, aged 78
Masham	Sept	7	Richard Strother, aged 84
Grimes Gill		9	Thomas Ascough, aged 42
Gollinglith	Oct	6	John Metcalfe, aged 66
Masham		8	Mary Linton, wid, poor, aged 75
Spelderbanks		24	Jane wf Marmaduke Wintersgill, aged 89
Fearby	Nov	17	John Blackburn, aged 83
Breary Banks		17	Sarah wf Robert Theakstone, aged 71

Breary Banks		22	Jane Smith, spr, aged 64
Ellingstring		28	Robert Walker, bach, aged 72
High Ellington	Dec	20	Ann wf John Jackson, aged 66
Clotherholme, pa. Ripon		24	Stephen Moseley, aged 78

37 Burials in 1793

[p. 99]

Burials 1794

Masham	Feb	2	William s William and Elizabeth Beckwith, poor, aged 1
Masham		13	Mary Walker, wid, poor, aged 84
Masham		22	Ann Bell, spr, aged 62
Masham	Mar	6	Elizabeth Walker, spr, aged 27
Swinton Mill		7	Hannah wf John Woodd, poor, aged 33
Spelderbanks		8	Marmaduke Wintersgill, aged 78
Masham		11	Roger Heslington, wdr, aged 86
Masham	Apr	10	Thomas s John and Sarah Chapman, aged 20
Healey Mill		22	Margaret d Lawrence and Elizabeth Heap, infant
Fairthorn		27	Thomas s Thomas and Amy Scaife, aged 30
Masham		30	Jane Hodgson, spr, poor, aged 54
Masham		30	Ann d George and Ann Truthwaite, poor, aged 13
Lobley Hole	May	10	John Lodge, aged 87
Ilton		13	Joseph s John and Esther Dummil, aged 1
Masham	June	5	Elizabeth wf John Banks snr, poor, aged 77
Masham		14	John Kidd, aged 68
Masham		19	Francis s Francis and Elizabeth Terry, aged 8
Masham		30	Dorothy Thompson, wid, aged 82
Masham	July	4	Hannah Harker, wid, poor, aged 39
Masham		10	Abigail wf Thomas Dowson, aged 53
Sykes House in Nidderdale		25	Catharine Hutchinson, wid, aged 90
Masham		27	Elizabeth Metcalfe, wid, poor, aged 100
Masham		28	Isabella Croft, wid, poor, aged 70
Masham	Aug	7	Stephen Siddal, aged 44
Masham		8	Stephen s Stephen and Mary Siddal, aged 6
Masham		15	Henry Thompson, aged 75
Masham		16	Mary d Matthew and Mary Gill, aged 17
Masham	Sept	1	Thomas s Judith Beverley, pauper, aged 19
Masham		7	Ann d Henry and Dorothy Croft, aged 3
North Cote	Oct	11	Mary d John and Margaret Boston, infant
Masham		29	Barbara wf William Doxford, aged 30
Masham	Nov	17	Hannah Taylor, wid, aged 72
High Ellington		22	Ann wf John Wilkinson, snr, aged 75

Ilton		24	Mary d Ralph and Elizabeth Prest, infant
Masham	Dec	5	Ann Body, wid, aged 88

35 Burials in 1794

[p. 100]

Burials 1795

Masham	Jan	6	Edward Blackburn, wdr, aged 84
Masham		12	Thomas s John and Dorothy Vitty, aged 1
Masham		14	Anthony Sturdy, aged 71
Masham		20	Thomas Almon, aged 58
Howe		24	John s Daniel and Eleanor Ianson, aged 29
Summerside		24	Elizabeth King, wid, aged 83
Masham		25	Mary d George and Isabella Clarkson, aged 2
Masham		27	Christopher Merriweather, poor, aged 48
Ellingstring	Feb	24	Christopher Hinley, poor [*no age given*]
Burton Constablery		28	Elizabeth wf Thomas Emlah, aged 32
Nutwith Cote	Mar	3	Henry Kendrew, aged 84
Burton Constablery		8	Tabitha wf Thomas Edmondson, aged 60
Warthermarske		11	Thomas Theakstone, aged 72
Masham		13	Hannah wf William Imeson, aged 72
Masham		15	John Richmond, wdr, aged 74
Masham		15	Rachel Hutchinson, wid, aged 75
Low Roomer		19	Joseph s Richard and Elizabeth Topham, aged 5
Swinton		21	Isabel wf Thomas Metcalfe, aged 80
Low Roomer		22	Elizabeth wf Richard Topham, aged 38
Masham		26	Mary wf Benjamin Siddal, aged 42
Sykes House		28	Ann Ashton, wid, aged 69
Ilton	Apr	3	Judith wf Robert Ruecroft, aged 73
Masham		4	Jane d William and Barbara Doxford, aged 1
Masham		18	Hannah d Thomas and Dorothy Leathley, aged 3
Masham		19	Lawrence Carter, wdr, aged 82
Masham		19	George s George and Isabella Clarkson, infant
Masham		21	James Vayro, wdr, aged 28
Colsterdale		25	Thomas s William and Mary Wintersgill, aged 3
Healey		27	Catharine d Francis and Elizabeth Glew, aged 13
Masham	May	2	Mary Beckwith, wid, aged 97
Swinton		12	Thomas Bradberry, aged 59
Swinton		18	Ann d Thomas and Margaret Bradberry, aged 25
Masham		31	Robert Plews, aged 60
Masham		31	Dorothy Hardy, aged 78
High Ellington	[*no date*]		Ann d John and Mary Durham, aged 2
Sykes House	Aug	30	Frances d Ralph and Ann Coldbeck, aged 5
Masham		30	Mary d Thomas and Frances Hutchinson, aged 11
Warthermarske	Sept	1	William s John and Catharine Hodgson, infant

Healey Cote		9	Ann Smorthwaite, wid, aged 79
Swinton	Oct	19	Matthew Dennison, aged 72
Masham		22	Ann d William and Mary Brewster, infant
Fearby		27	Thomas Hodgson, bach, aged 88
Fearby		29	Mary wf John London, aged 74

[p. 101]

Masham	Nov	2	William s Thomas and Elizabeth Drummer, infant
Masham		5	Mary d Robert and Esther Robinson, infant
Masham		11	John Reynard, aged 73
Masham		11	Mary Metcalfe, aged 67
Masham		14	Jane wf Richard Pickersgill, aged 55
Masham		24	Thomas s Thomas and Mary Sturdy, aged 3
Masham		24	Ann wf Richard Hanley, aged 82

50 Burials in 1795

Burials 1796

Masham	Jan	2	Jane wf William Ward, aged 25
Low Ellington		4	George Fenwick, aged 22
Masham		16	Anthony Thwaites, wdr, aged 93
Masham		23	Ann Smith, wid, aged 77
Fearby		23	Elizabeth Cundale, wid, aged 77
Masham	Feb	12	Jane wf Robert Smith, aged 51
Howe		24	Eleanor wf Daniel Ianson, aged 78
Healey Mill	Mar	13	Elizabeth d John and Emma Marsden, aged 15
Fearby		27	Mary Scurrah, aged 22
Foxholme	Apr	2	William Reynard, aged 55
Masham		6	Elizabeth wf William Beckwith, aged 48
Sourmire		9	Matthew s Mark and Elizabeth Hutchinson, aged 18
Masham		16	Thomas s Mary Siddal, aged 10
Masham	May	16	Ann wf Thomas Almon, aged 36
Masham	June	4	Jane d Stephen and Mary Siddal, aged 5
Masham	July	23	Margaret d Thomas and Frances Hutchinson, aged 16
Healey		29	John Vitty, wdr, aged 77
Masham		31	Sarah wf Robert Rayley [*no age given*]
Burton Constablery	Aug	6	Edward s Edward Gee, aged 14
Masham		7	Robert Slater, aged 21
Masham		12	Edward s Robert and Margaret Atkinson, aged 16
Healey	Sept	10	John Ascough, jnr, aged 30
Burton Constablery		12	James s Anderson and Mary Langstaff, aged 5
Masham		16	Thomas Craggs, wdr, aged 94
Masham		25	George Nicholson, aged 60

Ramshaw Mill	Nov	29	Ann Bellerby, wid, aged 80
High Ellington	Dec	9	John Wilkinson, aged 91
Masham		16	Mary Hodgson, aged 84
Warthermarske		19	Joseph s Mark and Elizabeth Barker, infant
Healey Pasture		26	Barnabas s Mary Walker, aged 33

30 Burials in 1796

[p. 102]

Burials 1797

Masham	Jan	1	Jonathan s John and Elizabeth Roundale, aged 20
Halton, pa. Whitchurch		4	Edmund s Edmund and Sarah Kanell [*no age given*]
Masham		8	Henry Leeming, aged 55
Fairthorn		11	Thomas Scaife, aged 82
Masham	Mar	11	Elizabeth Kay, spr, aged 83
Burton Constablery		17	Mary d Hannah Harker, aged 13
North Cote		26	Ann wf John King, aged 47
Masham		29	Hannah wf Matthew Carter, aged 39
Fearby	Apr	15	Ann wf John Hutchinson, aged 48
Masham		23	Roger Bolland, bach, aged 84
Masham		26	Frances Wilson, wid, aged 80
Fearby		27	John s Ralph and Mary Edon, aged 18
Burton Constablery	[*no date*]		William s Michael Foster, aged 10
Healey Mill	[*no date*]		Ann d Lawrence and Elizabeth Heap, aged 2
Masham	May	16	Elizabeth Clark, wid, aged 58
Fearby		31	Ann d Thomas and Bridget Taylor, aged 5
Swinton	June	9	Esther [*altered from* Elizabeth] Dennison, wid, aged 78
Masham	July	16	Robert Walker, aged 75
Masham		27	Matthew s Matthew and Hannah Carter, infant
Fearby		31	Christopher s Thomas and Jane York, aged 4
Masham	Aug	10	Mary Strangways, wid, aged 77
Healey		15	John Reed, bach, aged 42
Masham	Sept	25	Frances d Thomas and Mary Kaye, aged 18
Howe	Oct	10	Daniel Ianson, wdr, aged 75
Ilton		25	William Imeson, aged 78
Ilton		27	Alice wf Thomas Casling, aged 65
Masham		28	Leonard Mudd, aged 55
Ilton	Nov	19	Mary wf John Metcalfe, aged 49
High Ellington		24	Frances Ballan, wid, aged 76
Masham		24	Susanna Gains, wid, aged 91
Burton Constablery		28	William s William and Elizabeth Gatenby, aged 19
Swinton Mill	Dec	6	Thomas Dawson, aged 89
Swinton Mill		7	Isabel Dawson, aged 75

194

Masham		9	Jane Bell, wid, aged 71
Burton Constablery		10	Richard Spence, aged 73
Masham		17	Elizabeth Aire, wid [*no age given*]

36 Burials in 1797

[p. 103]   **Burials 1798**

Masham	Jan	4	Margaret d Thomas and Margaret Martindale, aged 27
Masham		4	Matthew Metcalfe, aged 75
Masham		30	Jane d Henry and Elizabeth Lofthouse, aged 4
Masham	Feb	5	Grace wf Thomas Metcalfe, aged 66
Ellingstring		20	Leonard Wilkinson, aged 60
Aldburgh	Mar	9	James Hutton esq., d. Mar 2, aged 60
Masham		16	Elizabeth d Thomas and Mary Kay, aged 30
Burton Constablery	Apr	1	Richard s Matthew and Mary Wilson, aged 1
Masham		1	Mary Leeming, wid, aged 65
Masham		4	Frances wf Thomas Hebdin, aged 68
Burton Constablery		6	Christopher s Christopher and Jane Hansom, aged 1
Healey		18	Elizabeth d George and Elizabeth Raw, aged 1
Swinton		27	Matthew Jackson, aged 72
Masham	May	1	Ann wf Richard Smith, aged 59
Masham		2	George illeg s Jane Gill, infant
Swinton		6	Sarah Sturdy, wid, aged 66
Fearby		10	Christopher Imeson, aged 80
Fearby		13	William Spence, aged 74
Ellington	June	4	Alice Coldbeck, wid, aged 75
Healey		19	William Simpson, aged 86
Masham		29	Mary Towler, wid, aged 76
Ilton	July	13	Catharine wf William Greathead, aged 55
Masham		22	Thomasin Urwin, wid, aged 75
Burton		25	James s William and Mary Stringer, aged 1
Masham	Aug	18	Thomas Hartley, aged 37
Burton		31	Margaret d William and Elizabeth Gatenby, aged 12
Masham	Sept	4	John s Anthony and Mary Urwin, infant
Burton		15	Margaret d Christopher and Jane Hansom, aged 13
Masham		21	Deborah d Thomas and Mary Banks, aged 1
Colsterdale	Oct	3	Esther Graham, wid, aged 76
Gollinglith	Nov	28	Mary Metcalfe, wid, aged 73
Fearby	Dec	7	Ann wf Thomas Rider, aged 43
Swinton		22	William Morton, aged 56

33 [*annual total*]

[p. 104]   **Burials 1799**

Healey Mill	Jan	11	Joseph Lancaster, aged 59
Ilton	Feb	22	John Smith, pauper, aged 89
Masham	Mar	9	William Imeson, wdr, aged 76
Masham		11	Thomas Court, aged 58
Ripon		24	Mary wf Joseph Ridley, aged 42
Healey		29	John Carter, aged 70
Masham		31	Sarah d John and Mary Beckwith, aged 2
Moorhead	Apr	10	Esther Pickersgill, wid, aged 87
Masham		12	Ann wf Anthony Ingelby, aged 55
Ellingstring		30	Esther wf Thomas Carter, aged 29
Ellington	May	16	Charlotte d Thomas and Ann Morrel, infant
Masham		23	William Terry, aged 80
Masham		25	John Chapman, aged 80
Masham	June	1	John Robinson, jnr, aged 62
Masham		6	Martha d Matthew and Mary Gill, aged 18
Burton Constablery		10	Elizabeth d Francis Kitchen, aged 45
Masham		10	Jane d John and Beatrice Plews, aged 14
Masham		20	Mary d John and Henrietta Baines, infant
Burton	July	23	John s Christopher and Jane Hanson, aged 12
Fearby		27	Jane Imeson, wid, aged 68
Masham	Aug	4	William s John and Henrietta Baines, aged 13
Foxholme		24	Dorothy Walker, wid, aged 80
Ellington	Sept	3	Margaret Winn, wid, aged 86
Grewelthorpe		19	Sarah wf George Pickersgill, aged 32
Masham		29	John Roundale, aged 64
Masham	Oct	18	John Croft, aged 80
Masham		21	Francis Thompson, aged 57
Masham		21	Thomas Dawes, gent, aged 65
Burton Constablery		23	John Brown, aged 12
Healey		26	Sarah wf Richard Thompson, aged 61
Masham	Nov	6	Jane d John and Mary Heslington, infant
Masham	Dec	7	John Gill, aged 69
Colsterdale, pa. East Witton	[*no date*]		Mary wf Thomas Wintersgill, aged 70
Round Hill		14	Thomas Atkinson, aged 79
Ellingstring		17	Jeremiah Metcalfe, aged 74

35 [*annual total*]

[p. 105]   **Burials 1800**

Masham	Jan	6	Robert Raley, aged 76
Healey		21	William Hodgson, aged 79
Ilton		22	Elizabeth Oliver, wid, aged 62

Masham	Feb [*blank*]		Thomas s Thomas and Mary Durham, infant
Masham		14	Ann d Peter and Sarah Plews, infant
Ilton		14	Elizabeth Smith, wid, aged 89
Burton Constablery		19	John Harker, aged 21
Breary Banks	Mar	12	[*blank*] wf George Smith, aged 85
Masham		13	Hannah Beckwith, spr, aged 80
Ellington		14	Mary wf Francis Lambert, aged 62
Masham		16	John s Robert and Elizabeth Atkinson, infant
Fearby		19	William Duffield, aged 79
Warthermarske		27	Ruth Ward, wid, aged 77
Masham	Apr	8	Elizabeth Thompson, aged 20
Masham		26	Mrs Phillis Harrison, spr, aged 68
Masham	May	14	Hannah d Thomas and Hannah Clarkson, aged 2
Ellingstring		15	Elizabeth d Jeremiah Metcalfe, aged 15
Grewelthorpe	June	18	Robert Jackson, aged 33
Fearby		25	Mary Rider, wid, aged 58
Kex Moor		28	Henry s John and Mary Rodwell, infant
Low Mains	July	4	Timothy Rider, aged 77
Fearby		10	Joseph Burnistone, aged 61
Masham		11	Sarah wf John Theakstone, aged 75
Healey		11	George s George and Elizabeth Raw, infant
Ilton		16	Robert Ruecroft, aged 84

Visitation held at Masham July 30 Revd W. Lawson Commissary

Round Hill	Aug	1	Thomasin Atkinson, wid [*no age given*]
Masham		13	John Robinson, aged 90
Low Ellington		17	Christopher s Christopher and Mary Lambert, aged 3
Swinton		27	Margaret Bradberry, wid, aged 67
Quarry House		31	Mary Stoney, wid, aged 83
Ilton	Oct	1	Thomas Jackson of Grewelthorpe late of Ilton, aged 81
Breary Banks		6	Elizabeth wf Thomas Jackson, aged 72
Fearby		9	Jane wf Matthew Terry, aged 27
Fearby		25	Sarah Bell, wid, aged 73
Grewelthorpe	Nov	2	Christopher Pickersgill, aged 55
Masham		9	The Revd John Wrather s Mr Samuel Wrather, aged 25
Masham		10	Elizabeth Atkinson, wid, aged 77
Masham	Dec	27	Catharine Hutchinson, wid, aged 86
Healey		28	Richard Hall [*no age given*]

39 [*annual total*]

[p. 106]   **Burials 1801**

Fearby	Jan	3	Ann Wintersgill, spr, aged 80

[*no place*]		5	James illeg s Ann Mudd, aged 1
Fearby		7	Thomas Carter, wdr, aged 58
Masham		10	Ann d John and Mary Hargrave, aged 2
North Cote		14	Elizabeth d Christopher and Mary Procter, aged 1
Ilton		23	[*blank*] Cartman, wdr, aged 86
Fearby		23	Mary Jackson, wid, aged 92
Masham		26	William s John and Mary Hutchinson, aged 1
Masham		31	Elizabeth d John and Mary Hargrave, aged 3
Summerside	Feb	3	Peter Burrill, bach, aged 81
Masham		21	Mary wf Ralph Pybus, aged 50
Masham		23	David s James and Alethea Nicholson, infant

[*End of Register*]

[Parish Register PR/MAS.1/10]

A Marriage Register Book for the Parish of Masham taking place at Lady Day 1754. Robt. Radclyffe, Curate

[p. 1]   **Marriages 1754**

June   17   Thomas Clarkson, servant, and Mary Robinson, wid, btp, banns (June 2, 9, 16), by R.R., both mark. W: William Rodwill, Thomas Spink
July   4   John London, tailor, and Mary Breary, spr, btp, banns (June 16, 23, 30), by R.R., both sign. W: Robert Blackbourn, John Harland
                Banns of Thomas Langdale of Masham and Priscilla Lickers of Walmgate [Walmsgate *sic*], York, publ. June 30, July 7, 14, by R.R.
Sept   14   Thomas King, husbandman, and Margaret Whorl(e)ton, spr, btp, banns (Aug 11, 25, Sept 1, by R.R.), by Richard Thistlethwaite, vicar of Well, both mark. W: John Whorlton, William Thirkill
[p. 2]
                Banns of Paul Parr and Ann Auton publ. Aug 25, Sept 1, 8, by R.R.
                Banns of Richard Simison and Ann Moor publ. Sept 15, 22, 29, by R.R.
                Banns of Thomas Barker and Dorothy Thompson publ. Oct 20, 27, Nov 3, by R.R.
                Banns of George Medley and Margaret Wardrop publ. Nov 3, 10, 14 [*sic*], by R.R.

[p. 3]   **Marriages 1755**

Jan   14   George Smith, husbandman, and Dorothy Ianson, spr, btp, banns (Dec 22, 29 1754, Jan 5), by R.R., both mark. W: John Carter, Robeart Jackson

MARRIAGES

May 19 John Kidd of Kirkby Malzeard, servant, and Margaret Banks of Masham, spr, banns (Apr 6, 13, 20), by R.R., he signs, she marks. W: Thomas Lonsdale jnr, Edw[ar]d Durham

20 John Jackson, wdr, and Mary Banks, spr, btp, banns (May 4, 11, 18), by R.R., both mark. W: Abraham Illingworth, Mary Hanley

June 14 John Myers of Well, shoemaker, and Ann Robinson of Masham, spr, banns (May 25, June 1, 8), by R.R., both sign. W: Deborah Robinson, Mary Hanley

[p. 4]

July 12 Edward Place, shoemaker, and Frances Williamson, spr, btp, banns (June 22, 29, July 6), by R.R., he signs, she marks. W: Mary Hanley, Abra[ha]m Illingworth

Oct 5 Anthony Ballan, husbandman, and Frances Eden, wid, btp, lic, by R.R., both sign. W: Christ[opher] Jackson, William Thirkill

21 Thomas Gell of Thirsk, tanner, and Jane Horseman of Masham, spr, lic from the Dean and Chapter of York, by R.R., both sign. W: W[illia]m Horsman, W[illia]m Leadley

22 William Malcolm, gardener, and Elizabeth Minion, serving maid, btp, banns (Oct 5, 12, 19), by R.R., both sign. W: John Rushton, Isabel Robinson

[p. 5]

Dec 11 William Wheatley of Tanfield, cooper, and Elizabeth Lacy of Masham, spr, banns (Oct 26, Nov 2, 9, by R.R.), by E.M., both sign. W: W[illiam] Lacy, Henry Cundall

Nov 20 John Hutchinson, husbandman, and Mary Leadley, spr, btp, banns (Oct 19, 26, Nov 2), by R.R., both sign. W: Hannah Leadley, John Walker, George Leathley

17 Joseph Atkinson, husbandman, and Ellen Scaife, spr, btp, banns (Nov 2, 9, 16), by R.R., both mark. W: Matthew Hutchinson, William Thirkill

24 Henry Lupton, serving man, and Julian Winn, spr, btp, banns (Nov 2, 9, 16), by R.R., both mark. W: William Lupton, Margret Winn

[p. 6]

25 Thomas Wintersgill, husbandman, and Mary Jackson, spr, btp, banns (Nov 9, 16, 23), by R.R., both sign. W: Thomas Jackson, Ann Jackson

Dec 21 Thomas Casling, labourer, and Alice Blackburn, spr, btp, banns (Nov 30, Dec 7, 14), by R.R., both mark. W: Tho[ma]s Jackson, Tho[ma]s Taylor

Marriages 1756

Mar 11 Jacob Towler, tailor, and Frances Wood, spr, btp, banns (Nov 30, Dec 7, 14 1755, by R.R.), by Richard Thistlethwaite, vicar of Well, he signs, she marks. W: William King (mark), William Thirkill)

Jan 24 Thomas Atkinson, labourer, and Thomasin Burril, spr, btp, banns (Dec 21, 28 1755, Jan 4), by R.R., both mark. W: Matthew Burell, Sarah Burill

[p. 7]

22 William Joy, tailor, and Martha Arnett, spr, btp, banns (Jan 4, 11, 18), by R.R.,

both mark W: Matthew Wardrop, William Thirkill

20   John Tanfield of Burneston, co. York, gent, and Catharine Beckwith of Masham, spr, lic, by R.R., both sign (*she signs* Katherine), W: Mary Beckwith, W[illia]m Beckwith

Banns of William Bain and Martha Sargeson publ. Jan 11, 18, 25, by R.R.

Banns of John Gill and Isabel Cardass publ. Jan 11, 18, 15, by R.R.

[p. 8]

Feb 14   George Spence of Coverham, husbandman, and Catharine Smorthwaite of Masham, spr, banns (Jan 25, Feb 1, 8), by R.R., he marks, she signs. W: Ann Jackson, Edward Smorthit

Apr 19   Joseph Acres of Kirkby Malzeard, husbandman, and Ellen Barker of Masham, spr, banns (Mar 28, Apr 4, 11), by R.R., both mark. W: Tho[mas] Talyor, Abraham Illingworth

22   Revd Robert Radclyffe, clerk, and Mary Wrather, spr, btp, lic, by Richard Thistlethwaite, vicar of Well, both sign. W: Eliz[abeth] Wrather, Tho[ma]s Wrather

May 18   Adam Barns of Aysgarth, joiner, and Sarah Hagstone of Masham, spr, banns (May 2, 9, 16), by R.R., he signs (Barnes), she marks. W: Tho[ma]s Hagston, John Bolland jnr

[p. 9]

24   Robert Theakstone, husbandman, and Sarah Burrill, spr, btp, banns (May 9, 16, 23), by R.R., both sign (he signs Thekston). W: Peter Burrell, John Bolland jnr

Banns of Anthony Sturdy and Elizabeth Ingram publ. May 23, 30, June 6, by R.R.

Banns of Christopher Walker and Mary Teasdale publ. May 23, 30, June 6, by R.R.

Sept 5   Henry Hodgson, woolcomber, and Rebecca Dobson, spr, btp, banns (Aug 15, 22, 29), by R.R., both sign. W: George Medley, William Heslington

[p. 10]

Nov 28   Hugh Robinson, labourer, and Esther Lofthouse, spr, btp, banns (Nov 7, 14, 21), by R.R., both mark. W: Jefferay Clarkson, David Bell

Dec 15   Matthew Crags, servant, and Ann Coats, spr, btp, banns (Nov 21, 28, Dec 5), by R.R., both mark. W: John Jackson, John Ballun

26   James Illingworth, woolcomber, and Mercy Body, spr, btp, banns (Nov 28, Dec 5,12), by R.R., both sign (she signs Boddy). W: George Robinson, William Body

Marriages 1757

May 12   John Taylor, tailor, and Ann Bell, spr, btp, banns (Apr 17, 24, May 1), by R.R., both mark. W: John Richmond, Tho: Taylor

[p. 11]

19   William Fawcett of East Witton, joiner, and Barbara Ascough of Masham, spr, banns (May 1,8, 15), by R.R., he signs (Fawcit), she marks. W: Ann Smorthit,

William Thirkill

30   Peter Jackson, husbandman, and Ann Barker, spr, btp, banns (May 8, 15, 22), by R.R., both sign. W: John Carter, Thomas Wintersgill

31   John Wilkinson, carpenter, and Ann Barker, spr, btp, banns (May 8, 15, 22), by R.R., both sign. W: George Barker, Peter Robinson

Aug 7   Mark Towler, shoemaker, and Docea Windrass, spr, btp, banns (July 24, by L.H., July 31, Aug 7, by R.R.), by R.R., both sign (she signs Doce). W: Peter Carter, Esther Carter

[p. 12]

16   Henry Storey, joiner, and Ellin Raper, spr, btp, banns (July 24, by L.H., July 31, Aug 7, by R.R.), by R.R., both sign. W: John Rogerson, Thomas Storey, Joanna Storey

23   Henry Thompson, tailor, and Alice Clapham, spr, btp, banns (Aug 7, 14, 21), by R.R., he signs, she marks. W: John Jackson, William Thirkill
Banns of Thomas Tayler and Eleanor Scowthrop publ. Aug. 7, 14, 21, by R.R.
Banns of John Jackson and Ann Bucktin publ. Aug 7, 14, 21, by R.R.

[p. 13]   Banns between William Toler and Martha Robinson publ. Aug 21, 28, Sept 4, by R.R.
Banns between John Robinson and Margaret Dunn publ. Aug 21, 28, Sept 4, by R.R.

26   Thomas Metcalfe of Masham, blacksmith, and Grace Hammond of Grinton, spr, lic, by R.R., he marks, she signs. W: Ann Elerton, Wm. Heslington

Nov 21   Edward Durham, chandler, and Ann Beecroft, spr, btp, lic, by R.R., both sign. W: Wm Durham, William Thirkill, Robert Crow

[p. 14]   **Marriages 1758**

Jan 3   Thomas Jackson, wdr, and Ann Thirkhill, spr, btp, banns (Dec 18, 25 1757, Jan 1), by R.R., both sign (she signs Thirkil). W: Joseph Jackson, George Leathley

10   Thomas Wilkinson, farmer, and Mary Banks, spr, btp, banns (Dec 18, 25 1757, Jan 1), by R.R., he signs, she marks. W: John Banks, Thomas Banks

10   George Leadley, gent, and Catherine Thirkill, spr, btp, lic, by R.R., he signs, she marks. W: Richard Jaques, Thos. Jackson, Thomas Jackson

Feb 6   John Ballan, husbandman, and Ann Jackson, spr, btp, lic, by R.R., both sign. W: Chris. Jackson, Thomas Ballan

[p. 15]

7   Thomas Bradberry, blacksmith, and Margaret Thwaites, spr, btp, banns (Jan 22, 29, Feb 5), by R.R., he signs, she marks. W: John Taylor, Tho[ma]s Croft

14   Caleb Powell, gent, and Elizabeth Thirkill, spr, btp, banns (Jan 29, Feb 5, 12), by R.R., both sign. W: Thos. Thirkill, William Thirkill
Banns between Joseph Rayley and Ann Prest publ. Feb 5, 12, 19, by R.R.
Banns between Thomas Theackston and Mary Verity publ. Feb 12, 19, 26, by R.R.

[p. 16]   Banns between Joseph Rayley and Ann Dowson publ. May 7, 14, 21, by R.R.

May 16 Daniel Ianson, husbandman, and Ellen Plews, spr, btp, lic, by R.R., both sign.
W: John Carter, Robert Ianson
Banns between Thomas Firth and Ann Hall publ. May 28, June 4, 11, by R.R.
Banns between John Butterfield and Esther Stephenson publ. June 18, 25, July
2, by R.R.

[p. 17]
Aug 8 Robert Jackson, husbandman, and Thomasin Burril, spr, btp, banns (July 9, 16,
23), by R.R., both sign (she signs Burrell). W: John Richmond, Tho[ma]s
Clarkson

Sept 21 Francis Thompson of Tanfield, firkiner, and Deborah Robinson of Masham,
spr, banns (Sept 3, 10, 17), by R.R., both sign. W: Wm Terry, Abraham
Illingworth
Banns between Luke Spence and Sarah Fokingbridge publ. Sept 3, 10, 17, by
R.R.

Oct 10 James Hamleton, miller, and Hannah Rodwell, spr, btp, banns (Sept 24, Oct 1,
8), by R.R., both mark. W: Mary Calvert, Abraham Illingworth

[p. 18]
Nov 21 Henry Scaife, husbandman, and Elizabeth Blades, spr, btp, banns (Oct 2 [*sic*],
29, Nov 5), by R.R., both mark. W: John Plews, William Allianson

Dec 27 Edward Smorthet, husbandman, and Jane Pickard, spr, btp, banns (Oct 29, Nov
5, 12), by R.R., both sign (Smorthit). W: Thos. Jackson, Timothy Rider

Nov 28 Robert Plews, husbandman, and Mary Maichel, spr, btp, banns (Nov 5, 12, 19),
by R.R., both mark. W: William Stora, Jane Clarkson
Banns between George Cowper and Mary Horseman publ. Nov 12, 19, 26, by
R.R.

[p. 19]
Dec 19 Thomas Beckwith, blacksmith, and Ann Jackson, spr, btp, banns (Dec 3, 10,
17), by R.R., both sign. W: Aaron Jackson, William Beckwith

Marriages 1759

Feb 3 Thomas Beecroft, farmer, and Catherine Horseman, spr, btp, banns (Jan 14, 21,
28), by R.R., both mark. W: Fras. Smith, Jno. Smith

15 Robert Walker of East Witton, collier, and Mary Lye of Masham, spr, banns
(Jan 21, 28, Feb 4), by R.R., both mark. W: Thom[a]s Jackson, Robt. Towler

21 Michael Clarkson of East Witton, husbandman, and Rebecca Burril of Masham,
spr, banns (Feb 4, 11, 18 by R.R.), by W.L., both sign (she signs Rebekah
Buriell). W: William Whitelock, William Thirkill

[p. 20]
Mar 15 Thomas Gill of Masham, husbandman, and Ann Blakestone of Kirkby
Malzeard, wid, lic, by R.R., both mark. W: John Theakston, John Thwaites

May 10 Thomas Jackson, bach, and Elizabeth Metcalfe, spr, btp, banns (Apr 15, 22, 29
by R.R.), by W.L., both sign (she signs Metcalf). W: James Metcalf, William
Metcalf

| | 13 | Thomas Gill, bach, and Jane Thwaites, spr, btp, banns (Apr 22, 29, May 26 by R.R.), by A.P., both mark. W: Tho: Bridberry, William Thirkill |
| July | 24 | John Warrenner, servant, and Susannah Gains, spr, btp, banns (July 8, 15, 22 by R.R.), by W.L., both mark. W: Geo. Pickersgill (mark), William Thirkill |

[p. 21]

Sept	25	John Carter, mason, and Frances Smith, spr, btp, banns (Sept 9, 16, 23 by R.R.), by W.L., he marks, she signs. W: William Thirkill, Abra: Illingworth
Oct	2	William Joy of [Thornton] Watlass, tailor, and Mary Beckwith of Masham, spr, banns (Sept 16, 23, 30), by R.R., both mark. W: William Beckwith, Samuel Beckwith
	6	Richard Hall, miner, and Sarah Stott, spr, btp, banns (Sept 16, 23, 30), by R.R., he marks, she signs (Stot). W: John Stott, William Thirkill
	17	William Fennick of Masham, husbandman, and Ann Kendray of West Tanfield, spr, lic, by R.R., he marks, she signs. W: William Thirkill, Martin Brown

[p. 22]

	18	William Beckwith, gent, and Prudence Horner, spr, btp, banns (Sept 30, Oct 7, 14), by R.R., both sign. W: Jno. Lonsdale, John Lonsdale jnr
Nov	22	Robert Smith, bach, and Margaret Iveson, spr, btp, lic, by J.W., he signs, she marks. W: William Thirkill, Robert Wardrop
	22	Thomas Geldard, husbandman, and Mary Kendray, spr, btp, banns (Sept (*sic*) 21, 28, Nov 4, by R.R.), by J.W., both mark. W: William Thirkill, William Geldard
Dec	5	William Temple, husbandman, and Esther Lofthouse, spr, btp, banns (Nov 18, 25, Dec 2), by R.R., both sign. W: Thos. Plews, Wm Thirkill

[p. 23]

| | 20 | Joseph Bartle, comber and weaver, and Margaret Lye, spr, btp, banns (Nov 25, Dec 2, 9), by R.R., both mark. W: John Ascough, Christopher Lightfoot |

Marriages 1760

May	10	William Teasdale of East Witton, husbandman, and Mary Smith of Masham, spr, banns (Apr 20, 27, May 4), by R.R., he signs, she marks. W: Ann Smorthit, William Thirkill
	15	John Harrison of Kirkby Malzeard, husbandman, and Mary Beckwith of Masham, spr, banns (Apr 27, May 4, 11), by R.R., he signs (Harison), she marks. W: Wm Craven, William Thirkill
	20	George Barker, husbandman, and Ann Hutchinson, spr, btp, banns (Apr 27, May 4, 11), by R.R., both sign. W: John Wilkinson, Matthew Hutchison

[p. 24]

| July | 24 | James Hamilton of Masham, an Out Pensioner of Chelsea Hospital, and Jane Steward of Masham, wid, banns (June 15, 22, 29), by R.R., he marks, she signs. W: John Plummer, William Thirkill |
| | 27 | John Bayns, servant, and Ann Dawson, spr, btp, banns (July 6, 13, 20), by R.R., he signs, she marks. W: William Imeson, Thos. Clarkson |

| Aug | 4 | Thomas Edmondson of Hauxwell, husbandman, and Tabitha Fawnes of Masham, spr, banns (July 6, 13, 20), by R.R., both mark. W: Robert Plummer, Jonas Metcalfe |
| | 8 | William Brignall, shoemaker, and Hannah Jackson, spr, btp, lic, by R.R., both sign. W: Thos. Wrather, William Thirkill |

[p. 25]

	14	William Heslington, grocer, and Mary Wrather, spr, btp, banns (July 27, Aug 3, 10), by R.R., both sign. W: Thos. Wrather, Wm Rodwill
Sept	20	Thomas Spence, husbandman, and Ann Teesdale, spr, btp, banns (Aug 17, 24, 31), by R.R., both mark. W: Wm Rodwill, Matthew Thompson
	29	Matthew Gill, woolcomber, and Mary Metcalfe, spr, btp, banns (Sept 7, [1]4, 21), by R.R., both sign. W: Thomas Jackson, James Metcalfe
Nov	23	John Snell, husbandman, and Jane Hebdin, spr, btp, banns (Oct 26, Nov 2, 9), by R.R., he signs, she marks. W: Wm Thirkill, Abr: Illingworth

[p. 26]

	24	Matthew Jeff, husbandman, and Ann Pearson, spr, btp, banns (Nov 2, 9, 16), by R.R., both mark. W: John Weighell, Matw: Thompson
	25	Christopher Walker of Tanfield, husbandman, and Hannah Wallis of Masham, spr, banns (Nov 2, 9, 16), by R.R., both mark. W: John Richmond, John Kilvington
Dec	1	James Nicholson of Grinton, mason, and Ann Prest of Masham, spr, banns (Nov 16, 23, 30), by R.R., both mark. W: Thomas Brown, William Thirkill

Marriages 1761

| Feb | 1 | Thomas Alman, husbandman, and Elizabeth Beckwith, spr, btp, banns (Jan 11, 18, 25), by R.R., both mark. W: Pebera Bson (*sic*), Will: Thirkill |

[p. 27]

	12	Gabriel Kay, labourer, and Sarah Deaken, btp, banns (Jan 25, Feb 1, 8), by R.R., both mark. W: Will. Thirkill, Wm Glew
Mar	12	Matthew Taylor of Masham, husbandman, and Catherine Imeson, spr, of Bedale, lic, by R.R., both sign. W: Joseph Denham, John Denham
Apr	28	William Ryder of East Witton, husbandman, and Easter Carter of Masham, spr, lic, by R.R., both sign (she signs Esther). W: Jane Plews, John Croft
May	3	Benjamin Akers, mason, and Ann Harland, spr, btp, banns (Apr 12, 19, 26), by R.R., both sign. W: John Harland, Will. Thirkill

[p. 28]

	5	Archibald Stewart and Diana Kendal, spr, btp, lic, by R.R., he signs, she marks. W: George Metcalf, Matthew Thompson
	6	Matthew Hagston, carrier, and Ann Banks, spr, btp, lic, by R.R., he signs, she marks. W: John Pickersgill, John Banks
	11	Thomas Spence of Tanfield, servant, and Margaret Nicholson of Masham, spr, banns (Apr 12, 19, 26), by R.R., both mark. W: Edwd. Nicholson, Will: Thirkill

| | 12 | George Firby, woolcomber, and Elizabeth Thwaites, spr, btp, banns (Apr 12, 19, 26), by R.R., both mark. W: George Thornberry, Henry Hodgson |

[p. 29]
	30	William Bradley, husbandman, and Dinah Blackburn, wid, btp, banns (Apr 12, 19, 26), by R.R., he signs, she marks. W: Matthew Thompson, Richard Thompson
June	11	John Carter, husbandman, and Jane Plews, spr, btp, banns (May 24, 31, June 7), by R.R., both sign. W: William Ryder, Thomas Carter
	11	Edward Nicholson of Masham, saddler, and Susanna Thomas of Kirklington, spr, lic, by R.R., both sign. W: Margaret Thwaites, John Richmond
	29	James Bartle, woolcomber, and Elizabeth Greathead, spr, banns (Apr 12, 19, 26), by R.R., both mark. W: John Ascough, Abraham Illingworth

[p. 30]
July	14	John Metcalfe, husbandman, and Mary Smith, spr, btp, banns (June 28, July 5, 12), by R.R., he signs, she marks. W: William Thirkill, Edwd. Metcalfe
Nov	11	John Suttill of Kirkby Malzeard and Elizabeth Metcalfe of Masham, spr, lic, by R.R., he signs, she marks. W: Edwd. Metcalfe (mark), William Thirkill
Dec	10	George Nicholson, mason, and Jane Graham, spr, btp, banns (Dec (*sic*) for Nov 15, 22, 29, by R.R.), by R.H., both sign. W: Ben. Severs, Robert Bell
	17	John Harland, tailor, and Mary Bearby, spr, btp, banns (Nov 29, Dec 6, 13), by R.R., both sign. W: Wm Pickard, Matthew Imeson

[p. 31]   **Marriages 1762**

Jan	21	William Hudson, labourer, and Mary Walker, spr, btp, banns (Jan 3, 10, 17), by R.R., he signs, she marks. W: Matw. Thompson, Thos. Terry
Feb	9	William Metcalfe, husbandman, and Ruth Kendrew, spr, btp, banns (Jan 24, 31, Feb 7), by R.R., both sign (he signs Metcalf). W: James Bolland, Henry Kendrew
Apr	12	Matthew Imeson, husbandman, and Christiana Hodgson, spr, btp, banns (Mar 14, 21, 28), by R.R., both sign. W: Augustine Hodgson, Elizabeth Imeson
May	12	Jonas Metcalfe and Phyllis Spence, btp, banns (Apr 25, May 2, 9), by E.M., both sign. W: Matthew Wardrop, William Thirkill

[p. 32]
| | 11 | Edward Gill of Kirkby Malzeard and Ann Craggs of Masham, lic, by E.M., he signs, she marks. W: Matthew Thompson, William Thirkill |

Banns between Matthias Burrell of Masham and Ann Wood of Kirkby Malzeard publ. May 2, 9, 16, by E.M.

| | 31 | John Metcalf and Sarah Bell, btp, banns (May 9, 16, 23 by E.M.), by R.H., both mark. W: Thomas Jackson, Robert Bell |
| Aug | 5 | Christopher Marshal and Mary Smithson, btp, banns (July 18, 25, Aug 1), by E.M., he marks, she signs. W: William Thirkill, Nicholas Cunliffe |

[p. 33]
Banns between John Burnet and Ann Wintersgill, btp, publ. Sept 12, 19, 26, by E.M.

Dec	2	William Bane of Well and Mary Thwaites of Masham, banns (Nov 7 by R.H., Nov 14, 21 by E.M.), by R.H., he marks, she signs. W: Mary Calvert, William Thirkill
Nov	30	Thomas Kitchingman of Ripon, esq., and Mary Beckwith of Masham, lic, by R.H., both sign. W: John Lister, William Thirkill
Dec	30	William Wrather and Elizabeth Beckwith, btp, lic, by E.M. , both sign. W: Wm Heslington, William Thirkill

[p. 34]   **Marriages 1763**

May	4	Mark Towler and Sarah Towler, btp, banns (Jan 16, 23, 30), by E.M., both mark. W: William Thirkill, James Towler (mark)
Feb	14	Joseph Burrill and Elizabeth Calvert, btp, banns (Jan 30, Feb 6, 13), by E.M., both sign. W: Chrisr. Ripley, Mary Calvert
Apr	25	William Appleton of Topcliffe and Elizabeth Horseman of Masham, banns (Mar 20, 27, Apr 3), by E.M., both sign. W: Jeffrey Horsman, George Cooper
	17	William Pybus and Deborah Glew, btp, banns (Mar 27, Apr 3, 10), by E.M., he marks, she signs. W: Geo. Imeson, William Thirkill

[p. 35]

	25	William Imeson and Mary Gill, btp, banns (Apr 3, 10, 17), by E.M., he signs, she marks. W: William Malthouse, William Thirkill
	20	Moses Jackson and Mary Rodwill, btp, banns (Apr 3, 10, 17), by E.M., he signs, she marks. W: Thomas Court, Henry Rodwill
	25	Thomas Scafe and Amy Metcalfe, btp, banns (Apr 10, 17, 24), by E.M., he signs, she marks. W: James Rucroft, Peter Burrell
	28	William Robinson and Hannah Metcalfe, btp, banns (Apr 10, 17, 24), by E.M., both mark. W: Samuel Beckwith, Thomas Bell
[p. 36]		Banns between Richard Pearson of Masham and Ann Wetherill of Bedale publ. Apr 24, May 1, 8, by E.M.
May	24	Christopher Dawson of Masham and Mary Nelson of Kirkby Malzeard, lic, by E.M., both sign. W: Peter Rogers, Gilbert Rogers
June	27	Robert Smith and Jane Thwaites, btp, banns (June 12, 19, 26, by E.M.), by R.R., both sign. W: Margaret Thwaites, Joshua Smith
Aug	14	Robert Wintersgill and Jane Coates, btp, banns (July 3, 10, 17), by E.M., both mark. W: Robert Wintersgill (mark), William Thirkill
	21	Robert Metcalfe and Alice Robinson, btp, banns (July 31, Aug 7, 14), by E.M., both mark. W: William Thirkill, George Thornberry
[p. 37]		
	22	John Nelson and Catherine Walker, btp, banns (Aug 7, 14, 21), by E.M., both sign. W: Joshua Aked, William Thirkill
	22	Thomas Robinson and Izabel Hamilton, btp, banns (Aug 7, 14, 21), by E.M., both mark. W: John Rider, William Thirkill
Oct	3	Anthony Plews and Mary Thwaites, btp, lic, by E.M., he marks, she signs. W: William Thirkill, Mary Tindal (mark)

MARRIAGES

Dec 1 Anthony Hill and Ann Smith, btp, banns (Nov 13, 20, 27), by E.M., both sign. W: John Hill, William Thirkill

[p. 38]

30 George Bowness and Elizabeth Machell, btp, banns (Dec 11, 18, 25), by E.M., he signs, she marks. W: Robert Bowness, William Thirkill

Marriages 1764

Jan 23 Timothy Rider and Esther Barker, btp, lic, by E.M., he signs, she marks. W: Ste: Maudesley, George Pybus

Feb 2 Robert Smith and Ann Elsworth, btp, banns (Dec 11, 18, 25, by E.M.), by W.L., he signs, she marks. W: Richard Ripley, William Atkinson

3 Noble Tarbuton of Ripon and Ann Pratt of Masham, lic, by R.R., he signs, she marks. W: Wm Harrison, Barnit Metcalf

[p. 39]

13 John Gill and Margaret Ripley, btp, banns (Dec 11, 18, 25, by E.M.), by T.D., both mark. W: John Hill, William Thirkill

Mar 12 Thomas Wilson and Hannah Ascough, btp, banns (Feb 12, 19, by W.L., Feb 26, by E.M.), by E.M., he signs, she marks. W: Caleb Powell, Francis Dighton

Feb 27 George Dobson of Well and Ann Burrill of Masham, banns (Feb 12, 19, by W.L., Feb 26, by E.M.), by E.M., both mark. W: R.(?) Strother, Henry Hodgson

May 31 William Brinkley and Grace Burnett, btp, banns (Apr 22, 29, May 6), by E.M., both mark. W: William Thirkill, Thomas Hutchinson jnr (mark)

[p. 40]

7 William Umpleby and Sarah Mudd, btp, banns (Apr 22, 29, May 6), by E.M., both mark. W: John Kirby, William Thirkill

June 8 Barnet Metcalfe and Rosamund Atkinson, btp, lic, by E.M., he signs, she marks. W: Wm Heslington, Simon Wrather

27 John Pickersgill and Mary Wilks, btp, banns (June 3, 10, by E.M., June 17, by W.L.), by E.M., both sign. W: Jane Wintersgill, John Wintersgill

26 William Harrison and Mary Thwaites, btp, banns (June 10, by E.M., June 17, by W.L., June 24, by E.M.), by E.M., both sign. W: Anthony Thwaites, William Thirkill

[p. 41]

July 5 Leonard Mudd and Jane Body, btp, banns (June 17, by W.L., June 24, July 1, by E.M.), by E.M., both sign. W: Francis Brotherton, Edward Robinson

Aug 9 George Atkinson and Ann Bateman, btp, banns (June 24, July 1, 8), by E.M., both sign. W: William Stephenson, Edward Horsman

July 9 George Blades and Elizabeth Dobson, btp, lic, by E.M., he signs, she marks. W: Benjamin Grange, Thomas Alexander

31 William Beckwith and Mary Naylor, btp, banns (July 8, 15, 22), by E.M., both sign. W: William Stephenson, Ben Severs

[p. 42]

Aug	1	John Pickersgill and Elizabeth King, btp, lic, by E.M., he signs, she marks. W: Elizabeth Moises, Ann King (mark)
Sept	5	Joseph Thorp and Mary Gill, btp, lic, by E.M., he signs, she marks. W: Matthew Gill, William Thirkill
	26	Thomas Wilson and Mary Longthorn, btp, banns (Sept 9, 16, 23, by E.M.), by T.D., he marks only. W: William Thirkill
Nov	25	Richard Pickersgill and Jane Ledly, btp, banns (Oct 7, 14, 21), by E.M., he marks, she signs. W: Henry Thompson, Benjamin Grange

[p. 43]

	3	David Greenhow of Kirkby Malzeard and Mary Calvert of Masham, banns (Oct 14, 21, 28), by E.M., both sign. W: William Thwaits, Joseph Burrill
	24	Joseph Thorns and Dorothy Wardrop, btp, banns (Dec 9, 16, by W.L., Dec 23, by E.M.), by E.M., both sign. W: John Carlile, Thomas Bell

Marriages 1765

Banns between Adam Barns of Masham and Mary Walker of East Witton publ. Jan 6, 13, 20, by E.M.

Apr	8	Robert Atkinson and Margaret Hamilton, btp, banns (Mar 17, 24, 31), by E.M., both sign. W: Barnet Metcalf, Matthew Gill

[p. 44]

May	8	Edward Elsworth of Ripon and Mary Hagston of Masham, banns (Apr 7, 14, 21), by E.M., both sign. W: Dorothy Thorns, George Hagston
Apr	30	Robert Auton of Kirklington and Dorothy Ascough of Masham, banns (Apr 14, 21, 28), by E.M., both sign. W: John Auton, John Pickersgill
May	28	Francis Brotherton and Jane Clarkson, btp, banns (May 12, 19, 26), by E.M., both sign. W: Jefferay Clarkson, Edward Robinson
		Banns between Simon Wrather of Masham and Margaret Beckwith of [Thornton] Watlass publ. May 19 by E.M., May 26 by W.L., and June 2 by H.M.

[p. 45]

June	24	Benjamin Severs and Isabella Robinson, btp, lic, by E.M., both sign. W: Edward Horsman, William Thirkill
July	16	Anthony Lister of Bedale and Katherine Beckwith of Masham, lic, by T.D., both sign. *No witnesses*
Sept	3	John Carlile and Mary Clarkson, btp, banns (Aug 18, 25, Sept 1), by E.M., both sign. W: Francis Brotherton, Joseph Thorns
	26	Thomas Broad and Elizabeth Heslington, btp, banns (Sept 8 by E.M., Sept 15 by W.L., Sept 22 by E.M.), by T.D., both sign. W: John Heslington, William Thirkill

[p. 46]

	30	George Merginton of Catterick and Dorothy Bell of Masham, banns (Sept 15, 22, 29, by E.M.), by T.D., both sign. W: George Robinson, Matthew Hanley
Nov	21	William Exelby of Well and Barbara Hall of Masham, lic, by E.M., both sign.

W: Chrisr. King, John Raynoldson

Dec 2   Peter Hammond and Mary Brown, btp, banns (Nov 17, 24, Dec 1), by E.M., he signs, she marks. W: Mark Nesam, Ralph Siddall

23   John Place of Well and Ann Bell of Masham, banns (Dec 8, 15, 22), by E.M., both mark. W: David Bell, George Merginton

[p. 47]   **Marriages 1766**

Banns between Jeffrey Horseman of Masham and Eleanor Pickersgill of Tanfield publ. Apr 6, 20, 27, by E.M.

May 20   Joseph Kirkley and Elizabeth Teal, btp, banns (May 4, 11, 18), by E.M., he marks, she signs. W: George Plews, Caleb Powell

Banns between Ralph Siddall of Masham and Bridget Chapelhow of Wensley publ. May 11, 18, 25, by E.M.

Aug 10   Robert Blackbourn and Elizabeth Wynne, btp, banns (July 20, 27, Aug 3, by E.M.), by H.M., he signs (Blackburn), she marks. W: Thos. Jackson, Peter Carter

[p. 48]

20   George Plews of Masham and Ann Bland of Kirkby Malzeard, lic, by E.M., both sign. W: Matthew Bland, William Beckwith

Sept 1   William Atkinson of Masham and Ellen Atkinson of Kirkby Malzeard, banns (Aug 17, by H.M., Aug 24, 31, by E.M.), by E.M., both mark. W: George Burniston, Caleb Powell

Banns between Christopher Mallaby of Masham and Susanna Coats of Kirkby Malzeard publ. Sept 7 by T.G., Sept 14 by E.M., Sept 21 by T.G.

Oct 9   Peter Robinson and Jane Daggit, btp, banns (Sept 21, 28, Oct 5, by T.G.), by T.D., both sign. W: John Richmond, Tom Pickersgill

[p. 49]

14   Joseph Muffet and Elizabeth Croft, btp, banns (Sept 28, Oct 5, 12, by T.G.), by T.D., he signs, she marks. W: James Wilkinson, Joseph Thorn

Nov 23   Henry Wynne of Thornton Steward and Prudence Wilson of Masham, banns (Oct 26, Nov 2, by E.M., Nov 9, by T.G.) by E.M., both sign. W: Chris. Rudd, Caleb Powell

24   Thomas Finley and Dorothy Walburn, btp, banns (Nov 9, by T.G., Nov 16, 23, by E.M.), by E.M., both mark. W: Caleb Powell, Wm Powell

25   George Clark and Elizabeth Wilson, btp, banns (Nov 9, by T.G., Nov 16, 23, by E.M.), by E.M., both mark. W: Thos. Clarkson, Caleb Powell

[p. 50]

27   Jonathan Roundill and Ann Kendrew, btp, banns (Nov 9, by T.G., Nov 16, 23, by E.M.), by E.M., he marks, she signs. W: Henry Charnack, Henry Kendrew

Dec 14   John Wintersgill and Deborah Spence, btp, banns (Nov 23, 30, Dec 7), by E.M., he signs, she marks. W: Jefferay Clarkson, Caleb Powell

20   John Emerson and Esther Towler, btp, banns (Nov 30, Dec 7, 14, by E.M.), by R.R., he marks, she signs. W: Elisabeth Towler, Matthew Towler (mark)

22   Thomas Ascough and Isabel Topham, btp, banns (Dec 7, 14, 21), by E.M., both mark. W: James Rucroft, Mathew Askew

[p. 51] **Marriages 1767**

Mar   3   Francis Mallaby and Sarah Blackbourn, btp, banns (Feb 8, 15, 22), by E.M., both sign (she signs Blackburn). W: William Rodwill, Thos. Jackson
Banns between Edward Blackburn of Masham and Isabella Collier of Ripon publ. Apr 19, 26, May 3, by E.M.

Aug   8   John Thwaites and Elizabeth Durham, btp, banns (June 21, 28, by H.M., July 5, by E.M.), by E.M., both sign. W: James Calvert, Christopher Durham

2   William Shepherd and Ann Tunstal, btp, banns (July 19, 26, Aug 2), by E.M., both mark. W: Jane Metcalf, Abraham Ellingworth (mark)

[p. 52] Banns between Richard Wilkinson of Kirkby Malzeard and Jane Bland of Masham publ. Oct 25, Nov 1, 8, by E.M.

Dec 22   John Pratt and Hannah Steel, btp, banns (Nov 1, 8, 15), by E.M., both mark. W: Thomas Jackson, Caleb Powell

Nov 19   Robert Walton and Mary Tenant, btp, banns (Nov 1, 8, 15), by E.M., both mark. W: Anthony Stelling, Caleb Powell

23   John Pybus and Ann Wood, btp, banns (Nov 1, 8, 15), by E.M., both mark. W: Edward Croft, Matthew Jackson

[p. 53]
26   Leonard Ryder of East Witton and Sarah King of Masham, lic, by E.M., both sign. W: Jane Eden, Abraham Ellingworth (mark)

Marriages 1768

Apr 19   Benjamin Grange and Frances Wilson, btp, banns (Apr 3, 10, 17), by E.M., he signs, she marks. W: Wm Terry, George Grange

May 3   Francis Wardrop, tailor, and Margaret Ward, spr, btp, banns (Apr 17, 24, May 1, by E.M.), by T.G., both mark. W: John Ward, Abram Illingworth

23   George Wintersgill and Elizabeth Ripley, btp, banns (May 8, 15, 22), by E.M., both mark. W: John Richmond, Abraham Ellingworth (mark)

[p. 54]
June 27   Thomas King and Dorothy Tunstal, btp, banns (June 12, 19, 26), by E.M., he signs, she marks. W: Francis Mallaby, Christopher Summers

July 22   John Burnet of Masham and Elizabeth Kirby of Kirkby Malzeard, banns (June 19, 26, July 3), by E.M., he signs, she marks. W: Caleb Powell, Robt Kirby (mark)
Banns between William Kay of Masham and Mary Scot of Kirkby Malzeard publ. Aug 28, Sept 4, 11, by E.M.
Banns between John Theakston of Masham and Jane Spence of Kirkby Malzeard publ. Oct 16, 23, 30, by T.G.

[p. 55]
Nov 24   James Bradley of Colne and Mary Moor of Masham, banns (Nov 6, 13, 20), by E.M., both sign. W: Jacob Towler, Caleb Powell

Marriages 1769

Feb 13   John Croft and Ellen Lee, btp, banns (Jan 29, Feb 5, by E.M., Feb 12, by T.G.), by R.R., both mark. W: Robt. Boyce, Caleb Powell
Banns between Robert Imeson of Masham and Elizabeth Walton of Bedale publ. Mar 5, by T.G., Mar 12, 19, by E.M.

Apr 17   John Roundall and Elizabeth Kendrew, btp, banns (Apr 2, 9, 16), by E.M., both sign. W: Henry Kendrew, Caleb Powell

[p. 56]
18   George Gouthwaite and Hannah Metcalf, btp, banns (Apr 2, 9, 16), by E.M., he signs, she marks. W: John Jackson, Thomas Topham

24   Michael Windall of Ripon and Margaret Clarkson of Masham, banns (Apr 9, 16, 23), by E.M., both sign. W: Thomas Langdale, Wm Windale

May 6   William Walker and Dorothy Walker, btp, banns (Apr 16, 23, 30), by E.M., both mark. W: Caleb Powell, Abraham Illingworth

3   William Floor of Masham and Elizabeth Iley of Southburn, lic, by E.M., he signs, she marks. W: John Iley, Caleb Powell

[p. 57]
15   John Auton of Kirklington and Elizabeth Ascough of Masham, lic, by E.M., both sign. W: George Ascough, Christopher Auton
Banns between Ralph Prest of Masham and Elizabeth Nicholson of Kirkby Malzeard publ. July 9, 16, 23, by E.M.

Aug 17   Thomas Carter of Masham and Mary Dowson of East Witton, banns (July 30, Aug 6, 13), by E.M., both sign. W: Thomas Smorthit, Thomas Dowson

Nov 2   Anthony Beneson and Mary Gregory, btp, banns (Oct 15, 22, 29, by E.M.), by R.R., both mark. W: Anthony Stelling, Caleb Powell

Marriages 1770

[p. 58]

Jan 25   William Smith and Jane Carter, btp, banns (Dec 10, 17, 24), by E.M., he signs, she marks. W: Caleb Powell, Henry Rodwill

Feb 20   Joseph Burneston and Isabel Edon, btp, banns (Feb 4, 11, 18), by E.M., both sign. W: John Ballan, Ralph Edon

22   Thomas Smorthit and Dorothy Cundall, btp, lic, by E.M., both sign. W: John Cundall, Chr. Dawson
Banns between John Barker of Masham and Elizabeth Leeming of Ripon publ. Mar 4, 11, 18, by E.M.

[p. 59]
Apr 23   Anthony Ingleby and Ann Whitelock, btp, lic, by E.M., he marks, she signs.

W: William Stephenson, Caleb Powell

May 10 Richard Thompson of East Witton and Isabel Hunter of Masham, lic, by E.M., he signs, she marks. W: Thomas Jackson, Caleb Powell

Banns between George Bradley and Mary Jackson, btp, publ. Apr 29, May 6, 13, by E.M.

June 7 William Lightfoot and Edith Durham, btp, banns (May 20, by E.M., May 27, by T.G., June 3, by E.M.), by R.R., both sign. W: Christopher Durham, Thomas Lightfoot

[p. 60]

16 Samuel Beach of Birmingham, diocese of Lichfield and Coventry, wdr, and Hannah Simpson of Masham, spr, lic, by T.G., both sign. W: R. Beckwith, Caleb Powell

26 George Ascough and Mary Durham, btp, banns (June 10, 17, 24, by T.G.), by R.R., both sign. W: Christopher Durham, Elizabeth Thwaits

July 5 Peter Carter and Esther Pickersgill, btp, lic, by E.M., both sign. W: Thomas Smorthit, Caleb Powell

Aug 20 John Chapman and Sarah Morris, btp, banns (July 22, 29, Aug 5), by E.M., he signs, she marks. W: Richd. Thompson, Thomas Topham

[p. 61] Banns between Christopher Spence of the chapelry of Muker and Mary King of Masham publ. July 29, Aug 5, 12, by E.M.

Sept 2 Robert Rider and Mary Jackson, btp, lic, by E.M., both sign. W: William Geldart, Leonard Mudd

Oct 11 Thomas Dawson of Coverham and Ann Hodgson of Masham, lic, by E.M., he signs, she marks. W: Thomas Jackson, Roger Paley

Banns between John Ward of Masham and Jane Pearson of [Thornton] Watlass publ. Oct 28, Nov 4, 11, by E.M.

[p. 62]

Nov 29 William Geldart and Margaret Yeoman, btp, banns (Nov 11, 18, 25), by E.M., he signs, she marks. W: Henry Charnack, Thomas Geldart

Dec 19 Emanuel Lye and Ann Plews, btp, lic, by E.M., he signs, she marks. W: John Pickersgill, Elizabeth Terry

Marriages 1771

Nov (*sic*, for

Jan) 19 Michael Hammond and Elizabeth Ward, btp, banns (Dec 9, 16, 23), by E.M., both mark. W: Caleb Powell, Flora Illingworth

Mar 6 Thomas Jackson and Mary Winn, btp, lic, by R.R., he signs, she marks. W: George Jackson, Caleb Powell

[p. 63]

Apr 15 John Metcalfe and Mary Walker, btp, banns (Mar 31, Apr 7, 14), by E.M., he signs, she marks. W: Caleb Powell, Wm Walker (mark)

Banns between Richard Whitelock of Masham and Eleanor Walton of Bedale publ. Mar 17, 24, 31, by E.M.

MARRIAGES

Banns between Thomas Dowson of Masham and Ann Grange of Ripon publ. Mar 17, 24, 31, by E.M.

Apr 22   Robert Jeff of Ripon and Mary Jackson of Masham, banns (Apr 7, 14, 21), by E.M., both sign. W: Ann Ballan, George Renard

[p. 64]

May 15   Christopher Merryweather and Jane Park, btp, banns (Apr 28, May 5, 12), by E.M., both mark. W: George Thornberry, Caleb Powell

20   Thomas Nelson and Ellen Robinson, btp, banns (May 5, 12, 19), by E.M., both sign. W: Leonard Hodgson, Thos. Jackson

Banns between Ralph Pattison of Masham and Esther Walker of East Witton publ. June 23, 30, July 7, by E.M.

Sept 3   David Walker and Elizabeth Bowes, btp, banns (Aug 18, 25, Sept 1), by E.M., he signs, she marks. W: William Harrison, Abraham Illingworth

[p. 65]

Nov 21   Richard Thompson and Hannah Craggs, btp, banns (Oct 27, Nov 3, 10), by E.M., both mark. W: Thomas Metcalf, Caleb Powell

Marriage 1772

July 26   Thomas Wrather and Ann Metcalf, btp, banns (Oct 6, 13, 20), by E.M., both mark. W: Caleb Powell, George Thornberry

Marriage 1771

Dec 3   David Walker and Ann Smorthit, btp, banns (Nov 17, 24, Dec 1), by E.M., he marks, she signs. W: Robert Smorthit, James Syckes

Marriages 1772

Jan 14   Jeffrey Clarkson and Ann Croft, btp, banns (Dec 29, Jan 5, 12, by E.M.), by T.G., both sign. W: Edward Croft, Mary Casey

[p. 66]

27   Thomas Dawson and Ann Grindale, btp, banns (Jan 12, 19, 26), by E.M., he signs, she marks. W: Thomas Burnet, Mary Metcalfe

Apr 20   Christopher Cartman of Topcliffe and Catherine Imeson of Masham, banns (Mar 22, 29, Apr 5), by E.M., he marks, she signs. W: William Glew, John Richmond

May 11 ⸰   John Peploe and Catherine Wood, btp, banns (Apr 26, May 3, 10), by R.R., he signs, she marks. W: Caleb Powell, Abraham Illingworth

Banns between William Swanby of Croft and Mary Mallaby of Masham publ. Apr 26, May 3, 10

[p. 67]

June	4	Henry Lupton, wdr, and Isabel Raley, spr, btp, banns (May 10, 17, 24), by T.G., both mark. W: Mary Metcalfe, Mary Wrather
May	28	Anthony Thwaites, husbandman, and Elizabeth Beck, spr, btp, banns (May 10, 17, 24), by T.G., both sign. W: Henry Beck, Ann Beck
June	9	Christopher Allinson of Burton Leonard and Elizabeth Terry of Masham, banns (May 24, 31, June 7, by T.G.), by E.M., both sign. W: Rd. Terry, Jno. Jackson
Aug	12	Matthew Park of Kirkby Fleetham and Frances Fletcher of Masham, banns (July 26, Aug 2, 9), by E.M., both mark. W: Matthew Worth, Abraham Illingworth

[p. 68]

Sept	7	Thomas Jackson and Phebe Barker, btp, banns (Aug 9, 16, 23), by E.M., both mark. W: Caleb Powell, Elisabeth Askew
	27	Marmaduke Hammond and Elizabeth Burton, btp, banns (Sept 6, 13, 20), by E.M., he marks, she signs. W: Caleb Powell, Abra: Illingworth
	22	Benjamin Siddall and Mary Astwood, btp, banns (Sept 6, 13, 20, by E.M.), by R.R., both sign. W: William Stephenson, George Hagston
		Banns between Andrew Metcalf of Ripon and Mary Lightfoot of Masham publ. Sept 6, 13, 20, by E.M.

[p. 69]

Nov	23	Robert Frank of Kirkby Malzeard and Rachel Hutchinson of Masham, banns (Nov 8, 15, 22), by E.M., both mark. W: William Bramley, Jonathan Tunsdale, Ann Bucktin
Dec	1	George Fenwick and Mary Alderson, btp, banns (Nov 8, 15, 22, by E.M.), by R.R., he signs, she marks. W: George Wilson, Caleb Powell
	3	Christopher Jackson and Mary Pickard, btp, banns (Nov 15, 22, 29), by E.M., both sign. W: Tim. Rider, Edward Smorthit
	22	Francis Linton of Ripon and Ann Houseman of Masham, banns (Dec 6, 13, 20), by E.M., both sign (she signs Housman). W: John Linton, John Horsman
[p. 70]		Banns between John Tempest of Masham and Elizabeth Birtwhistle of Skipton publ. Dec 13, 20, 27, by E.M.

Marriages 1773

		Banns between William Robinson of Ripon and Mary Metcalfe of Masham publ. Dec 20, 27, Jan 3, by E.M.
Jan	26	Robert Lancaster of Wath and Ann Robinson of Masham, banns (Dec 27, Jan 3, 10, by T.G.), by E.M., both mark. W: John Wells, Thos. Jackson
Mar	30	John Plews and Ann Buckden, btp, banns (Mar 14, 21, 28), by E.M., both sign (she signs Bucktin). W: Henry Bolland, Henry Kendrew

[p. 71]

Apr	1	Henry Leeming of Well and Mary Bonson of Masham, banns (Mar 14, 21, 28), by E.M., he signs, she marks. W: James Wilkinson, Benjamin Grange
	13	George Wilson and Esther Craggs, btp, banns (Mar 28, Apr 4, 11), by E.M., he signs, she marks. W: Henry Kendrew, Thomas Burnet, Thomas Banks

May	12	Thomas Robinson of Kirkby Malzeard and Mary Ripley of Masham, banns (Apr 25, May 2, 9), by E.M., both mark. W: John Banks, Caleb Powell
	27	Anthony Oliver and Elizabeth Neesom, btp, banns (May 9, 16, 23), by E.M., he signs, she marks. W: Matthew Jackson, Joseph Atkinson

[p. 72]

June	15	George Knowles of West Tanfield and Ann Spence of Masham, lic, by E.M., both mark. W: William Frankland, Caleb Powell
Oct	30	Robert Tempest and Elizabeth Horner, btp, banns (Sept 26, Oct 3, 10), by E.M., both mark. W: Jane Pickersgill, ?Anthon(y) Thwaites
	28	George Wintersgill and Elizabeth Simpson, btp, banns (Oct 10, 17, 24), by E.M., both mark. W: John Ascough, John Vitty
		Banns between Jeremiah Metcalfe and Margaret Graham, btp, publ. Nov 7, 14, 21

[p. 73]

		Banns between Benjamin Ellwood of Finghall and Elizabeth Fryar of Masham publ. Nov 14, 21, 28, by E.M.
Dec	9	George Jackson, bach, and Jane Edon, spr, btp, lic, by T.G., both sign. W: Abraham Edon, Caleb Powell

Marriages 1774

Jan	13	John Frier of Northallerton and Esther Wilson of Masham, banns (Dec 19, 26, Jan 2), by E.M., he signs, she marks. W: Thos. Clarkson, Michael Lee
		Banns between James May and Gertrude Prior, btp, publ. Jan 2, 9, 16, by E.M.

[p. 74]

	25	John Theakston and Sarah Horseman, btp, lic, by E.M., he signs, she marks. W: Thos. Clarkson, Caleb Powell
Apr	4	Thomas Ascough and Jane Atkinson, btp, banns (Jan 30, Feb 6, 13, by T.G.), by E.M., he signs, she marks. W: Caleb Powell
	28	Thomas Metcalf and Elizabeth Kendall, btp, banns (Apr 10, 17, 24), by E.M., both sign. W: Thomas Barrows, George Kendall
May	9	James Lancaster and Jane Trees, btp, banns (Apr 24, May 1, 8), by E.M., both sign. W: Thomas Bridberry, Mary Stoney

[p. 75]

June	2	Leonard Hodgson and Elizabeth Simpson, btp, banns (May 15, 22, 29), by E.M., he signs, she marks. W: Thomas Dawson, Thos. Jackson
July	9	Thomas Dixon, clerk, of Kirkby Ravensworth and Ann Jackson of Masham, lic, by E.M., both sign. W: Tho. Greenbank, John Jackson
		Banns between John Houseman of Masham and Jane Beckwith of the chapelry of Middlesmoor publ. July 17, 24, 31
Aug	23	Christopher Smith of Bedale and Esther Blackburn of Masham, banns (Aug 7, 14, 21), by E.M., he signs, she marks. W: Saml. Wilkinson, Catherine Porter

[p. 76]

Nov	8	Edmund Barker, husbandman, and Esther Beck, spr, btp, banns (Oct 23, 30, Nov 6, by E.M.), by T.G., both sign. W: Henry Beck, Anthony Thwaites

	15	Peter Ballan of Masham, bach, and Elizabeth Brown of [Thornton] Watlass, wid, lic, by T.G., both sign. W: William Ballan, Caleb Powell
	22	Thomas Barrows and Catherine Metcalf, btp, banns (Nov 6, 13, 20), by E.M., he signs, she marks. W: George Kendall, Thos. Yeadon
	24	Edward Crofts and Ann Hardy, btp, banns (Nov 6, 13, 20), by E.M., he signs, she marks. W: Jeffery Clarkson, Margaret Thompson

[p. 77]

	24	John Berwick and Jane Burneston, btp, banns (Nov 6, 13, 20), by E.M., both mark. W: David Ashton, Benjamin Jackson
Dec	10	Jeremiah Metcalf and Elizabeth Emerson, btp, banns (Nov 13, 20, 27), by E.M., both mark. W: John Buckle, Caleb Powell
	7	Peter Hutchinson and Mary Ashbridge, btp, banns (Nov 20, 27, Dec 4), by E.M., he signs, she marks. W: John Atkinson, Caleb Powell

Banns between James Towler of Masham and Dorothy Nornavel of South Otterington publ. Nov 27, Dec 4, 11, by E.M.

[p. 78]

Marriage 1775

Jan	2	George Thackwray of Spennithorne and Ellen Simpson of Masham, banns (Dec 4, 11, 18), by E.M., both mark. W: Caleb Powell, Abraham Illingworth

Marriage 1774

Dec	12	Edward Horsman and Elizabeth Imeson, btp, lic, by E.M., both sign. W: Jo: Lonsdale, Thos. Imeson

Banns between John Ascough of Masham and Mary Reynard of the chapelry of Middlesmoor publ. Dec 11, 18, 25, by E.M.

Marriages 1775

Jan	31	Mark Barker and Elizabeth Ward, btp, banns (Jan 15, 22, 29), by E.M., both sign. W: Joseph Horner, Caleb Powell

[p. 79]

Feb	9	William Jeff and Elizabeth Thwaites, btp, banns (Jan 22, 29, Feb 5), by E.M., both mark. W: John Jackson, Robert Jeff
	16	John Clarkson and Jane Robson, btp, banns (Jan 29, Feb 5, 12), by E.M., he signs, she marks. W: Robert Crew, James Proudfoot
	21	Thomas Burnet and Margaret Alderson, btp, banns (Feb 5, 12, 19), by E.M., he signs, she marks. W: John Jackson, Caleb Powell
Mar	9	Christopher Clarke and Hannah Jackson, btp, banns (Feb 9, 16, Mar 5), by E.M., both mark. W: R. Bolland, Caleb Powell

[p. 80]

Aug	3	Matthew Barker and Esther Towler, btp, lic, by E.M., both mark. W: Robt. Imeson, Abraham Illingworth
	6	George Graham and Mary Kearton, btp, lic, by E.M., both sign,. W: William Medcalf, Caleb Powell
		Banns between Charles Atkinson of Masham and Jane Mirfeld of Ripon publ. Aug 20, 27, Sept 3, by E.M.
Nov	4	William Morton and Elizabeth Myers, btp, lic, by E.M., both sign. W: Elizabeth Danby, Caroline Danby
[p. 81]		
	6	Thomas Myers of Hampsthwaite and Mary Lightfoot of Masham, lic, by E.M., both sign. W: Thomas Lightfoot, Joseph Myers
Dec	3	William Joy and Elizabeth Gill, btp, banns (Nov 5, 12, 19), by E.M., both mark. W: Caleb Powell, Abraham Illingworth
Nov	30	Thomas Banks of Bedale and Elizabeth Trees of Masham, lic, by E.M., both sign. W: Matth[e]w Thompson, Peter Trees
Dec	5	Michael Frier, husbandman, and Ann Mallaby, spr, btp, banns (Nov 19, 26, Dec 3), by T.G., he marks, she signs. W: Caleb Powell, John Willson
[p. 82]		
	26	John Thirkill of St Andrew, Holborn and Jane Wrather of Masham, lic, by E.M., both sign. W: Jno: Lonsdale, John Theakston

Marriages 1776

Apr	9	Thomas Thompson of Middleham and Alice Thompson of Masham, banns (Mar 10, 17, 24), by E.M., both sign. W: Richd. Strother, Geo. Langdale
	11	Thomas Lightfoot and Mary Stoney, btp, banns (Mar 24, 31, Apr 7), by E.M., both sign. W: Wm Lightfoot, Robert Stoney
		Banns between Thomas Cundal of Masham and Ann Stephenson of Kirkby Malzeard publ. Mar 24, 31, Apr 7, by E.M.
[p. 83]		
	11	Matthew Jackson and Ann Lodge, btp, lic, by E.M., both sign. W: John Lodge, Thos. Jackson
	23	William Bollum and Mary Hodgson, btp, banns (Apr 7, 14, 21), by E.M., he signs, she marks. W: George Bollum, Caleb Powell
May	16	Thomas Westmoreland of Darlington and Elizabeth Hunter of Masham, banns (Apr 14, 21, 28), by E.M., he signs, she marks. W: Richd. Thompson, William Wesmorland
	21	Henry Lupton of Masham and Elizabeth Haughton of Thornton Watlass, banns (Apr 28, May 5, 12), by E.M., both mark. W: Tho: Greenbank, Caleb Powell
[p. 84]		
July	11	Henry Rodwill and Rachel Porter, btp, banns (June 23, 30, July 7), by E.M., he signs, she marks. W: Henry Bolland, Isaac Illingworth
	20	James Shaw of West Tanfield and Ann Nicholson of Masham, banns (June 30, July 7, 14), by E.M., he marks, she signs. W: William Parker, William Booth

Oct   10   George Fenwick and Margaret Banks, btp, banns (Sept 22, 29, Oct 6), by
                E.M., he marks, she signs. W: John Plewes, John Jackson

      17   Edward Robinson of Ripon and Dinah Lobley of Masham, banns (Sept 29, Oct
                6, 13), by E.M., he signs, she marks. W: Matthew Burrell, Barnabas Bolland

[p. 85]

      21   John Jackson and Elizabeth Bowness, btp, banns (Oct 6, 13, 20), by E.M., both
                mark. W: John Richmond, Margret Terry

Nov   14   Thomas Clark and Margaret Kay, btp, banns (Oct 27, Nov 3, 10, by E.M.), by
                J.L., both mark. W: John Lennox, Abraham Illingworth
                Banns between William Plews of Thornton Watlass and Margaret Henderson
                of Masham publ. Nov 10, 17, 24, by E.M.

Dec   2   John Anderson of Kirkby Malzeard and Margaret Longstaff of Masham, banns
                (Nov 10, 17, 24), by E.M., he signs, she marks. W: Caleb Powell, Barnit
                Metcalf

[p. 86]

      14   Matthew Craggs and Hannah Mallaby, btp, banns (Nov 17, 24, Dec 1, by
                E.M.), by R.R., both mark. W: Hannah Mallabie, Caleb Powell

      26   James Abbot of Wath and Ann Thornberry of Masham, banns (Dec 1, 8, 15),
                by E.M., both sign. W: Geo. Gouthwaite, Caleb Powell

Marriages 1777

Jan   2   Joseph Mallaby of Masham and Jane Marchbanks of Aysgarth, lic, by E.M.,
                both mark. W: Matthew Jackson, Peter Jackson

Mar   10   Arthur Ash and Mary Gill, btp, banns (Jan 26, Feb 2, 9), by E.M., both mark.
                W: Caleb Powell, Abraham Illingworth

[p. 87]   Banns between Thomas Stuart of Masham and Sarah Horner of Coverham
                publ. Feb 16, 23, Mar 2, by E.M.

      31   George Metcalf and Jane Mallaby, btp, banns (Mar 16, 23, 30), by E.M., he
                marks, she signs. W: John Wilson, Caleb Powell

Apr   21   John Thorp and Mary Johnson, btp, banns (Apr 6, 13, 20), by E.M., both mark.
                W: Catherine Smith, Caleb Powell

May   1   William Hardisty and Mary Craggs, btp, banns (Apr 13, 20, 27), by E.M., both
                mark. W: Caleb Powell, Abraham Illingworth

[p. 88]

      27   Charles Atkinson of Ripon and Elizabeth Richmond of Masham, banns (May
                11, 18, 25), by E.M., both mark. W: John Richmond, Matthew Imeson

July   5   Charles Kendall, bach, of Masham and Mary Calvert of Coverham, lic, by T.G.,
                both sign. W: John Webster, George Kendall

      26   Ralph Pybus of Kirklington and Mary Mallaby of Masham, banns (June 29, July
                6, 13), by E.M., both mark. W: Francis Mallaby, William Pybus

Sept   22   George Tanfield and Judith Ruecroft, btp, banns (Sept 7, 14, 21), by E.M., he
                signs, she marks. W: Peter Jackson, Robt. Ruecroft

[p. 89]   Banns between Isaac Illingworth of Masham and Mary Buck of Kirkby

Malzeard publ. Oct 5, 12, 19, by E.M.

Nov 27   Thomas Harrison of Danby Wiske and Jane Hanley of Masham, banns (Nov 9, 16, 23), by E.M., both sign. W: Richard Hanley, Thomas Simpson

Marriages 1778

Feb 4   Francis Glew and Elizabeth Ascough, btp, lic, by E.M., both sign. W: Dorothy Theakston, John Pickersgill

26   John Reed and Elizabeth Thwaites, btp, lic, by E.M., both sign. W: Henry Bolland, John Chapman

[p. 90]

Mar 3   John Bellerby and Esther Herring, btp, banns (Feb 8, 15, 22), by E.M., both mark. W: Caleb Powell, Robert Atkinson

3   Ralph Edon and Mary Cundall, btp, banns (Feb 15, 22, Mar 1), by E.M., both sign. W: Abraham Edon, Thomas Cundall

Apr 20   William Herring and Rachel Pratt, btp, banns (Apr 5, 12, 19), by E.M., both mark. W: Caleb Powell, Robert Atkinson[1]

May 5   William Rider and Polly Theakston, btp, banns (Apr 19, 26, May 3), by E.M., both sign. W: Jonathan Bland, Caleb Powell

[p. 91]

June 2   Edward Blackburn and Deborah Thompson, btp, lic, by E.M., he signs, she marks. W: Caleb Powell, Robert Atkinson

Aug 3   Anthony Urwin and Mary Ruecroft, btp, banns (June 7, 14, 21), by E.M., both mark. W: John Ascough, John Richmond

June 29   Thomas Robinson of Burneston and Ann Hannam of Masham, banns (June 14, 21, 28), by E.M., he signs, she marks. W: John Pickersgill, John Richmond

July 20   George March and Ann Urwin, btp, banns (July 5, 12, 19), by E.M., he signs, she marks. W: Thomas Harrison, Caleb Powell

[p. 92]   Banns between Francis Thompson of Masham and Ann Blackburn of Ripon publ. Nov 1, 8, 15, by E.M.

Banns between James Metcalfe of Masham and Jane Bacon of Wensley publ. Nov 8, 15, 22, by E.M.

Dec 1   George Shaw and Mary Wilson, btp, banns (Nov 15, 22, 29), by E.M., both mark. W: George Wilson, James Towler

10   John Plews and Beatrice Duffeld, btp, banns (Nov 22, 29, Dec 6, by E.M.), by J.W., he signs, she marks. W: Joseph Akers, Caleb Powell

[p. 93]

14   William Carter and Elizabeth Emerson, btp, banns (Nov 29, Dec 6, 13), by

---

[1]   Note inserted here, addressed to E.M. about the publication of their banns: 'Revd Sir, Willm Herring has lived with me since Martinmas last and Rachel Pratt about five weeks at my house at Millstone bank. Your hum: servt. Jno. Bellerby,   March 28 '78.'

17   E.M., he signs, she marks. W: Caleb Powell, Robert Atkinson
Joseph Atkinson and Elizabeth Pickersgill, btp, banns (Nov 29, Dec 6, 13), by E.M., he signs, she marks. W: Caleb Powell, Robert Atkinson

Marriages 1779

Feb 4   William Ballan and Mary Ballan, btp, lic, by E.M., both sign. W: Benjamin Jackson, Caleb Powell

25   Joseph Dumville of Thornton Watlass and Elizabeth Atkinson of Masham, banns (Feb 7, 14, 21), by E.M., both mark. W: Joseph Atkinson, John Richmond

[p. 94]

Mar 1   Thomas Walker and Lydia Jackson, btp, banns (Feb 14, 21, 28), by E.M., both sign. W: Benjamin Jackson, Caleb Powell

9   William Clarkson of Kirkby Malzeard and Ann Fountain of Masham, banns (Feb 14, 21, 28), by E.M., he signs, she marks. W: Ben Severs, John Richmond

8   John Fenwick and Ann Robinson, btp, banns (Feb 21, 28, Mar 7), by E.M., he marks, she signs. W: Samuel Robinson, Caleb Powell
Banns between John Calvert of Masham and Izabel Pickersgill of Kirkby Malzeard publ. Feb 28, Mar 7, 14, by E.M.

[p. 95]

Apr 6   James Metcalf of Kirkby Malzeard and Jane Smithson of Masham, banns (Mar 7, 14, 21), by E.M., he signs, she marks. W: Mattw. Metcalf, John Day
Banns between Joseph Maynard and Mary Naylor, btp, publ. Mar 7, 14, 21, by E.M.

27   Peter Trees and Rachel Metcalf, btp, banns (Apr 11, 18, 25), by E.M., both sign. W: Geo. Nicholson, Joseph Akers

5   John Denison and Catharine Parker, btp, banns (Mar 21, 28, Apr 4), by E.M., both sign. W: William Denison, Caleb Powell

[p. 96]

27   James Towler and Ann Wilson, btp, banns, by E.M., he signs, she marks. W: Thomas Croft, Thomas Fletcher

June 7   Thomas Towler of East Witton and Hannah Gill of Masham, banns (May 16, 23, 30), by E.M., he signs, she marks. W: Caleb Powell, Thomas Burnett
Banns between George Robinson and Isabel Carter, btp, publ. June 6, 13, 20

July 13   George Truthit and Ann Hutchinson, btp, banns (June 27, July 4, 11), by J.W., both mark. W: Robert Rider, Caleb Powell

[p.101]

Aug 2   John Leeming, miller and bach, aged 22, and Mary Lye, spr, aged 25, banns, by E.M., both sign. W: Caleb Powell, John Lye

23   Thomas Thwaites, innholder and bach, aged 21, and Catharine Bainbridge, spr, aged 25, lic, by E.M., both sign. W: Edward Moises jnr, John Chapman

Sept 4   Thomas Clarke, miller and bach, aged 19, and Rosamond Ashton, spr, aged 19,

		banns, by E.M., both sign. W: Benjamin Siddall, Caleb Powell
	20	Thomas Robinson, carpenter and bach, aged 25, and Sarah Kendrew, spr, aged 28, banns, by E.M., both sign. W: Richd. Taylor, Jas. Metcalfe
Oct	4	William Lupton, linen weaver and wdr, aged 60, and Margaret Windall, wid, aged 53, banns, by E.M., both sign. W: Robert Atkinson, John Richmond
	12	William Hartley, cooper and bach, aged 25, and Elizabeth Kay, spr, aged 30, banns, by E.M., both sign. W: John Banks, Caleb Powell
	25	Richard Bowes, blacksmith and bach, aged 21, and Mary Johnson, spr, aged 28, banns, by E.M., both sign. W: John Gowland, Barnabas Towler
Nov	22	Charles Rumfitt, husbandman and bach, aged 22, and Ann Jackson, spr, aged 34, banns, by E.M., both sign. W: Robert Jeff, Caleb Powell
Dec	13	John Kaye, husbandman and wdr, aged 47, and Isabella Ascough, wid, aged 50, banns, by E.M., both sign. W: John Richmond, Robert Atkinson
	30	John London, tailor and bach, aged 24, and Jane Pickard, spr, aged 25, banns, by E.M., both sign. W: Tim: Rider, Edward Smorthit

Marriages 1780

Jan	11	Matthew Thompson, labourer and bach, aged 28, and Sarah Sturdy, spr, aged 22, banns, by E.M., both sign. W: Thomas Sturdy, Caleb Powell
	24	Thomas Metcalf, husbandman and bach, aged 21, and Sarah Neesham, spr, aged 20, banns, by E.M., both sign. W: Mattw. Metcalf, Caleb Powell
	24	Peter Jackson, woolcomber and bach, aged 28, and Ann Vitty, spr, aged 25, banns, by E.M., both sign. W: John Vitty, Matthew Metcalf
[p.102]		
Apr	10	Joseph Rayner, husbandman and bach, aged 27, and Ann Plews, spr, aged 31, banns, by E.M., both sign. W: Thos. Plews, Caleb Powell
May	15	Charles Reynard, husbandman and bach, aged 24, and Martha Hutchinson, spr, aged 34, banns, by E.M., both mark. W: Caleb Powell, Robt. Wright
June	20	John Ridley, joiner and bach, aged 25, and Mary Terry, spr, aged 23, lic, by R.R., both sign. W: James Metcalfe, Caleb Powell
Oct	28	John Berry, husbandman and bach, aged 27, and Elizabeth Bellerby, spr, aged 24, banns, by E.M., he marks, she signs. W: Jno. Pickersgill, Saml. King
Nov	23	Thomas Metcalf, husbandman and bach, aged 25, and Sarah Ward, spr, aged 20, banns, by E.M., both sign. W: Mark Barker, Caleb Powell
Dec	26	Simon Thompson, cooper and bach, aged 36, and Isabella [*illegible*], spr, aged 40, banns, by E.M., both sign. W: Thomas Judson, Samuel King
	30	Isaac Towler, shoemaker and bach, aged 24, and Mary Carmichal, spr, aged 29, banns, by E.M., both sign. W: Roger Bolland snr, Edmund Ward
	30	Peter Pearson, husbandman and bach, aged 51, and Elizabeth Metcalf, wid, aged 25, lic, by E.M., both sign. W: Chas. Kendall, John Kendall

Marriages 1781

Feb	26	Joseph Handley, husbandman and bach, aged 20, and Mary Rider, spr, aged 20, banns, by T.T., he signs, she marks. W: John Rider, Caleb Powell
Apr	16	Edward Rudd, tailor and bach, aged 30, and Judith Metcalf, spr, aged 22, banns, by E.M., both sign. W: William Parker, John Hutchinson
	24	Matthew Jackson, husbandman and bach, aged 54, and Mary Harland, wid, aged 46, banns, by E.M., he signs, she marks. W: John Holmes, Caleb Powell
May	21	Joseph Maynard, husbandman and bach, aged 27, and Mary Prest, spr, aged 25, banns, by E.M., both mark. W: Aaron Jackson, Jno. Richmond

[p.103]

July	1	Richard Boynton, tailor and bach, aged 24, and Isabel Richmond, spr, aged 26, banns, by E.M., both mark. W: Chrisr. Boynton, Jno. Richmond
Aug	14	William Astwood, carpenter and bach, aged 24, and Mary Gill, spr, aged 24, banns, by E.M., he signs, she marks. W: Benjn. Siddall, Caleb Powell
Sept	25	William Bradberry, clockmaker and bach, aged 19, and Isabella Ramsey, spr, aged 19, banns, by E.M, he signs, she marks. W: John Clarkson, John Richmond
Oct	8	Thomas Parker, husbandman and bach, aged 40, and Mary Wrather, spr, aged 28, lic, by E.M., both sign. W: Sam. Wrather, Wm Heslington
Nov	19	William Alchin, miller and bach, aged 22, and Elizabeth Nicholson, spr, aged 20, banns, by E.M., both sign. W: Wm Jones, Henry Bolland

Marriages 1782

Apr	5	Thomas Brown, husbandman and bach, aged 40, and Ann Geldart, spr, aged 22, banns, by E.M., he marks, she signs. W: Thos. Geldart, Caleb Powell
July	11	Peter Barker, husbandman and bach, aged 21, and Esther Wilson, spr, aged 28, banns, by E.M., both sign. W: John Wilson, George Kendall
Oct	10	Jno. Baines, surgeon and bach, aged 21, and Henrietta Hardcastle, spr, aged 21, lic, by E.M., both sign. W: T. Hardcastle, Jno. Baines snr
	18	Matthew Lakin, groom and bach, aged 47, and Margaret Hunton, spr, aged 47, lic, by T.G., both sign. W: Edward Horsman, S. Mills
Nov	23	John Ballan, butcher and bach, aged 25, and Isabella Blackburn, wid, aged 36, lic, by E.M., both sign. W: Henry Bolland, M. Blackburn
	23	George Wilkinson, husbandman and bach, aged 24, and Hannah Mallaby, spr, aged 27, banns, by E.M., both sign. W: Henry Thompson, Caleb Powell
	26	John Banks, husbandman and bach, aged 23, and Ann Hardy, spr, aged 24, banns, by E.M., both mark. W: Henry Croft, Caleb Powell
Dec	3	Charles Bainbridge, mason and bach, aged 27, and Ann Jackson, spr, aged 23, banns, by E.M., both sign. W: Thos. Jackson, William Tomson

[p.104]

	16	Thomas Scaife, husbandman and bach, aged 21, and Eleanor Howred, spr, aged 25, banns, by E.M., both mark. W: Mattw. Metcalfe, Caleb Powell

Marriages 1783

Feb	1	Robert Raley, labourer and wdr, aged 55, and Sarah Horsman, spr, aged 40, banns, by E.M., both mark. W: Caleb Powell, John Reply
	27	Christopher Wilson, husbandman and bach, aged 25, and Sarah Reynard, spr, aged 21, banns, by E.M., he signs, she marks. W: Mark Hutchinson, William London
May	13	John Wood, labourer and bach, aged 20, and Jane Sedgwick, spr, aged 25, banns, by E.M., he signs, she marks. W: Caleb Powell, Robert Atkinson
July	15	Henry Scaife, labourer and wdr, aged 46, and Ann Pybus, wid, aged 39, banns, by E.M., both mark. W: Ellen Scaife, Caleb Powell
Sept	18	Stephen Siddall, wheelwright and bach, aged 34, and Mary Gill, spr, aged 24, banns, by E.M., he signs, she marks. W: George Clarkson, Caleb Powell
	25	Charles Steer, clerk and bach, aged 24, and Jane Hardcastle, spr, aged 22, lic, by E.M., both sign. W: Thomas Hardcastle, Jas. Steer
Oct	7	Robert Bellerby, husbandman and bach, aged 22, and Mary Herring, spr, aged 18, lic, by E.M., both mark. W: Samuel King, Caleb Powell
	13	William Pybus, weaver and bach, aged 33, and Sarah Hebden, spr, aged 32, banns, by E.M., both sign. W: Thos. Hebden, John Little
	28	Peter Hanley, farmer and bach, aged 21, and Betty Jackson, spr, aged 18, lic, by E.M., both sign. W: Matt. Jackson, Simon Hanley
[p.105]		
Nov	15	William Petty, servingman and bach, aged 30, and Mary Robson, spr, aged 30, lic, by E.M., both sign. W: Susanna Mills, M. Senior
	20	George Kendall, farmer and bach, aged 29, and Mary Theakstone, spr, aged 20, lic, by E.M., both sign. W: Charles Kendall, John Barras
Dec	1	Henry Scafe, servingman and bach, aged 23, and Mary Pickersgill, spr, aged 19, banns, by E.M., he signs, she marks. W: Jno. Allinson, William Pickersgill
	2	George Lye, farmer and bach, aged 23, and Prudence Lye, spr, aged 24, banns, by E.M., he signs, she marks. W: John Lye, Mary Plews

Marriages 1784

Apr	14	John Abbot, badger and bach, aged 26, and Dorothy Fawbert, spr, aged 31, banns, by E.M., both mark. W: John Williamson, Michael Hammond
July	25	Francis Whorlton, tailor and wdr, aged 45, and Catharine Robinson, spr, aged 28, banns, by E.M., he signs, she marks. W: Caleb Powell, Thomas Carter
	26	Michael Walker, labourer and bach, aged 26, and Ann Snell, spr, aged 29, banns, by E.M., he marks, she signs. W: Thomas Harrison, Caleb Powell
Aug	9	Michael Hamond, basketmaker and wdr, aged 33, and Mary Metcalf, spr, aged 22, banns, by E.M., both sign. W: John Wilson, Caleb Powell
Sept	7	Arthur Ashe, labourer and wdr, aged 30, and Ann Astwood, spr, aged 35, banns, by E.M., he marks, she signs. W: Joseph Akers, William Astwood
	29	Thomas Johnson Hopper, servant and bach, aged 21, and Hannah Slee, spr,

aged 23, banns, by E.M., both mark. W: Isaac Towler, John Richmond

[p.106]

Oct 30   Christopher Walker, coalminer and bach, aged 27, and Dorothy Smith, spr, aged 24, banns, by E.M., both mark. W: Frans. Smith, Edman Jackson

Nov 9   Cornelius Plews, cordwainer and bach, aged 24, and Ann Brockhill, spr, aged 26, banns, by E.M., he signs, she marks. W: George Brockel, John Brockel

20   Thomas Imeson, farmer and bach, aged 50, and Mary Ascough, spr, aged 34, lic,. by E.M., he signs, she marks. W: Chr. Ascough, Caleb Powell

Dec 16   Thomas Craggs, husbandman and bach, aged 25, and Mary Cooke, spr, aged 23, banns, by E.M., both mark. W: John Cook, Chris. Lambert

Marriages 1785

Jan 18   Henry Fryer, husbandman and wdr, aged 60, and Eliza: Davy, spr, aged 40, banns, by E.M., he signs, she marks. W: Wm Lightfoot, Richard Hanley

24   Benjamin Akers, mason and bach, aged 25, and Elizabeth Beckwith, spr, aged 25, banns, by T.G., both sign. W: Wm. Beckwith, Joseph Akers

Feb 8   Jonathan Wood, gardener and bach, aged 21, and Mary Ianson, spr, aged 22, lic, by T.T., both sign. W: Anthony Hammond, John Carter

Mar 28   James Parcevill, music master and wdr, aged 50, and Ann Plews, wid, aged 50, lic, by E.M., both sign. W: Isabella Croxe, Jno. Richmond

June 6   Joseph Herring, husbandman and bach, aged 19, and Elizabeth Tempest, spr, aged 30, banns, by E.M., he marks, she signs. W: Caleb Powell, Robert Atkinson

July 1   Robert Bellerby, butcher and bach, aged 29, and Sarah Taylor, spr, aged 21, lic, by E.M., both sign. W: Esther Baker, John Richmond

[p.107]

Oct 15   Thomas Durham, grocer and bach, aged 21, and Mary Blackburn, spr, aged 21, lic, by E.M., both sign. W: John Durham, Catharine Blackburn

24   John Wood, labourer and wdr, aged 23, and Hannah Dawson, spr, aged 25, banns, by E.M. jnr, he signs, she marks. W: Caleb Powell, Christopher Dawson

Nov 7   Mark Parkinson, bricklayer and bach, aged 23, and Sarah Smithson, spr, aged 27, banns, by E.M., he signs, she marks. W: Jno. Richmond, Robert Atkinson

23   Thomas Allison, labourer and wdr, aged 34, and Dorothy Warrener, spr, aged 22, banns, by E.M., he signs, she marks. W: Caleb Powell, Robert Atkinson

Dec 8   Anthony Ballan, husbandman and bach, aged 24, and Ellen Cundall, spr, aged 23, lic, by T.G., both sign. W: Abraham Edon, Matthew Cundall

8   John Vitty, miller and bach, aged 33, and Dorothy Longstaf, spr, aged 20, banns, by T.G., both sign. W: Richd. Machell, Bryan Vitty

Marriages 1786

Feb	2	James Walker, butcher and bach, aged 48, and Mary Hanley, spr, aged 45, lic, by E.M., both sign. W: Richard Hanley, James Teasdale
May	17	Anthony Robinson, husbandman and bach, aged 21, and Ann Hakin, spr, aged 22, banns, by E.M., both sign. W: Antho: Thompson, Mark Stott
June	24	Peter Reid, gardener and bach, aged 33, and Hanna Metcalf, spr, aged 29, lic, by E.M., both sign. W: Ns. Carter, Caleb Powell
July	4	Thomas Stainthorp, husbandman and bach, aged 21, and Elizabeth Hodgson, spr, aged 35, lic, by T.G., he signs, she marks. W: Molly Metcaf (*sic*), Thos. Jackson
	18	Henry Ripley, carpenter and bach, aged 23, and Jane Vitty, spr, aged 27, lic, by E.M., both sign. W: John Ascough, Thomas Vitty
Aug	5	John Richmond, schoolmaster and bach, aged 28, and Esther Parker, spr, aged 23, banns, by E.M., he signs, she marks. W: George Harker, Robert Atkinson

[p.108]

	17	William Robinson, hosier and bach, aged 23, and Mary Firby, spr, aged 21, banns, by E.M., he signs, she marks. W: Caleb Powell, Thomas Burnet
Nov	25	Richard Smith, labourer and wdr, aged 50, and Ann Poppleton, maid, aged 42, banns, by E.M., both mark. W: Matthew Carter, John Carter

Marriages 1787

Feb	12	John Robinson, wool stapler and bach, aged 26, and Frances Wilson, spr, aged 21, lic, by E.M., both sign. W: William Dinsdale, Matthew Carter
Apr	10	Thomas Falshaw, farmer and bach, aged 27, and Eleanor Ibbotson, spr, aged 28, banns, by E.M., both sign. W: John Hutchinson, James Falshaw
May	1	Nicholas Carter, husbandman and bach, aged 36, and Elisabeth Lightfoot, spr, aged 36, lic, by J.S., both sign. W: William Morton, Matthew Carter
	5	William Duxford, miller and bach, aged 25, and Barbara Banks, spr, aged 24, banns, by E.M., both mark. W: John Jackson, Joseph Towler
	19	Richard Hanley, farmer and bach, aged 39, and Elizabeth Henessy, wid, aged 42, lic, by E.M., both sign. W: John Jackson, Caleb Powell
Aug	2	George Nicholson, husbandman and bach, aged 25, and Susanna Astwood, spr, aged 25, lic, by T.G., both mark. W: Wm Astwood, Caleb Powell
	13	Thomas Ascough, husbandman and bach, aged 30, and Mary Nelson, spr, aged 29, banns, by T.T., he signs, she marks. W: Thomas Nelson, Thos. Wintersgill
Oct	2	Edward Moises, clerk and bach, aged 25, and Mary Baxies, spr, aged 22, lic, by E.M. snr, both sign. W: James Hutton, Watson Moises
	2	Richard Nussey, carpenter and bach, aged 21, and Ann Crabtree, spr, aged 21, banns, by E.M., he signs, she marks. W: Thos. Leathley, Caleb Powell

[p.109]

Nov	10	Richard Hall, husbandman and wdr, aged 47, and Mary Scaife, spr, aged 22, banns, by E.M., he marks, she signs. W: Caleb Powell, Robert Atkinson

Dec 18   James Falshaw, farmer and bach, aged 28, and Peggy Theakston, spr, aged 21, banns, by T.G., both sign. W: William Rider, Thos. Falshaw

24   William Pickersgill, husbandman and bach, aged 25, and Jane Thorpe, spr, aged 20, banns, by E.M., both mark. W: Thos. Lightfoot, Thos. Towler

Marriages 1788

Jan 28   William Walburn, miller and bach, aged 25, and Jane Urwin, spr, aged 26, banns, by E.M., both mark. W: Joseph Towler, Caleb Powell

Mar 20   Matthew Elseworth, labourer and bach, aged 34, and Eleanor Robinson, spr, aged 35, banns, by E.M., he marks, she signs. W: Caleb Powell, John Robinson (mark)

June 5   George Kendall, farmer and wdr, aged 30, and Esther Carter, spr, aged 21, lic, by T.G., both sign. W: Charles Kendall, John Carter

Aug 12   Richard Morland, clockmaker and bach, aged 27, and Sarah Wilson, spr, aged 23, banns, by E.M., he signs, she marks. W: John Ascough, William Lambert

26   William Baynes, carpenter and bach, aged 32, and Sarah Wood, spr, aged 32, banns, by E.M., he signs, she marks. W: John Metcalf, Willm. Beckwith

Oct 28   George Fletcher, labourer and bach, aged 35, and Elizabeth Richardson, spr, aged 33, banns, by E.M., both mark. W: John Chapman, James Towler

[p.110]

Marriages 1789

May 4   Thomas Wintersgill, husbandman and bach, aged 30, and Ann Leathley, spr, aged 27, banns, by J.B., both sign. W: Geo. Wintersgill, Geo. Leathley

12   William Cartwright, husbandman and bach, aged 30, and Ann Brignall, spr, aged 26, banns, by J.B., both mark. W: Caleb Powell, Thos. Brignall

30   George Dawson, shoemaker and bach, aged 22, and Mary Akers, spr, aged 26, banns, by E.M., both sign. W: Christopher Dawson, John Chapman

June 11   William Bell, blacksmith and bach, aged 32, and Ann Thompson, spr, aged 29, lic, by E.M., both sign. W: Ann Horsman, John Sayer

July 2   Caleb Powell, plumber and bach, aged 20, and Dorothea Soulby, spr, aged 22, lic, by E.M., both sign. W: Caleb Powell, Mattw. Imeson

Oct 20   Thomas Jackson, carpenter and bach, aged 25, and Mary Ballan, wid, aged 28, lic, by E.M., both sign. W: Matthew Carter, John Chapman

27   Matthew Kearton, shoemaker and bach, aged 27, and Frances Chapman, spr, aged 27, banns, by J.B., he signs, she marks. W: Francis Mallaby, Thomas King

Nov 24   Joseph Burniston, weaver and wdr, aged 51, and Ann Bradley, spr, aged 42, banns, by E.M., he signs, she marks. W: Thomas Jackson, Caleb Powell

24   Thomas Sturdy, husbandman and bach, aged 28, and Mary Hammond, spr, aged 22, banns, by E.M., he signs, she marks. W: Richard Hanley, George Grundill

MARRIAGES

| | 24 | George Roe, husbandman and bach, and Elizabeth Hodgson, spr, banns, by E.M., both mark. W: John Carter, Caleb Powell |
| Dec | 5 | Richard Braithwaite, husbandman and bach, aged 22, and Elizabeth Mallaby, spr, aged 26, banns, by J.B., both mark. W: Geo. Wilkinson, John Mallaby |

[p.111]

| | 8 | Thomas Haslop, tanner and bach, aged 25, and Isabell Horsman, spr, aged 20, lic, by J.B., both sign. W: Jno. Baines, Caleb Powell |
| | 31 | George Grundill, husbandman and bach, aged 22, and Elizabeth Coldbeck, spr, aged 22, banns, by J.B., he signs, she marks. W: Chrisr. Pickersgill, Richard Hanley |

Marriages 1790

Jan	11	Ralph Walker, husbandman and bach, aged 25, and Mary Burrell, spr, aged 21, banns, by J.B., both sign. W: George Graham, Jno. Richmond
Feb	16	Thomas Carter, husbandman and bach, aged 25, and Esther Rider, spr, aged 21, banns, by J.B., both sign. W: George Kendall, John Carter
Mar	1	Thomas Leathley, shoemaker and bach, aged 30, and Dorothy Leeming, spr, aged 22, banns, by J.B., he signs, she marks. W: Mattw. Metcalf, Thos. Theakston
	16	John Heslington, maltster and bach, aged 35, and Mary Metcalf, spr, aged 31, lic, by J.B., both sign. W: Edwd. Horsman, Robt. Imeson
Apr	8	Nenian Procter, tanner and bach, aged 28, and Elizabeth Jackson, spr, aged 23, lic, by J.B., both sign. W: Matthew Jackson, Thos. Jackson
	26	William Atkinson, labourer and wdr, aged 46, and Ann Graham, spr, aged 48, banns, by J.B., both mark. W: John Shields, Benjn. Siddall
May	10	William Rayner, husbandman and bach, aged 24, and Molly Issett, spr, aged 24, banns, by J.B., both sign. W: Eneas Pattison, Thos. Vitty
	11	Robert Wintersgill, shoemaker and bach, aged 24, and Ann Sedra, spr, aged 20, banns, by J.B., both sign. W: Geo. Wintersgill, Thomas Almone
July	3	William Fielden, woolcomber and bach, aged 30, and Mary Charnack, spr, aged 18, lic, by J.B., both sign. W: Robt. Wardell, Caleb Powell
	11	William Thompson, husbandman and bach, aged 29, and Ann Lye, spr, aged 25, lic, by J.B., he signs, she marks. W: Willm. Fielden, Caleb Powell

[p.112]

Aug	9	Richard Thompson, labourer and wdr, aged 39, and Sarah Thornton, spr, aged 45, banns, by J.B., he signs, she marks. W: Caleb Powell, Robert Atkinson
	17	Stephen Wintersgill, wheelwright and bach, aged 29, and Jane Gill, spr, aged 28, banns, by J.B., both sign. W: Miles Rainforth, Henry Hamilton
	19	Henry Weare, gent and bach, aged 30, and Ann Tanfield, spr, aged 21, lic, by J.B., both sign. W: Dorothy Tanfield, Tho: Dawes
Sept	20	Joseph Towler, miller and bach, aged 24, and Isabella Myers, spr, aged 22, banns, by J.B., he signs, she marks. W: John Jackson, Henry Loftus
	30	Thomas Rider, farmer and wdr, aged 37, and Ann Jackson, wid, aged 36, lic,

by J.B., both sign. W: Thos. Vitty, John Ascough

Oct 11 Henry Loftus, brewer and bach, aged 28, and Elizabeth Pickersgill, spr, aged 23, banns, by J.B., both sign. W: Thos. Jackson, Joseph Towler

Nov 8 William Thwaites, sievemaker and bach, aged 24, and Nell Brown, spr, aged 21, banns, by J.B., both sign. W: David Kay, John Plews

11 Richard Wells, farmer and bach, aged 26, and Ann Jackson, spr, aged 25, lic, by J.B., both sign. W: Thos. Jackson, Thos. Batty

22 John Thompson, husbandman and bach, aged 35, and Alice Slater, spr, aged 29, banns, by J.B., he signs, she marks. W: Thos. Metcalfe (mark), Caleb Powell

23 William Casling, labourer and bach, aged 28, and Jane Oselton, spr, aged 26, banns, by J.B., he signs, she marks. W: William Chandler, Caleb Powell

23 Jeremiah Metcalfe, farmer and wdr, aged 50, and Elizabeth Slie, spr, aged 23, banns, by J.B., both mark. W: Caleb Powell, Mattw. Slie (mark)

23 James Beck, husbandman and bach, aged 28, and P[r]udence Reynolds, spr, aged 24, banns, by J.B., he marks, she signs (Pudance). W: Joseph Rynard, Caleb Powell

[p.113]   **Marriages 1791**

Feb 20 John Huklaharland, surgeon and bach, aged 54, and Esther Smorthit, spr, aged 36, lic, by J.B., both sign. W: John London, Caleb Powell

Mar 4 John Braithwaite, plasterer and bach, aged 22, and Elizabeth Towler, spr, aged 21, lic, by J.B., he signs, she marks. W: James Metcalfe, William Thompson

Apr 28 John Wilkinson, butcher and bach, aged 21, and Mary Hill, spr, aged 21, lic, by J.B., both sign. W: James Blackburn, Peter Barker

Aug 20 Mark Towler, husbandman and bach, aged 24, and Elizabeth Drummer, spr, aged 23, banns, by J.B., both mark. W: George Dixon (mark), Caleb Powell *Duty paid.*

Oct 25 James Vayro, carpenter and bach, aged 25, and Margaret Kid, spr, aged 20, banns, by J.B., both sign. W: John Kid, John Horner

Nov 14 John Horner, carpenter and bach, aged 25, and Ann Hutchinson, spr, aged 21, banns, by J.B., both sign. W: John Varey, James Vayro

21 Robert Robinson, husbandman and bach, aged 26, and Esther Richmond, wid, aged 28, banns, by J.B., he marks, she signs. W: Matthew Carter, Francis Sturdy

22 George Wintersgill, husbandman and bach, aged 22, and Elisabeth Caul, spr, aged 25, banns, by J.B., both mark. W: Ralph Edon, Caleb Powell

26 John Jackson, husbandman and bach, aged 33, and Ann Reynard, spr, aged 29, banns, by J.B., he signs, she marks. W: Francis Sturdy, William Reynard

Dec 29 John Court, shoemaker and bach, aged 23, and Mary London, spr, aged 32, banns, by J.B., he signs, she marks. W: Wm London, Thomas Court

Marriages 1792

Feb 6 Matthew Jackson, saddler and bach, aged 26, and Jane Young, spr, aged 22, lic, by J.B., both sign. W: Edman Jackson, Thomas Pullen

6 George Clarkson, mason and bach, aged 35, and Isabella Ferguson, wid, aged 29, banns, by J.B., he signs, she marks. W: Jeffery Clarkson, Caleb Powell

9 James Blackburn, grocer and bach, aged 29, and Elizabeth Pickersgill, spr, aged 35, lic, by J.B., both sign. W: Chrisr. Pickersgill, Caleb Powell

14 Gabriel Kay, husbandman and bach, aged 30, and Elizabeth Herring, aged 18, banns, by J.B., both mark. W: Thos. Lightfoot, Mattw. Metcalf

Mar 18 John Ascough, farmer and bach, aged 26, and Hannah Heppel, spr, aged 20, lic, by J.B., both sign. W: John Heppel, George Ascough

20 James Metcalfe, husbandman and bach, aged 34, and Esther Scaife, spr, aged 21, banns, by J.B., both mark. W: Edman Jackson, Thomas Jackson

May 14 Christoper [*sic*] Hall, husbandman and bach, aged 24, and Hannah Brignall, spr, aged 24, banns, by J.B., he signs, she marks. W: John Richmond, Wm Cartwright (mark)

June 24 Mattw. Metcalf, husbandman and bach, aged 29, and Hannah Rodwell, spr, aged 27, lic, by J.B., both mark. W: Wm Horsman, Caleb Powell

25 Thomas York jnr, tailor and bach, aged 28, and Jane Imeson, spr, aged 24, lic, by J.B., both sign. W: Caleb Powell, Thomas Metcalfe (mark)

26 Edman Jackson, husbandman and bach, aged 30, and Mary Horsman, spr, aged 31, banns, by J.B., he signs, she marks. W: Peter Barker, Caleb Powell

Aug 16 Donkin Cameron, husbandman and bach, aged 21, and Isabella Roe, spr, aged 24, banns, by J.B., both mark. W: Esther Jackson, John Richmond

Sept 3 John Fletom, husbandman and bach, aged 26, and Susanna Warriner, spr, aged 30, banns, by J.B., both mark. W: John Witham, Caleb Powell

29 William Brewster, draper and bach, aged 27, and Mary Nattrass, spr, aged 29, lic, by J.B., he signs, she marks. W: Chrisr. Pickersgill, Caleb Powell *D[uty] Pd.*

Oct 9 Thomas Fletcher, husbandman and bach, aged 25, and Denas Thompson, spr, aged 28, banns, by J.B., both mark. W: Mattw. Metcalf, Mark Hutchinson

29 John Dallow, weaver and bach, aged 24, and Elisabeth Jackson, spr, aged 24, banns, by J.B., both sign. W: Peter Hanley, Matt. Jackson

Nov 22 John Hill, cordwainer and bach, aged 25, and Jane Coldbeck, spr, aged 20, banns, by J.B., he signs, she marks. W: Mattw. Metcalf, John Gill

26 William Woodd, labourer and bach, aged 23, and Mary Malaby, spr, aged 22, banns, by J.B., he marks, she marks. W: Mattw. Metcalf, Christr. Darnbrough

27 Joseph Warrener, labourer and bach, aged 27, and Mary Lye, spr, aged 23, banns, by J.B., both mark. W: Mattw. Metcalf, George Lye

Dec 27 William Harker, grocer and bach, aged 30, and Juliana Dockeray, spr, aged 30, lic, by J.B., both sign. W: Thos. Dockeray, Mary Dockeray

Marriages 1793

| Jan | 10 | H. Candler, attorney at law and bach, aged 29, and Mary Ascough, spr, aged 23, lic, by J.B., both sign. W: Fras. Barroby, Alice Twelwell(?), Ann Bowers |
| Apr | 22 | John Miller, husbandman and bach, aged 22, and Edith Emmerson, spr, aged 25, banns, by J.B., both mark. W: Mark Hutchinson, John Wilson |

[p.116]

July	2	James Hutton esq., bach, and Mary Hoyle, spr, lic, by J.B., both sign. W: Henry Bolland, Mary Bolland
Aug	24	John Hodgson, farmer and bach, aged 26, and Catharine Leathley, spr, aged 23, banns, by J.B., he signs, she marks. W: Thos. Hodgson, Wm Leathley
	26	John Walker, woolcomber and bach, aged 22, and Jane King, spr, aged 23, banns, by J.B., he signs, she marks. W: Chris. Spence (mark), Mattw. Metcalf
Sept	16	Robert Marsden, gent and bach, aged 24, and Elizabeth Wrather, spr, aged 27, lic, by J.B., both sign. W: W. Dawson, Jane Wrather, Lucinda Wrather, Chs. Hawksley Webb
Dec	7	Robert Hudson, husbandman and bach, aged 20, and Jane Rudd, spr, aged 22, banns, by J.B., he signs, she marks. W: Mattw. Metcalf, Robt Walker (mark)
	9	Thomas Drummer, blacksmith and bach, aged 22, and Fanne Hunter, spr, aged 20, banns, by J.B., both sign. W: Thomas Burnett, Caleb Powell

Marriages 1794

Jan	16	Barnard Bulcock, cotton spinner and bach, aged 18, and Ann Barnes, spr, aged 18, banns, by J.B., both mark. W: John Brug, Caleb Powell, Charles Dovenor
	20	Robert Walker, husbandman and bach, aged 22, and Mary Thorpe, spr, aged 21, banns, by J.B., he signs, she marks. W: Mattw. Imeson, Caleb Powell
Feb	3	Thomas Renwick, mason and wdr, aged 47, and Mary Edminton, spr, aged 44, banns, by J.B., he signs, she marks. W: George Nicholson, Caleb Powell

[p.117]

	13	John Hird, fellmonger and bach, aged 26, and Hannah Walker, spr, aged 33, lic, by J.B., both sign. W: Henry Hall, Caleb Powell
	27	John Wintersgill, husbandman and bach, aged 32, and Elizabeth Metcalf, spr, aged 29, lic, by J.B., both sign. W: Geo. Wintersgill, Mattw. Wintersgill
Mar	12	John Beckwith, miller and bach, aged 21, and Mary Metcalfe, spr, aged 21, lic, by J.B., both mark. W: Jas. Smith, Hannah Robinson
Apr	22	Thomas Whitaker, labourer and bach, aged 26, and Esther Barnes, spr, aged 23, banns, by J.B., both mark. W: Charles Dovenor, Charles Powell
May	19	John Ascough, butcher and bach, aged 23, and Anna Smorthit, spr, aged 22, lic, by J.B., both sign. W: Thos. Smorthit, Geo: Ascough
	24	Thomas Clarkson, mason and bach, aged 22, and Hannah Barnet, spr, aged 22, banns, by J.B., he signs, she marks. W: Stephen Luck, Caleb Powell
June	10	Joseph Burrill, clerk and bach, aged 30, and Lucinda Wrather, spr, aged 30, lic, by W.P., both sign. W: Jno. Grimston, Caleb Powell

	24	Luke Thornton, labourer and wdr, aged 50, and Esther Bellerby, wid, aged 50, banns, by J.B., both mark. W: Ben Jackson, Mattw. Metcalfe
July	14	John Boston, husbandman and bach, aged 20, and Marget [*sic*] King, spr, aged 21, lic, by J.B., he marks, she signs. W: Richd. Whitelock, Robart Atkinson
Aug	12	John Shields, gardener and bach, aged 33, and Sarah Duffield, wid, aged 34, lic, by J.B., he signs, she marks. W: Joseph Thompson, Caleb Powell
[p.118]		
Oct	20	Matthew Imeson, farmer and bach, aged 25, and Elizabeth Barker, spr, aged 27, lic, by J.B., both sign. W: Peter Hanley, Geo. Barker
Nov	9	Mathew Terry, millwright and bach, aged 29, and Jane Ascough, spr, aged 22, lic, by J.B., both sign. W: George Ascough, Wm. Lightfoot
Dec	1	Thomas Myers, carpenter and bach, aged 24, and Martha Furby, spr, aged 23, banns, by J.B., both mark. W: Caleb Powell, Anth.(?) Gill (mark)
	14	Benjamin Siddall, carpenter and bach, aged 20, and Elizabeth Johnson, spr, aged 23, banns, by J.B., he signs, she marks. W: Benjn. Grange, Caleb Powell
	29	William Ward, cordwainer and bach, aged 24, and J. Greenhow, spr, aged 24, banns, by J.B., both sign. W: Wm Atkinson, Caleb Powell

Marriages 1795

Jan	18	Edward Metcalf, husbandman and bach, aged 23, and Anna Wintersgill, spr, aged 23, lic, by J.B., both sign. W: Caleb Powell, Robt. Wintersgill
Feb	10	John Ramshaw, husbandman and bach, aged 21, and Jane Mallaby, spr, aged 23, banns, by J.B., he marks, she signs. W: Ralph Ramshaw (mark), Caleb Powell
Mar	26	William Hodgson, saddler and bach, aged 32, and Ellen Fryer, spr, aged 23, banns, by J.B., he signs, she marks. W: Matt. Jackson, George Windross
May	23	George Hartley, joiner and bach, aged 24, and Abigail Craggs, spr, aged 20, banns, by J.B., both sign. W: Jas. Metcalfe, Caleb Powell
[p.119]		
	27	Christopher Masdin, husbandman and bach, aged 24, and Mary Brignall, spr, aged 24, banns, by J.B., he signs, she marks. W: Ben Jackson, Mattw. Metcalfe
June	13	Peter Smith, bricklayer and bach, aged 23, and Frances Park, spr, aged 20, banns, by J.B., both mark. W: William Leming, Caleb Powell
July	22	George Clark, labourer and wdr, aged 29, and Esther Barker, spr, aged 20, banns, by J.B., both mark. W: Thos. Metcalfe (mark), Caleb Powell
Oct	24	George Windross, butcher and bach, aged 28, and Ann Geldart, wid, aged 42, lic, by J.B., both sign. W: Thos. Jackson, Mattw. Metcalfe
Nov	3	Miles Lonley, stuff weaver and bach, aged 25, and Mary Reynard, spr, aged 22, banns, by J.B., he signs, she marks. W: Caleb Powell, John Clark
Dec	17	Henry Harrison, gamekeeper and bach, aged 21, and Jane Greenhow, spr, aged 23, banns, by J.B., both sign. W: Thos. Dowson, Caleb Powell
	19	Charles Beckwith, labourer and wdr, aged 40, and Mary Thorpe, wid, aged 36,

banns, by J.B., both mark. W: Thos. Lightfoot, Caleb Powell

   30   Robert Wilson, clerk and bach, aged 35, and Ann Bowes, spr, aged 28, lic, by J.B., both sign. W: Edwd. Moises, Dorothy Bowes

Marriages 1796

Jan   18   Thomas Humble, husbandman and bach, aged 27, and Ann Barnes, spr, aged 26, banns, by J.B., both mark. W: Adam Barnes, Caleb Powell

[p.120]

Feb   1   Christopher Clark, woolcomber and bach, aged 22, and Esther Barningham, spr, aged 23, banns, by J.B., he signs, she marks. W: Jas. Metcalfe, Caleb Powell

   15   William Glew, farmer and bach, aged 21, and Ann Theakston, spr, aged 27, banns, by J.B., he marks, she signs. W: Nicolas Carter, Thos. Theakston

Mar   7   James Yates, wool sorter and bach, aged 20, and Ann Pickersgill, spr, aged 20, banns, by J.B., both sign. W: Henry Lofthouse, Geo. Yates

   7   James Edrington, husbandman and bach, aged 20, and Mary Topham, spr, aged 23, lic, by J.B., both mark. W: Caleb Powell, Robert Hudson

   29   John Hargreaves, woolcomber and bach, aged 26, and Mary Dowson, spr, aged 21, banns, by J.B., he marks, she signs. W: Wm Hartley, Saml. Margerison

   31   Christopher Hauxwell, husbandman and bach, aged 21, and Hannah Boys, spr, aged 23, lic, by J.B., he marks, she signs. W: Mattw. Metcalfe, Esmd. Barker

Apr   11   Abraham Edon, farmer and bach, aged 45, and Elizabeth Cundale, spr, aged 37, lic, by J.B., he signs, she marks. W: Nicholas Carter, Ralph Edon

   18   Peter Pratt, blacksmith and bach, aged 22, and Christiana Imeson, spr, aged 20, by J.B., both sign. W: John Imeson, Caleb Powell

May   2   Thomas Fawcet, husbandman and bach, aged 24, and Mary Dent, spr, aged 27, banns, by J.B., he marks, she signs. W: Caleb Powell, Thos. Stelling

   2   George Kitchen, cordwainer and bach, aged 27, and Margaret Gill, spr, aged 30, banns, by J.B., both mark. W: Wm Astwood, Caleb Powell

[p.121]

   7   Matthew Carter, farmer and bach, aged 36, and Hannah Lightfoot, spr, aged 38, lic, by J.B., both sign. W: Nicholas Carter, Caleb Powell

   17   John Smith, husbandman and bach, aged 27, and Sarah Metcalf, spr, aged 26, banns, by J.B., both sign. W: Jona^n. Roundall, Wm Smith

   23   Ralph Cumings, woolcomber and bach, aged 25, and Ann Harker, spr, aged 19, banns, by J.B., he signs, she marks. W: Caleb Powell, Jeffrey Clarkson (mark)

   28   George Imeson, blacksmith and bach, aged 35, and Esther Ward, spr, aged 36, lic, by J.B., both sign. W: Thos. Imeson, Nicholas Carter

Aug   17   William Dinsdale, blacksmith and bach, aged 24, and Mary Jackson, spr, aged 20, banns, by J.B., he marks, she signs. W: Mattw. Metcalfe, John Chapman

Sept   11   William Dickinson, gardener and bach, aged 21, and Esther Metcalf, spr, aged 21, lic, by J.B., both sign. W: John Wintersgill, Caleb Powell

| Dec | 3 | William Edmondson, husbandman and bach, aged 27, and Frances Johnson, spr, aged 21, banns, by J.B., he marks, she signs. W: Caleb Powell, Robart Atkinson |

Marriages 1797

Jan	12	Thomas Tomlin, tailor and bach, aged 26, and Ann Hutchinson, spr, aged 22, banns, by J.B., both sign. W: Mark Hutchinson, John Pickard
	23	Hugh Prest, husbandman and bach, aged 24, and Margaret Walker, spr, aged 26, banns, by J.B., he signs, she marks. W: Mattw. Metcalf, Robert Atkinson
	24	Robert Imeson, farmer and bach, aged 21, and Esther Whitelock, spr, aged 19, lic, by J.B., both sign. W: Richd. Whitelock, Caleb Powell
Feb	25	Thomas Smorthit, farmer and bach, aged 22, and Elizabeth Lightfoot, spr, aged 23, lic, by J.B., both sign. W: Wm. Morton jnr, John Lightfoot

[p.122]

May	13	William Willson, woolcomber and bach, aged 24, and Jane Rider, spr, aged 23, banns, by J.B., both sign. W: Thos. Carter, Mark Rider
	15	Christopher Collinson, blacksmith and wdr, aged 59, and Elizabeth Banks, spr, aged 42, banns, by J.B., both mark. W: Caleb Powell, Robt. Sadler
	29	William Ward, cordwainer and wdr, aged 27, and Elizabeth Hoult, spr, aged 24, banns, by J.B., he signs, she marks. W: Wm Atkinson, Saml. Margerison
July	18	John King, farmer and wdr, aged 51, and Margaret Judson, spr, aged 46, lic, by J.B., both sign. W: Chrisr. Pickersgill, Henry Procter
	18	Leo: Howson, gent and wdr, aged 39, and Easter Rider, spr, aged 26, lic, by J.B., both sign. W: Francis Croft, Caleb Powell
Aug	29	John Ponder, husbandman and bach, aged 20, and Elizabeth Edmondson, spr, aged 23, banns, by J.B., both mark. W: Peter Barker, Mattw. Metcalf
	29	John Emerson, husbandman and bach, aged 25, and Elizabeth King, spr, aged 19, banns, by J.B., both mark. W: Mattw. Metcalf, Wm Gill
Oct	30	William Taylor, woolcomber and bach, aged 27, and Elizabeth Wintersgill, spr, aged 20, banns, by J.B., both mark. W: James Wintersgill, Caleb Powell
Nov	20	George Wintersgill, farmer and bach, aged 36, and Isabella Hutchinson, aged 22, lic, by J.B., both sign. W: Peter Hanley, Thos. Tomlin
	23	Marmaduke Hauxwell, husbandman and bach, aged 21, and Jane Lye, spr, aged 19, banns, by J.B., he signs, she marks. W: Joseph Appelbey, Caleb Powell
	28	Andrew Brown, husbandman and bach, aged 32, and Jane Smith, spr, aged 26, banns, by J.B., both mark. W: Matthew Carter, Caleb Powell

[p.123]

Marriages 1798

| Feb | 13 | Ben: Jackson, yeoman and bach, aged 40, and Frances Edon, spr, aged 40, lic, by J.B., both sign. W: Abraham Edon, Robert Jeff |

| | 18 | William Lightfoot, farmer and bach, aged 25, and Esther Smorthit, spr, aged 23, lic, by J.B., both sign. W: Wm Morton jnr, John Lightfoot |

Apr 9 — John Jackson, farmer and bach, aged 30, and Jane Imeson, spr, aged 25, lic, by J.B., both sign. W: Dorothy Imeson, Margaret Imeson

15 — Mark Rider, farmer and bach, aged 28, and Sarah Ward, spr, aged 30, lic, by J.B., both sign. W: Nicholas Carter, Caleb Powell

30 — Bateman Atkinson, joiner and bach, aged 25, and Mary Storrah, spr, aged 23, banns, by J.B., he signs, she marks. W: George Clarkson, John Metcalf

May 1 — Leonard Barker, farmer and bach, aged 32, and Elizabeth Jackson, spr, aged 32, banns, by J.B., he marks, she signs. W: John Barker, Caleb Powell

1 — William Court, woolcomber and bach, aged 25, and Dorothy Clarkson, spr, aged 21, banns, by J.B., both sign. W: Chris. Court, Caleb Powell

12 — Joseph Clarkson, husbandman and bach, aged 26, and Mary Winn, spr, aged 27, banns, by J.B., both sign. W: Caleb Powell, Prudence Winn

22 — James Clark, husbandman and bach, aged 21, and Isabella Bage, spr, aged 22, banns, by J.B. both mark. W: Caleb Powell, Margaret Furby

28 — Thomas Morell, husbandman and bach, aged 30, and Ann Wilkinson, spr, aged 34, banns, by J.B., he signs, she marks. W: George Wilkinson, Thomas Jackson

[p.124]

June 2 — Samuel Platts, clothmaker and wdr, aged 30, and Mary Dent, spr, aged 29, lic, by J.B., both sign. W: George Clarkson, Christop: Baldwin

July 9 — William Stirk, husbandman and bach, aged 28, and Ann Taylor, spr, aged 20, banns, by J.B., he signs, she marks. W: M. Bolland, E.A. Dawes

14 — Roger Kirkbride, husbandman and bach, aged 21, and Hannah Robinson, spr, aged 21, banns, by J.B., he marks, she signs. W: Henry Lofthouse, Caleb Powell

22 — George Ascough, blacksmith and bach, aged 22, and Elizabeth Hutchinson, spr, aged 23, lic, by J.B., he signs, she marks. W: John Horner, Caleb Powell

Aug 27 — George Nelson, tailor and bach, aged 21, and Elizabeth Duffield, spr, aged 29, lic, by J.B., both sign. W: Caleb Powell, Robart Atkinson

Sept 9 — Robert Harrison, husbandman and bach, aged 29, and Dorothy Thompson, spr, aged 34, lic, by J.B., both sign. W: John Lye, Caleb Powell

Dec 3 — William Bearby, husbandman and bach, aged 25, and Jane Lobley, spr, aged 20, banns, by J.B., both mark. W: Matt. Jackson, Caleb Powell

10 — Matthew Spence, husbandman and bach, aged 22, and Mary Clark, spr, aged 22, banns, by J.B., both mark. W: John Court, Caleb Powell

10 — William Jackson, husbandman and bach, aged 25, and Elizabeth Place, spr, aged 25, banns, by J.B., both mark. W: Matt: Jackson, Caleb Powell

[p.125]

20 — Michael Bell, husbandman and bach, aged 27, and Ann Hall, spr, aged 20, banns, by J.B., both mark. W: Mattw. Metcalfe, Chr. Kendall

24 — John Metcalfe, husbandman and wdr, aged 46, and Ellen Reynard, wid, aged 46, banns, by J.B., he signs, she marks. W: Caleb Powell, Robt. Wintersgill

Marriages 1799

Jan	1	Thomas Metcalfe, weaver and bach, aged 34, and Elizabeth Prest, spr, aged 37, banns, by J.B., both mark. W: Caleb Powell, Geo. Nicholson (mark)
	1	George Wilson, woolcomber and bach, aged 24, and Elizabeth Fenwick, spr, aged 21, banns, by J.B., both mark. W: Caleb Powell, Saml. Margerison
Feb	2	Thomas Theakston, farmer and bach, aged 34, and Mary Lightfoot, spr, aged 22, lic, by J.B., both sign. W: Wm Morton, John Smorthit
Mar	25	John Hutchinson, woolcomber and bach, aged 22, and Mary Deighton, spr, aged 19, banns, by J.B., he signs, she marks. W: John Windross, Caleb Powell
Apr	14	Matthew Carter, farmer and wdr, aged 38, and Hannah Ward, spr, aged 34, lic, by J.B., both sign. W: Wm Morton, Ns. Carter
May	11	Thomas Turner, farmer and bach, aged 25, and Sarah Watson, spr, aged 28, lic, by J.B., both sign. W: John Jackson, Thos. Jackson
June	3	James Brown, husbandman and bach, aged 21, and Ann Alderson, spr, aged 22, banns, by J.B., he signs, she marks. W: John Wilson, Matt. Metcalfe

[p.126]

	15	John Carter, farmer and bach, aged 37, and Catharine Blackburn, spr, aged 32, lic, by J.B., both sign. W: Peter Carter, Robert Blackburn
July	11	Francis Walker, butcher and bach, aged 25, and Jane Gill, spr, aged 22, lic, by J.B., both sign. W: Mattw. Metcalf, Thomas Bray
Aug	31	James Dixon, carpenter and bach, aged 23, and Rachel Hall, spr, aged 23, banns, by J.B., he signs, she marks. W: John Horner, Christ: Horner
Sept	28	Matthew Wintersgill, miller and bach, aged 35, and Elizabeth Glew, spr, aged 20, lic, by J.B., he signs, she marks. W: Peter Carter, Caleb Powell
Nov	22	Marmaduke Croft, husbandman and bach, aged 23, and Jane Pickersgill, spr, aged 22, banns, by J.B., he signs, she marks. W: Thomas Croft, Caleb Powell
	23	Christopher Thompson, husbandman and bach, aged 20, and Jane Myers, spr, aged 22, banns, by J.B., both mark. W: Thomas Myers, Caleb Powell
	26	George Stelling, husbandman and bach, aged 30, and Mary Hagstone, spr, aged 25, banns, by J.B., both mark. W: Mattw. Hagston, Wm Beckwith
	27	Henry Wagget, husbandman and bach, aged 23, and Mary Craggs, spr, aged 38, banns, by J.B., both mark. W: George Hartley, Caleb Powell
Dec	17	William Topham, husbandman and bach, aged 21, and Emey Suttill, spr, aged 25, banns, by J.B., he marks, she signs. W: Caleb Powell, Henry Chapman

[p.127]

Marriages 1800

Mar	15	John Smorthit, farmer and bach, aged 22, and Hannah Lightfoot, spr, aged 21, lic, by J.B., both sign. W: Wm Horsman, Mattw. Metcalf
Apr	27	Peter Carter, farmer and bach, aged 28, and Ann Barker, spr, aged 25, lic, by J.B., both sign. W: Wm Morton, Nicholas Carter
Sept	1	Thomas Mainman, tailor and bach, aged 47, and Mary Siddall, wid, aged 40, banns, by J.B., both mark. W: Richard Hanley, Thos. Place

	16	George Morton, gent and bach, aged 22, and Elizabeth Ann Dawe(s), spr, aged 38, lic, by J.B., both sign. W: Wm Morton, Eliza Morton
	27	Henry Knowl, husbandman and bach, aged 37, and Martha Fisher, spr, aged 25, banns, by J.B., both mark. W: John Wilson, James Brown
Oct	7	George Clarkson, woolcomber and bach, aged 23, and Elizabeth Hammond, spr, aged 38, lic, by J.B., he signs, she marks. W; James Metcalfe, Matthew Clarkson
Dec	9	George Barker, farmer and bach, aged 33, and Mary Merryweather, spr, aged 28, lic, by J.B., both sign. W: Wm Morton, Edmd. Barker
	17	Peter Graham, husbandman and bach, aged 24, and Sarah Proctor, spr, aged 25, banns, by J.B., both sign. W: Thomas Ascough, Caleb Powell

INDEX OF NAMES

The symbol * after the page number indicates that the name occurs more than once on the page indicated. In this register the spelling of many surnames varies considerably , and it is not always easy to tell whether two names, phonetically similar, are in fact the same family name. In this index, each entry lists any variant spellings of the surname that have been encountered. Christian names also vary considerably in spelling, but in general they are indexed under the modern equivalent. In the case of the following Christian names, abbreviations have been used in this index as indicated:

Anth.	Anthony	Jos.	Joseph
Barb.	Barbara	Kath.	Katherine
Benj.	Benjamin	Laur.	Laurence
Cath.	Catherine	Lawr.	Lawrence
Chas	Charles	Leon.	Leonard
Chris.	Christopher	Magd.	Magdalen
Dan.	Daniel	Marg.	Margaret
Deb.	Deborah	Marj.	Marjorie
Dor.	Dorothy	Marm.	Marmaduke
Edmd	Edmund	Matth.	Matthew
Edwd	Edward	Mich.	Michael
Eliz.	Elizabeth	Nich.	Nicholas
Fred.	Frederick	Phil.	Philip
Geo	George	Richd	Richard
Humph.	Humphrey	Robt	Robert
Hy	Henry	Sam.	Samuel
Isab	Isabel	Steph.	Stephen
Jas	James	Thos	Thomas
Jeff.	Jeffrey	Wm	William

Abbot, Abbott, Ann 126, 218; Dor. 138, 223; Frances 126; Jas 126, 218; John 138*, 158, 223

Ackers, Acres, *see* Akers

Aire, Eliz. 195

Aked, Joshua 206

Akers, Ackers, Acres, Ann 108*, 140, 204; Benj. 62, 74*, 76*, 105, 108, 137, 140, 141, 144*, 146, 150, 154, 159, 162*, 182, 183, 204, 224; Eliz. 137*, 140, 141, 144, 146, 150, 154, 183, 224; Ellen 200; Hannah 62, 74, 105, 141, 162*, 183; Jane 71; Jos. 74, 150, 200, 219, 220, 223, 224; Marg. 136; Mary 136, 226; Richd 71; Thos 146; Wm 154

Alchin, Eliz. 222; Wm 222

Alderson, Aaron 58; Ann 63, 162, 235; Eliz. 58, 107, 165; Geo. 76, 104, 163, 169; Jane 110, 166; John 54, 169; Marg. 60, 216; Mary 57, 71, 107, 110, 116, 165, 166, 169*, 170, 181, 214; Ralph 54, 57, 60, 63, 71, 76, 104, 107, 110, 116*, 162, 163, 165, 166, 169*, 170*, 175; Thos 110, 169

Glover, Eliz. 118; Tabitha 118; Thos 118
Godsalve, Jos. 25; Rebecca 9; Thos 9, 25
Gouthwaite, *see* Gowthwaite
Gowland, John 221
Gowthwaite, Gouthwaite, Eliz. 118; Geo. 115, 118, 211, 218; Hannah 115, 118, 211; John
   115
Graham, Ann 67, 227; Esther 39, 137, 195; Geo. 67, 123, 124, 126, 129, 132*, 134, 137,
   138, 179, 190, 217, 227; Jane 205; John 67; Jonathan 134; Jos. 138; Marg. 123, 215;
   Mary 67, 123, 124, 126*, 129, 132, 134, 137, 138, 179, 190, 217; Peter 124, 161,
   236; Rebecca 129, 179; Sarah 236; Thos 39
Grainger, Jas 125; Mary 125; Nich. 125
Grange, Ann 114, 213; Beatrice 18; Benj. 114, 207, 208, 210, 214, 231; Ellen 15; Frances
   114, 210; Geo. 210
Grason, *see* Grayson
Gray, Grey, Ann 33; Jane 27; John 1*, 33, 35*, 101
Grayson, Grason, Ann 68; Mary 170
Greathead, Ann 184; Cath. 195; Dor. 73; Eliz. 15, 99, 205; Francis 15, 26; Wm 195
Greenbank, Revd Thos xii, 209*, 210*, 211*, 212*, 213, 214*, 215*, 216, 217, 218, 222,
   224*, 225*, 226*
Greenhow, Greenhough, David 208; J. 231; Jane 113, 231; Mary 113, 208
Greenwood, Barb. 16; Jane 72; John 147*; Mary 147
Gregg, Greg, Chris. 93; Eliz. 87; Marg. 100; Mary 23; Mr 23; Thos 31
Gregory, Mary 211
Grey, *see* Gray
Grime, Eliz. 161; Mary 65; Thos 65
Grimston, John 230
Grindale, Ann 13, 213; Geo. 113
Grundill, Grundal, Ann 145; Chas 148; Eliz. 142, 145, 148, 151*, 154, 227; Geo. 142*, 145,
   148, 151, 154, 159, 226, 227; Mary 154

Hagstone, Hagston, Ann 2, 40, 107*, 111, 114, 117, 122, 176, 204; Dor. 66, 105, 176, 181;
   Eliz. 9, 27, 41, 81, 151; Frances 45, 84, 171, 182; Geo. 41, 42, 45, 48, 52, 56*, 81,
   84, 167, 208, 214; Isab. 41, 52, 170; Jane 73; John 117; Mary 48, 122, 208, 235;
   Matth. 45, 105, 107, 111, 114*, 117, 122, 151, 176, 204, 235; Robt 6, 26; Sarah 40,
   200; Thos 2, 6, 9, 26, 27, 41, 42, 45, 66, 93, 111, 151, 181, 200
Hakin, Ann 225
Halfpenny, Eliz. 61, 96; Hy 77; Thos 61, 77, 96
Hall, Ann 18, 161, 202, 234; Barb, 208; Cath. 138; Chris. 146, 148, 155, 229; Eliz. 4, 23,
   120; Hannah 146, 148, 155*, 229; Hy 151, 156, 230; Jeremiah Metcalfe 156; John
   118, 120, 121, 124*, 125, 147, 171, 174; Marg. 140, 148; Mary 138, 140, 144, 147,
   151, 156, 225; Peter 13, 18, 77, 92; Rachel 118, 120, 121*, 124, 125*, 171, 174*,
   235; Richd 138, 140, 144, 147, 151, 181, 197, 203, 225; Sarah 181, 203; Thos 13, 77,
   118, 144, 146, 171; Wm 4, 5*, 23
Hamilton, Hamleton, Ann 111, 168; Ellen 175; Hannah 108, 111, 113, 117, 119, 123, 168,
   169, 202; Hy 227; Isab. 206; Jas 77, 104, 108, 111, 113*, 117, 119, 123, 165, 168,

169, 175, 202, 203; Jane 117, 203; Marg. 208; Mary 68, 104, 165; Matth. 21; Rachel 123; Thos 77, 119, 169; Wm 108, 185

Hammond, Ann 73; Anth. 224; Eliz. 73, 106*, 111, 120, 167, 177, 212, 214, 236; Frances 67; Grace 201; Hannah 175; Hy 156; Isab. 120; Jas 67; Jane 156, 163; John 76, 156; Marm. 60, 62*, 73, 76, 106, 111, 120, 167*, 214; Mary 112*, 115, 187, 209, 223, 226; Matth. 75, 100; Mich. 159, 176, 212, 223*; Peter 75, 112, 115*, 166, 187*, 209; Robt 60; Thos 111, 167; Thomasin 166

Hanley, Handley, Hanlah, Hanly, Ann 28, 57, 62, 67, 96, 163, 193; Betty 153, 223; Chris. 45, 161, 167; Deb. 53, 79; Eliz. 71, 135, 137, 139, 141, 143, 149, 153, 185, 225; Esther 53; Geo. 131; Jane 45, 60, 69, 101, 134, 219; John 32, 69, 75, 101; Jos. 131, 134, 137*, 158, 222; Marg. 50, 83; Mary 18, 31, 32, 131, 134, 135, 137, 161, 199*, 222, 225; Matth. 141, 208; Peter 135, 137, 139, 141, 143*, 149, 153, 185, 223, 229, 231, 233; Richd 18, 28, 32, 35*, 50, 53*, 54*, 57, 60, 62, 67, 75, 92, 96, 103, 163, 165, 193, 219, 224, 225*, 226, 227, 235; Sarah 33, 137, 185; Simon 24, 149, 223; Susanna 53, 92, 103; Thos 53, 139; Wm 160

Hannam, Ann 219

Hansom, Chris. 150*, 195*; Jane 150, 195*; Marg. 195; *see also* Hanson

Hanson, Chris. 196; Jane 196; John 196; *see also* Hansom

Hardcastle, Harkasel, Ann 67; Chas 10, 92; Charlotte 111; Eliz. 63, 97; Francis 91; Henrietta 104, 222; Jane 76, 223; John 61, 101; Marg. 19; Mary 22, 60, 68; Mercy 111; Richd 64, 99; T. 10, 222; Thos 4*, 22, 58, 84, 223; Wm 58, 59*, 60, 61, 63, 64, 76, 99, 101, 104, 111, 180

Hardisty, Eliz. 126; Mary 126, 218; Wm 126, 218

Hardy, Ann 158, 216, 222; Dor. 192

Hargrave, Ann 153, 198; Eliz. 198; John 153, 198*, Mary 153, 198*

Hargreaves, John 232; Mary 232

Harison, *see* Harrison

Harkasel, *see* Hardcastle

Harker, Ann 232; Geo. 225; Hannah 191, 194; John 197; Juliana 229; Mary 194; Wm 229

Harland, Harlan, Ann 13, 48, 184, 204; Frances 45, 86; Hannah 11, 73; Jane 16, 172; John 108, 178, 198, 204, 205; Marg. 23, 42; Mary 18, 108, 158, 205, 222; Peter 24; Sarah 35, 48; Thos 13, 15, 18, 35, 39, 42, 45, 86, 87, 108; Wm 8*, 11, 15, 16, 32, 39, 91

Harling, Martha 19

Harrington, Revd Robt 205*, 206*

Harrison, Harison, Abigail 108, 116, 168; Ann 18, 70, 131; Clement 49, 51, 53; Dor. 234; Edwin 73; Eliz. 108; Frances 51; Hy 231; Jane 174, 219, 231; John 54, 57, 70, 99, 120, 123, 203; Jos. 111; M. 14; Marg. 54, 99; Martha 108, 111, 115, 116, 120, 123, 125, 129, 168, 170, 174, 185; Mary 14, 129, 203, 207; Peter 4; Phyllis 197; Richd 53; Robt 49, 234; Sarah 73; T. 4; Thos 131*, 219*, 223; Troth 57, 91; Wm 108, 111, 115*, 116, 120, 123, 125*, 129, 168, 170*, 174, 185*, 207*, 213

Harte, Sam. 161

Hartley, Abigail 149, 231; Ann 77; Beatrice 138, 142, 144, 186, 188, 190; Christiana 138, 186; Eliz. 60, 129, 221; Geo. 149, 231, 235; John 144, 190; Mary 73, 107*, 113, 142, 188; Nanny 149; Thos 60, 63, 73, 77, 104*, 107, 113, 175, 195; Ursula 113; Wm 63, 129*, 138, 142, 144, 157, 186, 188, 190, 221, 232

Ingleby, Ingelby, Ann 123, 127, 196, 211; Anth. 123, 127, 196, 211; Dan. 121, 142, 150; Eliz. 121, 142, 150; Esther 127; Hannah 142; Mark 150; Walker 121; Wm 123
Ingram, Eliz. 200; Revd Goodricke xii, 73
Inman, Marg. 39; Mary 39; Thos 34
Issett, Molly 227
Iveson, Marg. 203; Wm 189

Jackson, Aaron 36, 37*, 40, 43, 45, 47, 50, 52, 55, 90, 99, 161, 167, 170, 202, 222; Abraham 133; Ann 5, 15, 52, 56, 64, 72, 103, 104, 106, 108, 109, 110, 112, 113, 115, 120, 125, 126, 130, 131, 145, 149, 153*, 157, 158, 161, 170, 173, 182*, 185, 190, 191, 199, 200, 201*, 202, 215, 217, 221*, 222, 227, 228*; Anna 149; Anth. 115, 162, 170; Ben 231*, 233; Benj. 61, 216, 220*; Betty 110, 223; Cath. 89; Chris. 22, 23, 36, 39, 42, 45, 47, 50*, 55, 57, 60, 61, 62, 64, 74, 84, 85, 92*, 95, 97, 98, 101, 102, 173, 174, 180, 186, 201, 214; David 106, 113, 139, 164, 169; Dor. 108, 177; Edmd 42, 144, 145, 148, 152, 161, 190, 224, 229*; Edwd 40, 80; Eliz. 12, 13, 15, 18, 23, 28, 36, 46, 57, 67, 71*, 78, 85, 97, 100, 103, 109, 110, 113*, 116, 120, 126, 130, 141, 145, 149, 160, 173, 182, 190, 197, 202, 218, 227, 229, 234*; Ellen 60, 97, 121, 174; Esther 7, 15, 52, 62, 74*, 120, 126, 165, 228; Frances 233; Geo. 41, 42, 43, 45*, 47, 50, 52, 55, 58, 61, 62, 64, 97, 99, 122, 125, 129*, 133, 135, 143, 149, 212, 215; Gillin/Gillian /Jillian 40, 161, 167; Hannah 45, 64,145, 204, 216; Harry 62; Hy 24, 118; Isab. 29; Jas 137; Jane 9, 45, 47, 64, 85, 98, 108, 122, 125*, 126, 129, 133, 144*, 146, 149, 152, 153, 154, 163, 173, 186, 188, 215, 229, 234; Jenny 102; John 6, 7, 8, 24, 58, 63, 71, 72, 97, 100, 103, 106*, 108, 109*, 110, 112, 113, 114, 115, 118, 126, 130*, 133*, 135, 137, 139, 141, 144, 145, 149, 153, 154, 164, 168, 169, 170, 171, 173, 177, 182, 190, 191, 199, 200, 201*, 214, 215, 216*, 218*, 225*, 228, 234, 235; Jos. 63, 125, 201; Lydia 42, 220; Marg. 16, 28, 66, 99; Martha 153; Mary 8, 15, 16, 22, 47*, 70, 77, 78, 101, 102, 106*, 108*, 110, 112, 113, 114, 115*, 118*, 120, 121, 125, 130*, 133, 135, 137, 139*, 141, 143, 144, 145*, 147*, 148*, 149, 152*, 160, 164*, 165, 168, 169, 171, 174*, 177, 182, 183, 190*, 198, 199*, 206, 212*, 213, 214, 222, 226, 229, 232; Matth. 5, 6, 7, 9*, 11*, 13, 15*, 24, 35, 36, 37, 40, 42, 51, 55, 79, 80, 109, 144, 146, 149, 153, 158, 161, 165, 169, 195, 210, 215, 217, 218, 222, 223, 227, 229*, 231, 234*; Moses 8, 16, 35, 50, 52, 90, 108, 112*, 115, 118, 121, 164, 172, 174, 182, 206; Peter 7*, 9, 16, 22, 28, 36, 58, 96, 99, 102, 103, 113, 130, 131, 157, 180, 181, 188, 201, 218*, 221; Phoebe 120, 214; Rebecca 56; Robt 37, 39, 50, 77, 89, 95, 98, 112, 113, 130, 139, 179, 183*, 197, 198, 202; Sarah 110*, 112*, 118, 152, 168; Thos 4*, 7, 8, 9*, 12, 15, 19, 36, 42, 44*, 45*, 46, 50*, 51, 52, 58, 67, 77, 79, 84*, 85, 96, 99*, 100*, 101, 103*, 104, 108, 109, 110*, 112, 113, 116*, 118*, 120*, 122, 130, 143, 146, 147, 152, 154, 164, 173, 174, 182, 183, 185, 189, 197*, 199*, 201*, 202*, 204, 205, 209, 210*, 212*, 213, 214*, 215, 217, 222, 225, 226*, 227*, 228*, 229, 231, 234, 235; Thomasin 185, 202; Ursula 19, 99; Wm xi, xii, 41, 61, 77, 97, 114, 120, 131, 139, 149, 234
James, Eleanor 84; John 61; Steph. 83; Thos 61, 98*; Wm 83, 84
Jaques, Ann 7, 29; Cath. 39, 97; Eliz. 25; Frances 166; John 7*, 9*, 12, 29, 32, 165; Mich. 11, 30; Richd 201; Robt 5*, 7, 11, 30*, 35, 39, 97, 165; Thos 12, 21, 81
Jeff, Ann 30, 106, 129, 155, 204; Benj. 125; Chris. 89; Eliz. 38, 125*, 129, 155, 216; John

261

154, 166, 171, 193, 198, 215, 225; Matth. 42, 162; Peter 36, 40, 42, 44, 47*, 49, 51, 83, 88, 89, 95, 113, 116, 120, 132*, 169, 170, 171, 172, 201, 209; Ralph 172; Richd 29, 31, 108, 174; Robt 144, 147, 150, 154, 193, 228; Sam. 220; Sarah 60, 181, 221; Simon 156; Thos 29, 32, 36, 41, 44*, 61, 62, 83, 85, 95, 108, 114, 126, 129, 134, 136, 143, 154, 156, 157, 174, 181, 206, 215, 219, 221; Thomasin 66, 166, 176; Wm 2*, 13, 15, 41, 42, 44, 46, 48, 50, 52, 53, 90*, 96, 100*, 108, 110, 114, 124, 125, 144, 159, 162, 164, 170*, 171, 181, 206, 214

Robison, Mary 19, 78

Robson, Jane 216; Mary 223

Rodwill, Rodwell, Anna 42; Eliz. 153; Ellen 60; Hannah 188, 202, 229; Hy 127, 184, 197, 206, 211, 217; Jane 55; John 124, 153, 197; Jos. 124, 127, 153; Mary 40, 93, 197, 206; Rachel 184, 217; Sarah 124, 127; Wm 1, 38*, 40, 42, 55, 60, 79*, 188, 189, 198, 204*, 210

Roe, Eliz. 145, 227; Geo. 145, 227; Isab. 229; Mary 145, 174

Rogers, Dor. 148*; Gilbert 206; John 148; Peter 206

Rogerson, Roginson, Ann 3, 26; John 35, 62, 162*, 201; Marg. 91; Mary 70, 169, 185; Richd 3, 26, 55, 79, 169; Thos 55, 59*, 62, 70, 162*, 169, 179

Rooking, Cath. 153*; John 153

Rose, Janet 28; Thos 30

Roundill, Roundale, Roundall, Roundell, Roundhall, Roundhill, Ann 209; Eliz. 115, 118, 119*, 123, 173, 186*, 194, 211; John 115, 118, 119, 123, 173, 186, 194, 196, 211; Jonathan 123, 194, 209, 232; Mary 118; Wm 115, 173

Rucroft, Ruecroft, Betty 112; Eliz. 60, 70, 98; Jacob 107, 135; Jas 62, 206, 210; Judith 72, 107, 112, 192, 218; Judy 74; Marg. 135*; Mary 38, 56, 94, 97, 102, 219; Phil. 38; Robt 56*, 60, 62, 72, 74, 94, 97, 98, 101, 102, 107, 112, 192, 197, 218

Rudd, Rud, Chas 131, 179; Chris. 2, 10, 14, 37*, 42, 82, 91, 101, 209; Dor. 10; Edwd 58, 131, 134, 139*, 142, 146, 151, 156, 158, 179, 186*, 222; Frances 2; Francis 31; Geo. 134; Hannah 146; Jane 70, 91, 117, 156, 230; John 82; Judith 131, 134, 139, 142*, 146, 151, 156, 179, 186, 222; Mary 58, 117, 171; Thos 151; Trothy 14; Wm 42, 82

Ruecroft, *see* Rucroft

Rumfitt, Ann 129, 221; Chas 129, 157, 221; Chris. 129

Rushton, Hy 169; John 199; Marg. 169

Russel, Jane 147; Mary 147; Robt 147

Ryder, Rider, Ann 62, 72, 143*, 146, 148, 151, 195, 227; Anth. 26; Chas 114; Dor. 151; Eleanor 92; Eliz. 148; Ellen 107, 111, 114; Esther 109, 111, 113, 115*, 116, 117, 120, 122, 124, 154, 159, 168, 175, 204, 207, 227, 233; Geo. 77, 118, 180; Hannah 55, 64, 94, 121; Jane 14, 44, 72, 100, 120, 127, 148, 164, 184, 233; Jenny 115; John 5, 8, 48, 52, 55, 57*, 59, 61, 62, 69, 75, 77, 88, 94, 100, 104, 206, 222; Jos. 61, 113, 148, 169; Joshua 148; Leon. 210; Marj. 57; Mark 57, 61, 64, 116, 154, 233, 234; Mary 69, 104, 114, 115, 117, 118, 121, 125, 127, 130, 135, 154, 158, 164, 180, 184, 190, 197, 206, 212, 222; Matth. 49, 114, 115, 124; Polly 219; Robt 5, 9*, 11, 14, 26*, 35*, 52, 59, 85*, 92, 100, 109, 117, 118, 121, 125, 127, 130, 135*, 154, 172, 180, 182, 184*, 212, 220; Sarah 154, 210, 234; Steph. 61; Thos 8, 26, 44, 47*, 48, 49, 52*, 55, 59*, 62, 86*, 88, 96, 97, 107, 111*, 114*, 122, 125, 143, 146*, 148, 151, 164, 168, 195, 227; Tim. 11, 75, 100, 109, 111, 113, 115, 116, 120, 122, 124, 168, 169, 175, 184, 197,

INDEX OF PLACES

The symbol * after the page number indicates that the name occurs more than once on the page indicated.

282

INDEX OF SUBJECTS, OCCUPATIONS AND TITLES

The symbol * after the page number indicates that the name occurs more than once on the page indicated.